CW01095604

THE
VICTORIAN NAVAL BRIGADES

THE
VICTORIAN NAVAL BRIGADES

Lieutenant Commander Arthur Bleby

Whittles Publishing

Published by
Whittles Publishing,
Dunbeath Mains Cottages,
Dunbeath,
Caithness KW6 6EY,
Scotland, UK
www.whittlespublishing.com

© 2006 Arthur Bleby

ISBN 1-904445-25-X

Typeset by
Sharon McTeir, Creative Publishing Services

Printed by Bell and Bain Ltd., Glasgow

CONTENTS

PREFACE

The genesis of this work lies back in my childhood when I received one of G A Henty's books as a Sunday School prize. The story in that book (and I cannot now remember its title) was centred on the adventures of two young brothers caught up in the events of the Indian Mutiny and contained a passing reference to HMS *Shannon* and Captain Peel's Naval Brigade. Years later I came across a copy of *The Devil's Wind* by Major General G L Verney, the reading of which stirred my memory of that long lost Sunday School prize and made me think that here was a subject about which I should like to know more.

My interest widened as I discovered that, beginning with the Crimean War and ending with the Boxer Rising, the Royal Navy had landed Naval Brigades to play a significant role in eleven of the Wars of the Empire and I could find no single book recording the efforts and adventures of these Naval Brigades. I was surprised to find that a Naval Brigade had fought in the Zulu War, was lucky enough to trace some long out of print contemporary accounts of the actions of the Naval Brigades, and had the temerity to write and submit to the Editor of the *Naval Review* an article on this subject. This article (the first I had ever written) was published. This encouraged me to research and submit further articles on the Naval Brigade in other wars. These articles are the substance of this book. I cannot claim that this work is comprehensive. There were at least three other Naval Brigades that were landed to take part in minor wars, two in South Africa and one in Burma. In Burma the Brigade was employed to crew the boats that carried the Army up the Irrawadi from Rangoon to Mandalay. Of the two in South Africa one was employed as a beach party and on bridge building and saw no action. The other marched and camped with the Army throughout the bush, guarded the camp when the rest of the column were out burning the villages of the rebellious natives and saw no real action.

Perhaps I should explain that 'Naval Brigade' was the generic term used to define a body of seamen and Royal Marines drawn from their ship or ships and landed for active service under the orders of an Army Commander. Numbers were immaterial since a Naval Brigade was not comparable with an Army Brigade, indeed it was not often even of battalion strength. Generally the armament of a Naval Brigade was made up of what was available from the parent ships from which the Brigade was drawn and what the Army Commander asked for as a supplement to the arms and equipment provided for his force. Except in the Second Boer War, naval uniform was worn and the naval ratings' headgear was a sennet hat with a cap ribbon embroidered with the name of the wearer's ship.

In the Crimea, and initially for Peel's Brigade in India, the Army required siege artillery. In Abyssinia, the Zulu war and the First Boer War the rocket was a potent weapon. The Gatling gun or its variant the Gardiner gun was the main weapon of the Naval Brigades in Egypt and the Sudan. In the Second Boer War the 12 pdr and 4.7 inch guns were dismounted from the ships and placed on improvised mountings. This allowed their use on land and gave the Army parity of range with the French and German guns with which the Boers were equipped.

When landed for service in a Naval Brigade the individual seaman was armed with a rifle and a cutlass-bayonet. When fixed as a bayonet it made the rifle very muzzle-heavy and even less accurate than it already was in the hands of the sailors. It could also be used as a sword using either point or edge. But it had other, if unofficial, uses. It was used as a machete for clearing bush, as an axe for cutting firewood, as a butcher's cleaver and the many other uses the ingenious sailor found for it.

It cannot be said that the seamen of the Naval Brigades were well trained in land warfare. Those that passed through HMS *Excellent*, the Naval Gunnery School at Whale Island, had received instruction in naval gunnery and gun drill and some elementary drill on the Parade Ground for forming fours and squares. They also received some rifle drill and a short course in practical musketry. The standard of marksmanship was not high. Those that had not passed through Whale Island were even less accomplished.

I have tried in this book to give some account of what the Naval Brigades were and what they did. But I should like to add something of what the men were like. Two quotations from contemporary accounts seem to me to give a better picture than I ever could.

Mrs Dubberley, an Army wife who smuggled herself through the port of Balaklava to be with her husband during the siege of Sevastopol, wrote after the dreadful Crimean winter:

> "There were no workmen, carpenters, joiners, builders, half as handy or so willing to assist as those of the Naval Brigade. There certainly was no camp in which more consideration for others, more real active help, has been offered to all than of the sailors; and their cheerfulness and willingness to labour encouraged and comforted all through the difficulties and sufferings of last winter."

Major General W C F Molyneux fought alongside the Naval Brigades in the Zulu War and again against Arabi Pasha in Egypt. His tribute is pithy:

> "Sailors are the best of comrades in rough times; nothing puts them out; I suppose because the ship is their home, and a run ashore is always and in any circumstances a holiday to them."

I think these quotations say it all.

ACKNOWLEDGEMENTS

I am indebted to Mr Atlee and his staff at the Helston Branch of the Cornwall County Library who obtained for me many of the books that I studied during the writing of this work. I would also like to thank the editors of the Naval Review, since their acceptance for publication of individual articles encouraged me to complete this entire text.

I am most grateful to my daughter, son-in-law and grandsons who between them keyed an electronic version of my typescript for submission to the publishing company.

Finally, I offer my heartfelt gratitude to my long-suffering wife for the support and understanding she has given me during my work on this book.

CHAPTER 1

THE CRIMEAN WAR

1854–1855

In 1850 Tsar Nicholas II, considering the Turkish Empire ripe for dissolution, propounded his own ideas of how it should be divided, to Russian advantage. His opinions and ideas were not shared by Great Britain and France. Through three years of diplomacy the Russians remained intransigent and when in the spring of 1853 the Turks, persuaded by Great Britain, politely rejected Russian proposals, a Russian army moved into the Turkish provinces of Moldavia and Wallachia (now a part of Romania). There were further efforts by Great Britain and France to mediate, backed by the passing of their fleets through the Dardanelles. But Turkey had thrown an army across the Danube and a Turkish squadron of frigates cruising in the Black Sea was, on 30th November 1853, destroyed at Sinope by the Russian Black Sea Fleet. By March 1854 it was obvious that there was no diplomatic solution and Great Britain and France sent an ultimatum to Russia demanding the evacuation of Turkish territory before 30th April. The Tsar made it known that he would not condescend to reply and war was officially declared on 27th March 1854.

The war aims were firstly to ensure the restoration of the status quo and then to inflict on Russia such a defeat as to deter further aggression. The overall strategy was twofold: maritime action against the Baltic and northern ports and trade of Russia, and military action to assist Turkey in ejecting the Russian invaders and then to strike the punitive blow.

A British army under Lord Raglan was formed piecemeal; battalions of infantry and regiments of cavalry, artillery and ancillary troops were staged forward through Malta, Gallipoli, and Scutari to Varna, on the Romanian coast. Here too the French army under Marshal St Arnaud assembled, bringing with it the cholera that was spread through both armies and both navies, killing many and debilitating many more.

Meanwhile the Turkish army had had some success against the Russians who fell back from the Danubian provinces. This success was achieved with very little British assistance, though a party of two officers and thirty seamen from HMS *Britannia* went inland to help bridge the Danube. Before doing so they manned some small gunboats on the river and played an important part in the capture of the river island of Rustchuk. Having built a bridge of boats in three weeks under fire, they sailed downstream to Silistria, which had withstood a Russian siege, destroying on the way the Russian riverbank forts.

With Turkish territory cleared of the invaders, it remained to strike hard at Russia and Sevastopol became the target. Sevastopol was the major Russian naval base in the Black Sea. It was not strongly fortified and it was considered within the power of the allied armies to seize the town before winter set in and to hold it against any Russian counter attack. Success would bring great benefits, namely secure and comfortable winter quarters for the armies and the capture or destruction of the Russian fleet. So, on 14th September the expedition sailed for the Crimea, landing unopposed, but not unobserved, three days later. The chosen landing place was at Kalamita Bay, 33 miles north of Sevastopol.

On 19th September everything was ready and the advance on Sevastopol began. After a brush with the enemy at the Bulganak River that afternoon, the river Alma, defended by the Russian army, was in sight at dusk on the 20th. Lord Raglan and Marshal St Arnuad conferred that night but could not agree on a plan for concerted action. Consequently, the battle of the Alma fought on 21st September developed into two uncoordinated actions. The French forces positioned on the right and flanked by the sea, advanced against the weaker wing of the Russians, drove them off and halted. The British army, with an unguarded left flank, defeated the bulk of the Russian infantry after hard fighting. When the Russians fell back the French refused to join in the pursuit.

On 23rd September the advance on Sevastopol continued with the intention of assaulting the city from the northern approach. When it was seen that such an attack required passage over Sevastopol harbour (a thousand yards of water protected by a strong fortification which prevented the Allied fleets from assisting in the crossing) the armies turned inland and marched round the city to establish a base at Balaklava and to attack Sevastopol from the south. The fleet sailed round and secured the port on 26th September as the advance guard of the armies reached the crest of the hills surrounding the harbour.

Sevastopol is built on the northeastern shoulder of a peninsular, with its northern face protected from the sea. Behind the town the land rises to a plateau, broken to the east by a number of ravines. The plateau falls precipitously to the valley of the Tchernaya and a flat and roadless plain. On the south of the peninsula, about ten miles distant surrounded by steep hills, lies the small port of Balaklava. On the northwestern tip of the land are two sheltered stretches of water with an easier approach to the plateau than that from Balaklava.

Balaklava was found to be too small to be the base port for both armies. It would have been logical, therefore, for the British army to have pushed on from Balaklava, taken the left flank and based itself on Kamiesh and Kasatch Bays. But Balaklava had been occupied by the Royal Navy and on the strong advice of Vice Admiral Lyons, Lord Raglan insisted on retaining this port for his base.

There were now differences of opinion on tactics. Lord Raglan considered, with justification, that Sevastopol would fall to an immediate assault. General Canrobert, to whom in his mortal sickness St Arnaud had surrendered the command of the French army, considered an artillery bombardment an essential preliminary to the infantry attack. Canrobert's opinion was shared by Lord Raglan's Senior Engineer Officer and, under persuasion, Lord Raglan deferred to his allies. For a fortnight, both inside and outside the city, there was a period of intense labour and preparation. The Russians, directed by Colonel Todleben (who showed himself a genius in fortification) strengthened their defences, digging trenches, constructing and improving strongpoints and siting their batteries. At the same time they passed into the city strong reinforcements from their field army, though the bulk of this remained to threaten the inadequately guarded right flank and the British supply lines. The French and British armies encamped on the plateau above Sevastopol and, while their siege trains were unloaded, began the digging of their own trenches, the construction of the sites for their batteries and the transportation of guns and ammunition to their chosen sites. The task of unloading the British transports fell to the Royal Navy, and working parties from the fleet struggled in the holds of the transports which were not 'combat loaded'. The confusion that bedevilled the port of Balaklava had begun.

Lord Raglan wished to augment his forces and, the Russians having sunk the major units of their fleet as blockships in Sevastopol harbour, the Royal Navy were anxious to find some active part to play in the siege. On 28th September a battalion of Royal Marines was formed from the detachments in the fleet and was landed to assist in the defence of Balaklava. Two days later this force was reinforced and reorganised into two battalions that occupied a position two miles long on the heights 1200 feet above the port. The position was strengthened by batteries of guns landed from the fleet and manned by the Royal Marine Artillery. Lord Raglan further requested that the Navy should provide guns and seamen to man them to augment his siege train. On 1st October the orders for the landing of the Naval Brigade were issued and by sunset the next day the men of the Brigade were encamped at the head of the gorge leading out of Balaklava.

The Naval Brigade, commanded by Captain Lushington assisted by Captains Peel and Moorsom, was made up of 18 lieutenants, 18 mates or midshipmen and 1000 seamen. They were to man 50 guns, 44 of which were 32 pdrs and six were 68 pdr Lancasters, guns with an oval, twisted bore, an early experiment in rifling. 150 rounds of shot and 30 shells were provided as the initial outfit for each gun. Each man was issued with a cutlass, and pistols with ten rounds were available for a third of the force. Each man landed with a complete change of clothing, a pilot coat and two blankets. They were also provided with haversacks and water bottles.

The Brigade's first night ashore under canvas was a short one. Reveille on 3rd October was at 0300, and after a parade at which each man was issued with a dose of quinine, they began the task of bringing the guns and ammunition up from Balaklava to the naval camp near the village of Kadakoi at the head of the gorge. Work began at 0430, and with two breaks totalling one and a half hours for breakfast and dinner, went on until 1930. What work! Although the artillery lent travelling carriages for the six Lancasters and a few of the 32 pdrs, these and the majority of the 32 pdrs on their 'trucks' (the small, solid, wooden wheels of their ship mountings) had to be hauled by manpower up the steep unmetalled track. It needed fifty one men for each gun, fifty on the drag ropes and a musician, fifer, fiddler or vocalist mounted on the gun to lead the chantey to which the team hauled away. Those not hauling guns were carrying ammunition — two men to each 112 lbs of powder, which was packed in a zinc container within a wooden box (a total weight of over 130 lbs and an awkward load to carry), plus one man to each 68 pdr shot or shell and one man to two 32 pdr shot or shell.

After six days camp was shifted to the plateau. Half of the Naval Brigade began to move the guns forward from the camp to the batteries and to install them in their firing positions. The other half continued to work from Balaklava to the camp bringing up the rest of the guns and ammunition. By 16th October, the eve of the first great bombardment, all the guns were sited and for each gun there was some 500 rounds of shot and shell – though the quantity of powder in the batteries and their ready use magazines would require replenishment.

The defences of Sevastopol were roughly U-shaped, running from the northwest through south to the northeast and were anchored by four major works: the Central Bastion in the middle of the west face, the Flagstaff Bastion roughly at the bottom of the U and on the east face the Redan and the Malakoff tower. The Central Bastion and the Flagstaff Bastion were mutually supporting, as were the Flagstaff Bastion and the Redan, and the Redan and the Malakoff. The Malakoff was the key to the whole position for it dominated the whole of the northeast face and the lie of the land was such that an assault could only be launched on the defences from the Flagstaff Bastion to the Malakoff. The French lay before the west face whilst the British faced the Redan and Malakoff. By the nature of the ground the French were

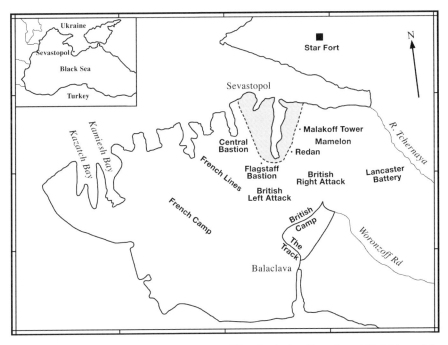

Defences of Sevastopol during the Crimean War, depicting French and British positions

able to dig deep trenches and their batteries were advanced close to the Flagstaff and Central Bastions. The British batteries were, perforce, at much greater range.

The British built two large batteries, the Left and Right Attack. The Left Attack were allocated the Flagstaff Bastion and Redan, and the Right Attack the Redan and Malakoff as their primary targets at ranges of between 1400 and 1700 yards. More than half the guns in each battery were manned by the Naval Brigade. Captain Moorsom commanded in the Left Attack and Captain Peel in the Right Attack and since they were manned from HMS *Queen* and HMS *Diamond* it was named the Koh-I-Noor Battery. The guns were dug in to a depth of two feet and protected by an embrasured wall of gabions and packed earth. Each gun was sited on a level platform of railway sleepers to facilitate running in and out and traversing. Magazines were made behind each battery for the storage of powder using, for the Right Attack, natural caves in the ravine behind the battery.

On 17th October the first attack on Sevastopol began. The plan was simple. There was to be a combined bombardment on all the Russian positions. When the opposition had been beaten down the French were to assault the Flagstaff Bastion and the British to make supporting attacks on the Redan and Malakoff. The general opinion throughout the armies was that Sevastopol would fall in a matter of hours.

[5]

Even the most pessimistic estimate by some of the older and more prudent officers was that the Russian resistance would last for 48 hours.

The Naval Brigade was organised into three watches, and at 0230 the first watch of guns' crews marched down to the batteries. The bombardment was to commence at 0630 when more than 100 heavy guns would open fire with, it was hoped, surprise and a devastating effect. The Russians, however, had detected the preparations and opened fire first. On time, at 0630, the combined artillery of the French and British armies opened fire and a very heavy artillery duel began. By about 0900 the Right Attack was running short of powder and Captain Peel sent an urgent message back to camp for every available man to take powder up to the battery. After this emergency resupply the battery was replenished with powder by the army a further three times during the day. On the first occasion three wagon loads of powder were brought up. One was left near the battery in full view of the Russians. Captain Peel and Lieutenant Douglas led the unloading party and brought in the powder under the Russian fire. The other two wagons were left behind the battery in an area in which the 'overs' were falling and so obviously dangerous that the sailors baulked at moving into it. The Commander of HMS *Queen* went out and struggled with the first box. Fired by his example the sailors joined him and with only one casualty all the powder was brought in. Later, when the army left another wagon of powder in the same place, it was exploded by a shell before anyone could reach it.

All was going well until about 1000 when the Russians hit the French magazine that blew up and devastated the French battery. This silenced the French guns and halved the force of the bombardment. It also prevented the French from making an assault. The Left Attack now came under a heavier concentration of fire but remained in action until late in the day when it had exhausted its ammunition. The Right Attack continued to bombard its target with great effect. At about 1400 hits were scored on the magazines of both the Redan and Malakoff which blew up; the Redan was reduced to three guns left firing and, by the end of the day, the Malakoff was reduced to only two. At dusk the firing ceased.

The French had hoped to be ready to reopen fire on the morning of 18th October, and the British batteries renewed their bombardment at first light. The French were not ready — the damage was so serious that they could not reopen fire until 20th October. The British continued the bombardment daily, but the Russian exertions each night, including the conscription of all the civilians in Sevastopol, quickly rebuilt and (from the resources of the naval arsenal) rearmed their works. As a consequence, when the French could reopen fire the Russian defences were almost as strong as they had been at the beginning of the bombardment. Nevertheless the bombardment was kept up until 24th October.

Any hopes of storming Sevastopol before winter set in were destroyed by the events of the next fortnight. On 25th October the Russian field army launched an attack on Balaklava that resulted in the battle of that name. Though the Royal

Marine Artillery Batteries on the heights above the port were engaged at long range, neither the Royal Marine battalions nor the Naval Brigade played any part in the battle.

On 26th October the Russians made a sortie from Sevastopol and attacked the British forces on the Inkerman flank close to a battery of two Lancaster guns, commanded by Mr Hewitt, Mate, RN, sited there to fire on shipping in the harbour below. Hewitt had a restricted view of the ground close to his battery and was engaging a Russian column that he could see to his right front. He could not see a Russian column advancing towards him on his right flank. Since others had seen this column and knew no support was available, orders were sent to Hewitt to spike his guns and retire. Whilst the order was being given to him Hewitt saw the head of the column on his right flank, in a position where he could not train his guns. He fired one gun so that the recoil brought the muzzle back clear of the embrasure, reloaded, trained right and ran the gun up with its muzzle against the earthen flank wall of the battery. As the messenger repeated the order Hewitt shouted "Retire – retire be damned – FIRE!" The shot and blast hurled a mass of stone and earth out fanwise into the faces of the advancing Russians who recoiled. A party of infantry appeared and charged the Russians who retired. Mr Hewitt received the Victoria Cross for his behaviour.

On 5th November the Battle of Inkerman was fought in patchy fog that greatly assisted the Russians to achieve surprise. The partial visibility and the scrubby, broken ground reduced the battle to a series of local, bloody encounters between, on the British side, bodies of men of no more than battalion strength and the Russian columns. At one time a Russian column was seen advancing towards the flank of the Right Attack that could be overrun. While six guns were moved to face the threat, preparations were made to spike the guns in the battery and the gun crews were shown their line of retreat. The Russians, however, changed the line of their attack and the head of the column entered dead ground and halted, leaving the tail exposed. At a range of between 1100 and 1500 yards the Naval Brigade guns engaged and destroyed the exposed Russians who stoically stood to be shot to pieces. The Redan and Malakoff batteries tried, unsuccessfully, to silence the guns of the Right Attack. By 1300 the destruction of the column was complete and there were no more targets to be engaged.

Captain Peel was not with his battery. Accompanied by his 'Doggie', Midshipman Daniels, he had gone towards the main battle to see what was going on. They became involved with the Guards Brigade fighting in and around a small redoubt named the Sandbag Battery. Collecting a party of soldiers together Peel and Daniels led them in bayonet charges on the Russians. For their bravery here, and on another occasion when they fought a fire in and saved a magazine of powder, both Captain and Midshipman were awarded the Victoria Cross.

Two companies of the Royal Marines had, a few days before, been attached to the Light Division and fought with distinction at Inkerman. Corporal Prettyjohn, RM, was awarded the Victoria Cross for his conduct, and Captain Hopkins, commanding the detachment, was named in Lord Raglan's despatch as distinguishing himself by his conduct.

On 10th November the weather, which had been deteriorating, finally broke and for four days there was continuous heavy rain and a strengthening wind. At about 0400 on 14th November the wind increased to hurricane strength. Within two hours the camp was reduced to a shambles. All but a very few tents, fortuitously pitched in the lee of stonewalls, were blown away. Wagons were overturned, the air was full of flying debris and it was impossible for a man to walk upright. At about noon the wind veered into the west and the sheeting rain became first sleet and then heavy snow. After a further two hours the wind began to moderate and the Naval Brigade started to salvage what it could. By nightfall the Naval Brigade had their lines in some sort of order.

The ships in Balaklava suffered much damage in the storm but the real disaster befell those loaded transports anchored off the port. Eight were driven ashore and sunk with a very heavy loss of life. The most serious losses were the two transports that carried the army's reserve of powder and the entire stock of winter clothing.

There was now no prospect of taking Sevastopol before the spring of 1855, so the French and British armies settled down to maintain the siege throughout the Crimean winter. The British army was singularly unsuitably equipped and organised to operate in the nightmarish conditions that it had to endure. In all weathers the men were required to guard the trenches by day, and by night to labour at digging new trenches, parallels and saps required for the prosecution of the siege. The debilitating effects of cholera were still present, scurvy had developed in October and the men, now in poor physical condition, were reduced to near exhaustion by their duties and the lack of adequate food and rest. All this when they were inadequately clothed and sheltered from the inclemencies of the weather.

Rations were basic: salt beef or salt pork, biscuit and rum were usually all that was available. There were no arrangements for cooking. Each man was issued his ration and expected to make his own culinary arrangements. There was very little fuel and the only cooking utensils available were the individual mess tins. It was next to impossible to cook the salt beef in these but the salt pork could be eaten raw. Coffee was issued, but as the berries were green and needed both roasting and grinding, for which there were no facilities, this was useless.

The Naval Brigade became the envy of the whole army. On 20th November they moved to a new campsite in a sheltered position next to the French camp. Captain Lushington borrowed 'well sinkers' from the army and, to provide ample pure water for his men, sank wells in the camp. Latrines were dug well away from the camp on the far side of an adjacent ravine and a suspension bridge, the footway made from the staves of shaken casks, was rigged to provide access. There was a central galley, manned by seamen detailed off as cooks. The heavy zinc liners from the ammunition boxes were utilised as camp kettles and harness casks. A hut for drying clothes and bedding was built and a hospital marquee erected. Captain Lushington obtained warm underwear and new shoes, at his own expense, from Constantinople, which were issued on repayment.

The Brigade remained in three watches and the guns were manned throughout the 24 hours. Before marching down to the batteries the men going on watch were issued with, and drank under supervision, hot cocoa or coffee. The relieved watch, on return to camp, were first taken to the drying hut where, under supervision, they shifted into warm, dry clothes. They were provided with a hot meal and allowed to turn in. There was a daily issue of quinine and lime juice which was also drunk under supervision, and a daily issue of rum. Carrying parties were marched down to Balaklava each day and brought back ammunition, rations and fuel. To the surprise of the army the naval officers in charge of the carrying parties brought back their individual loads.

The 14 mile round trip to Balaklava varied from difficult to extremely hazardous. The unmetalled track through the gorge, never maintained, had, through the constant traffic, been reduced to deep and viscous mud and was often deep in snow. It was marked by the carcasses of foundered transport animals, as well as broken wagons and abandoned supplies. Despite the difficulty of the trip there were sometimes advantages to be gained from making it. There were opportunities to make private purchases of, or to 'pick up', extra food and little luxuries.

The sailors were recognised as expert scroungers. The commanding officer of the French Regiment encamped beside the Naval Brigade paid a formal call on Captain Lushington to make a polite protest. Backed by the threat that, as he numbered among his men some of the most expert thieves in Paris, unless the sailors ceased their depredations, some morning they would wake to find half their camp had vanished. The report of the Sanitary Commissioners included the statement that the sailors were "by no means unwilling to appropriate to their service of his necessities whatever useful objects good fortune may throw in his way". Another tribute was to the sailor's "adaptability to new circumstances and his capability of suiting to his wants any new objects that falls into his possession".

It was not, however, a case of all take and no give. The sailors' peculiar skills were shared with the army and its camp followers. Off duty the sailors turned their hands to the repair of tents and uniforms, carpentry and other odd jobs that needed doing and were being left undone by the soldiery. Officers and civilians paid for the work, in part at least in rum, which was shared with any passing soldier. Mrs Duberly, diarist and one of the camp followers, wrote in her journal:

"There were no workmen, carpenters, joiners, builders, half as handy or so willing to assist as those of the Naval Brigade. There certainly was no camp in which more kind consideration for others, more real active help, has been afforded to all than in that of the sailors; and their cheerfulness and willingness to labour encouraged and comforted all through the difficulties and sufferings of last winter."

Christmas was no season of cheer for the army. No special provision had been made and due to a not unusual failure of the Commissariat many of the regiments on the plateau received no issue of provisions. The Naval Brigade, however, had hot meals and enjoyed some mild festivity. Then on 30th December, because they fetched them themselves, the Naval Brigade were issued with warm clothing. Each man received a sheepskin jacket, a fur cap and a pair of gloves. At this time too the Crimean Army Fund, organised from home and civilian run, started its operations and tea and other 'luxuries' became available at reasonable prices.

During January the officers of the Naval Brigade were duped by a Russian spy. A civilian, who spoke English with a slight northern accent and introduced himself as an army doctor, walked into the camp. He was entertained to lunch and then taken into the Right Attack where he was shown around, watched the re-venting of a gun and had his questions about the guns, magazines and organisation of the defences answered in full. He was guided to the advanced trenches where he wandered around. Suddenly he jumped over the parapet and bolted into the Russian lines which he reached unharmed.

Throughout the winter the guns were required to dominate the Russian batteries and to protect the men in the trenches. The army quickly found that, whilst a request for supporting fire passed through the chain of command took so long to be approved that the need had passed before action had been taken, a message to a naval battery brought an immediate and effective response. In February the batteries were re-armed and strengthened by the substitution of 68 pdr guns and Lancasters for some of the 32 pdrs.

Battle casualties and the ravages of the winter had greatly weakened the British army. The French, now predominant in numbers, added to their responsibility the covering of the Malakoff and the Mamelon, a new defence work built a quarter of a mile in advance of, and covering the Malakoff. These two works, because of their importance as the keys to the Russian defences, became the major objectives of the French army and French batteries were built to bombard them. However, they remained as targets for the Right Attack and during the first fortnight of March a steady fire was concentrated on the Mamelon.

The first major action of 1855 began on 9th April with a bombardment of all the Russian positions. The Russians were taken by surprise and it was half an hour before they opened fire in return. The surprising ability of the Russians to rebuild and re-arm their defences (Sevastopol had, as the arsenal of the Black Sea Fleet, an enormous stock of guns on which to draw) had been recognised. The siege train had therefore been reinforced by batteries of mortars that, it was thought, would drop shells with accuracy by night in the target areas and prevent repair. This tactic was not as successful as was hoped. An early mastery of the Russian batteries was established and on 11th April Captain Peel reported, "If the Allies intend to assault, a better opportunity than this will not offer. The fire of the Russian batteries of the Malakoff is completely crushed." Lord Raglan read Peel's report and remarked only, "Impossible, I fear." Nevertheless the bombardment continued until 18th April when the French had exhausted their ammunition. By this time all the major works of the Russians had been mastered and the Russians had massed infantry (which suffered 6000 casualties) to repel the assault that they thought certain.

It is conjectured that the failure to attempt an assault during this bombardment was due to direct interference by the French Emperor, Napoleon III. He wished to come to the Crimea, take personal command of the French army and claim the glory of the victory. The hands of the French commander-in-chief were tied by his covert instructions and if he could not order the French army to assault, Lord Raglan for the sake of the alliance would not act unilaterally. Finally the French commander-in-chief, General Canrobert, handed over his command to General Pelissier, though he remained in the Crimea as a divisional commander. Napoleon III was finally dissuaded from his venture.

The next assault was planned to take place in June. It was to be a two-staged attack: initially the French were to seize the Mamelon as a jumping off point for an attack on the Malakoff and the British were to seize the Quarries, a defensive position between their lines and the Redan. It was then intended to assault Sevastopol on 18th June in the hope that a successful combined operation on the anniversary of the Battle of Waterloo might serve to ameliorate French bitterness engendered by that defeat.

At 1400 on 6th June the allied artillery of some 550 guns spread over a five mile front opened fire on the Russian positions, with the naval batteries engaging their usual targets, the Redan, the Malakoff and the Mamelon. As the guns fell silent at dusk, mortars opened fire and at dawn the guns took over again. Early in the forenoon the batteries in the Malakoff and Mamelon ceased fire. The French, in divisional strength, advanced on the Mamelon and took it. The retreating Russians were brought under fire from the naval guns of the Right Attack and were driven back into the Malakoff where, reformed and reinforced, they destroyed an impetuous French Regiment that had followed them to the walls of the Malakoff. Under fire from the Right Attack the Russians counterattacked and drove the French from the Mamelon only to be thrown out again. The fighting swayed to and fro, with intermittent aid from the naval guns, until at dusk the French established themselves in the Mamelon. Under the cover of the guns of the Left Attack an English column seized the position in the Quarries and fought off the series of counterattacks delivered during the night. On the morning of 8th June both the Mamelon and the Quarries were secured.

The next six days were another period of unremitting labour. New trenches were dug, batteries were advanced and ammunition was stockpiled in readiness for the grand assault on 18ᵗʰ June. The agreed plan was for another grand bombardment throughout 17ᵗʰ June, mortar fire overnight, a further bombardment for two hours from dawn on 18ᵗʰ and a French assault on the Malakoff. The British assault on the Redan was to be launched by Lord Raglan, either in support of the French or to take advantage of their success.

Apart from their share in the bombardments, the Naval Brigade had obtained for themselves an active part in the assault. Three columns were to assault the Redan, one on each face and one in the centre. Each column was to be led by a party of sailors carrying ladders to facilitate the crossing of the trench, 15 feet wide and 11 feet deep that fronted the *glacis* of the work.

At daylight on 17ᵗʰ June the bombardment opened and continued throughout the day. By dusk the Russian return fire had been effectively silenced and there were great hopes that after a two-hour bombardment the next morning a successful assault would be launched. Then at 2000 General Pelissier informed Lord Raglan that he had changed his plan and would now launch his assault on the Malakoff at dawn next morning without further artillery preparation. Lord Raglan was unhappy at the proposal but he had to accept.

From the beginning the French attack went wrong. The Russians were alerted and ready, their batteries and trenches fully manned. One French column mistook the burning fuse of a mortar shell for the signal rocket and attacked early, the second jumped off on time and the third was delayed by half an hour. The uncoordinated attacks faltered and failed.

Lord Raglan was not aware of the full extent of the debacle. He saw that the French column on his immediate right was pinned down under artillery and musket fire and decided that he must give support. Accordingly he ordered the British assault to begin. The attacking columns moved forward into a hail of shot, shell and musketry. Captain Peel, who was in overall command of the Naval parties led the right hand column himself, shouting, "Come on sailors; don't let the soldiers beat you", and reached the *abatis* before being wounded. Three of the four other officers with this party were also wounded, as were all but nine of the sixty sailors. In the face of all difficulties one ladder was carried to the Russian works, only to be abandoned unused. The left hand column fared no better, all their officers were wounded and, though fewer sailors fell, no ladder reached the left face of the Redan. The centre column hardly advanced. The skirmishing line took cover before it had gone far and the ladder party perforce halted and went to ground, waiting under fire for the advance to continue. Finally they were recalled and under cover of the fire of the batteries they and the remnants of the other columns made their way back to their own trenches.

For the next two months the allied armies, now reinforced by an army from the Italian kingdom of Sardinia, reverted to the classic moves of siege warfare, advancing their sappers, parallels and batteries towards the defences and maintaining a steady fire to cover their operations. Lord Raglan died of cholera on 26th June and was succeeded in command by General Simpson, his chief of staff. Captain Lushington was promoted to Rear Admiral, awarded the KCB, and recalled. He was succeeded by Captain the Honorable Henry Keppel on 21st July. On 15th August the Russians made a final attempt to relieve Sevastopol and launched an attack by their field army of 60 000 towards the right flank of the main French position. In severe fighting a French division and the Sardinian army (which particularly distinguished itself) inflicted a heavy defeat on the Russians.

A new target now appeared for the Naval batteries. The Russians built a bridge of boats across Sevastopol harbour and it, and any daytime traffic, was engaged at long range. This was something of a diversion as at extreme range there was no real hope of destroying the bridge or of stopping the traffic. Within the British lines the Naval Brigade again showed its versatility by helping with the construction of a light railway from Balaklava to the camp, by roadmaking and by building huts for the army, though they themselves remained under canvas.

The French had advanced their trenches to within 25 yards of the Malakoff, and the British theirs to within about 200 yards of the Redan by the beginning of September. It was agreed to assault these works, after a three-day bombardment, on 8th September. The plan was much the same as that which had previously been tried and had failed. The French were to attack at noon on the 8th (they having discovered that at this time the Russians were changing watches in their defences which would temporarily be unmanned as the relieving watch did not move into the lines until the outgoing watch had marched out). The British assault was not to start until the Tricolour was hoisted in the Malakoff. The Naval Brigade was not to be allowed the honour of providing ladder parties for the British assault as it was believed (with good reason) that the sailors planned to abandon the ladders, arm themselves from dead and wounded soldiers and make their own assault.

The bombardment went as planned, and at noon the French made a dash into the Malakoff. Within ten minutes they had established a foothold and hoisted the Tricolour. Although there were moments when it seemed that they might be driven out, they held their ground and by dusk were secure in the possession of the work. The British attack went in as arranged, but over a greater distance and against an alerted defence. Disorganised by heavy casualties, the assaulting force breached the defences, established a small foothold and, for a while, held on against repeated and eventually overwhelming counterattacks. Lacking reinforcement they were eventually driven back. A renewal of the assault by the Highland Brigade was hastily planned for the next day. At about 2300 a very loud explosion was heard from the Redan and Sir Colin Campbell, the Brigade Commander, ordered a reconnaissance.

The Redan at sunrise, September 9th: removing the wounded
(Illustrated London News, October 6, 1855)

The Redan was found abandoned, its magazine blown up. Throughout the night there was a series of explosions from Sevastopol itself. In the morning it became apparent that during the night the garrison had marched away over the bridge of boats, which it had then destroyed. The city was found to be a charnel house.

Although Sevastopol had fallen, the war dragged on for another six months though there was little action and much boredom. The Naval Brigade did not remain ashore and on 16th September it was cheered through the camp as, headed by the bands of the 14th and 18th Regiments, it began its march back to re-embark. The Royal Marine Battalions remained, for the time being, with the army and in October took part in an amphibious operation to capture the fortress at Kimburn. It was a small, bloodless success.

During the period from 1st October 1854 to 16th September 1855 a total of 4,469 officers, seamen and Royal Marines had served ashore at some time. Five officers and 95 men had been killed and 38 officers and 437 men wounded. Four officers and six ratings were awarded the Victoria Cross as were one officer and two men of the Royal Marines.

On 17th September this General Order was issued from Army Headquarters:

The service for which the Naval Brigade was attached to this Army having been completed by the fall of Sevastopol, the force has been ordered to rejoin the Fleet.

The Commander of the Forces heartily thanks the officers, Petty Officers and seamen for the very efficient services they have rendered in the batteries, and on all occasions when their aid against the enemy was required; and he has to notice the patience and courage with which, side by side with the soldiers of the army, they have endured the dangers and hardships of nearly a year's duty in the trenches.

General Simpson cordially acknowledges the obligations he is under to Rear Admiral Sir Stephen Lushington, KCB, who so ably commanded the Brigade from its formation until his removal by promotion to higher rank, and to Captain the Hon. H. Keppel, RN, who succeeded him, and retained the command until the conclusion of this ever memorable siege.

Bibliography

Duberly, F. (1855) *Mrs Duberly's Journal*. Longman, Brown, Green and Longman
Eardley-Wilmot, S. (1898) *Life of Vice Admiral Lord Lyons GCB*. S Low, Marston and Co
Gifford, G. (1892) *Reminiscences of a Naval Officer*. (Publisher unknown)
Hibbert, C. (1961) *The Destruction of Lord Raglan*. Longmans
Higginson, G. (1916) *Seventy-one years of a Guardsman's Life*. John Murray
Keppel, H. GCB OM (1899) *A Sailor's Life under Four Sovereigns*. Macmillan
Kingslake, A.W. (1863) *The Invasion of the Crimea*. Blackwood
Lawson, G. (1968) *Surgeon in the Crimea*. Military Book Society
Lloyd, C. and Coulter, J. L. S. (1963) *Medicine and The Navy* Vol IV. Edinburgh
Montague, V. (1898) *A Middy's Recollection*. (Publisher unknown)
Sayer, F. (1857) *Despatches and Papers* (Ed. Sayer, F.). Harrison
Warner, P. (1972) *The Crimean War — A Reappraisal*. Taplinger
Wood, E. VC (1906) *From Midshipman to Field Marshall*. Methven
Wood, E. VC (1896) *The Crimea in 1854 and 1894*. Chapman and Hall

CHAPTER 2

THE INDIAN MUTINY

1857–1858

When the Indian Mutiny broke out at Meerut on 10th May 1857, the Royal Navy was embroiled with the Chinese on the Canton River. HMS *Shannon*, commanded by Captain William Peel VC, RN, was on passage to China carrying Lord Elgin to assume control of matters there. HMS *Shannon* had just arrived at Hong Kong when the news of the mutiny was received there and HMS *Pearl* was also in harbour. Lord Elgin decided that he should give what help he could in India and re-embarked in HMS *Shannon* to go to Calcutta to confer with the Governor General. A provisional 400-strong Battalion of Royal Marine Light Infantry was embarked in HMS *Shannon* and HMS *Pearl* who sailed in company for Calcutta, arriving off the mouth of the Ganges on 6th August after picking up further reinforcements at Singapore.

The situation in India was now very grave. A small force of British, Gurkhas and loyal Indians were on the ridge facing Delhi and with inadequate numbers and armament, particularly heavy artillery, were attempting to besiege and capture the city. The Residency at Lucknow was under siege by the mutineers, Cawnpur had fallen to the Nana Sahib with massacre and subsequent atrocity, and though retaken was tenuously held as the base for the relief of Lucknow.

The British strategy was firstly to capture Delhi, next to relieve the siege of the Residency in Lucknow and finally to destroy the remnants of rebellion. Concurrently it was necessary to secure the lines of communication, to prevent as far as possible the spread of rebellion and to preserve the lives of Europeans anywhere and at any time. Indeed this last objective was often the overriding factor so that, whilst men were desperately needed in front of Delhi, it had been necessary to concentrate a force to relieve Cawnpur (where it arrived too late) and then to march on to Lucknow. This force had broken through to the Residency but it was not strong enough to fight its way out with the besieged and had to remain as a reinforcement of the garrison and wait for further relief.

Even in Calcutta, the seat of government, the home of the Governor General of India and the port through which all reinforcements and sea borne supplies must come, there was apprehension at the possibility of a rising of the native population. The Royal Marine Battalion brought by HMS *Shannon* and HMS *Pearl* occupied the fort and HMS *Pearl* was berthed so as to cover the city with her guns and overawe the natives.

Captain Peel, meanwhile, formed a Naval Brigade from HMS *Shannon* and on 14th August set out with ten eight inch guns, two brass 'field pieces' and rocket tubes to join the force at Delhi to provide heavy artillery support. The Brigade was to proceed by river transport as far as Allahabad. Captain Peel and his officers embarked in the river steamer *Chunar* with his 450 men in one 'flat' with the guns, ammunition, clothing and medical comforts in a second. The launch and cutter from HMS *Shannon* were also taken. These flats were large dumb-lighters, of great beam but very shallow draught with a thatched canopy, and were used on the Ganges at all seasons. Whilst the flats were adequate for the seven-week river trip, the engines of the *Chunar* were in poor condition and after one day's steaming she was replaced. Her replacement was of too great a draught to go above Dinajpur and a third steamer had to be found to complete the trip.

Lieutenant Vaughan, First Lieutenant of HMS *Shannon*, had remained in Calcutta with the strange duty of recruiting men from the assembled merchant shipping, then training and bringing forward when ready, a further rifle company to add to the Naval Brigade. He raised nearly 100 men and on 18th September his party embarked for the trip to Allahabad where they arrived on 20th October. Meanwhile Captain Sotheby of HMS *Pearl* had, at the request of the Governor General, also formed a Naval Brigade and on 12th September started for the interior, to be followed on 12th October by a second party which also included a large number of merchant seamen.

Delhi fell to the besieging forces with bitter streetfighting between 14th and 20th September, but Generals Havelock and Outram, having fought their way into the Residency at Lucknow, remained besieged there. The new commander-in-chief, General Sir Colin Campbell, who had recently arrived in India, began the redeployment of his forces and the concentration of an array at Cawnpur for the next attempt to relieve Lucknow. *Shannon*'s Brigade took over the garrison at Allahabad and *Pearl*'s Brigade garrisoned Buxar. *Shannon*'s Brigade was to join the forces at Cawnpur for the relief of Lucknow. *Pearl*'s Brigade was to operate to the east of the River Ghaghara charged with the control of northwest Bengal, safeguarding the provinces of Gorukhpore and Faizabad.

Shannon's Brigade was organised as an artillery unit and two rifle companies. The mountings of the eight-inch guns brought up from the ship were unsuitable for use on land, so at Allahabad they were exchanged for six 24 pdr guns acquired from the Bengal Artillery. Each gun was drawn by a team of thirteen span of oxen and followed by an ammunition cart drawn by three span. An ammunition train followed the whole battery. When the 24 pdr guns were received it was found that, in accordance with local practice, they were not fitted with sights. Under Captain Peel's direction the three Engineer Officers with the Brigade made and fitted sights to the guns. With these it was Peel's boast that the guns were more accurate than any rifle. Peel made a further innovation. He trained his Brigade in the use of dragropes so that, in action, the guns could be manhandled about, sited and fired in the same way as, if a little more slowly than, light horsed artillery.

Captain Sotheby's training problems were very different. His Brigade was organised into infantry and a horsed battery of 'light field pieces' — four 12 pdr brass guns. The Brigade was combed for men who had experience of horses and they were given plenty of riding practice. Astonishingly quickly the sailors learnt to ride and gallop the guns about with the panache, if not the skill, of horse artillery. For the remainder of the Brigade it was a case of drill and musketry, literally musketry, for though the Marines were armed with Minie rifles, the sailors carried old muskets.

Throughout their campaigns the two Naval Brigades wore Naval uniform and kept Naval customs. The officers wore caps (with a neck flap attached) or a type of topee purchased privately, undress coats, white trousers and black shoes, sometimes with spurs, for all the officers bought horses or ponies. The ratings wore loose fitting, large collared blue shirts, open at the neck, over their loose blue trousers, sennet hats, wide brimmed and decorated with a narrow black hat ribbon on which some, at any rate, had embroidered their ship's name. By Captain Peel's orders the men of *Shannon*'s Brigade continued to shave and had to polish their boots each day. In *Pearl*'s Brigade shaving was generally discontinued. Before leaving Calcutta the Naval Brigades drew much equipment from the army. Tents and bedding, waterbottles, haversacks, waterproof clothing and even boots were supplied.

Each officer had a tent to himself, square, with a single pole, double roofed and lined with blue cotton. On opposite sides the upper roof spread into large eaves, under one of which the native servants slept. There were carpets for flooring and charpoys for beds. Similar, but less well-appointed tents were provided for the ratings on a scale of six men to a tent. In the field the tents were carried by elephant, the baggage in ox carts or by camel.

There was no lack of native servants. Each officer engaged a personal retinue, usually a bearer who acted as personal servant and head of household, a waterboy, a groom and a grass cutter for each horse that he owned. Each of the ratings' tents had its two or three servants and there were cooks and barbers as well. When in camp the officers were woken with a cup of tea and enjoyed the luxury of being shaved in bed, sometimes whilst still asleep! This was the usual routine for the Army in India — and the Naval Brigade enjoyed this part of the routine.

Rations were drawn from the Army. Fresh beef or mutton, fresh vegetables, rice, bread, biscuit or flour, and tea, coffee and sugar were usual but, when the circumstances dictated, salt beef and biscuit were all that was issued. The basic diet could be supplemented with fruit and fresh vegetables and anything else that fancy and depth of pocket would allow, purchased from the native bazaar that accompanied the Army wherever it went. Each morning young girls drove herds of goats through the camp, selling milk straight from the udder to anyone who wished to buy. Of course there was rum! Up spirits was piped daily and though the tot was often local arrack it was still swallowed with avidity. The officers enjoyed an occasional bottle of brandy, bought, when obtainable, from the bazaar.

The men of the Naval Brigades showed in full measure the sailors' partiality for pets and in short order dogs, cats, monkeys, parrots, guinea pigs, mongooses, pigs, goats and chickens were acquired. The goats and chickens were certainly required to earn their keep and supply fresh milk and eggs, but whether the pigs ended as roast pork is not known. However these pets certainly added to the singularity of the Naval Brigade in camp and on the march.

Shannon's Brigade on the march were a strange and un-military spectacle. Led by the ship's band and fiddlers, with mounted officers riding up and down the column, they rolled along singing sea shanties. First a rifle company, then the rum cart under guard, then the heavy guns drawn by elephants or oxen and the ammunition carts with pets everywhere on the guns and limbers and running under foot, then the native followers, baggage camels and assorted livestock and finally another rifle company bringing up the rear.

The Army took a great interest in these men "four feet tall, four feet wide with long hair and dragging heavy guns" as a future Field Marshal described them, and once they had been in action together had the greatest admiration for the sailors. In camp it was a popular diversion to watch *Shannon*'s Brigade at gun drill and in action nothing pleased the soldiers more than to have the Brigade with them. Regimental Bands often paid the Brigade the compliment of playing them into camp at the end of the days march. When it could, the Brigade returned the compliment and on one occasion a famous Highland Regiment was led into camp by six fiddlers from *Shannon* with a 'stamp and go'.

The Brigades were provided with very necessary assistance in coping with the difficulties of campaigning in India. Each Brigade was allocated two Army Officers, one to act as interpreter and the other as baggage master. These officers can have had no easy task and must have required much tact and lively senses of humour. Certainly there are nothing but laudatory references to their services.

Both *Shannon*'s and *Pearl*'s Brigades began their active participation in field operations at the end of October 1857. They were never to campaign together so each has a separate history. As *Shannon*'s Brigade took part in the main campaign their story will be told first.

HMS *SHANNON*'S NAVAL BRIGADE

On October 24th 1857, the first detachment of the Naval Brigade of 100 men under Lieutenant Vaughan (the First Lieutenant) with the guns marched from Allahabad for Cawnpur, followed four days later by Captain Peel with the second company, leaving in garrison a party of 150, including the sick and the band. The second detachment joined a convoy under the command of Lietenant Colonel Pownell of the 53rd Regiment marching up the Grand Trunk Road and on 31st October had camped after a march of twelve miles. In the afternoon intelligence came in that a rebel force was in the vicinity with the intention of either attacking Fatehpur or crossing ahead of the convoy to join the rebel forces around Lucknow. Camp was immediately broken up and the whole convoy marched on to Fatehpur, arriving at midnight.

The enemy were reported to be about 24 miles away near the village of Khujwa. Colonel Pownell decided to attack and a force of just over 500, including 100 men of the Naval Brigade and two 9 pdr guns of the Bengal Artillery, marched out at dawn. At about 1400 the force was advancing up the road, the advance guard in skirmishing order followed by the rest of the force in column, when the enemy were seen positioned on either side of the road down which three guns were sited to fire:

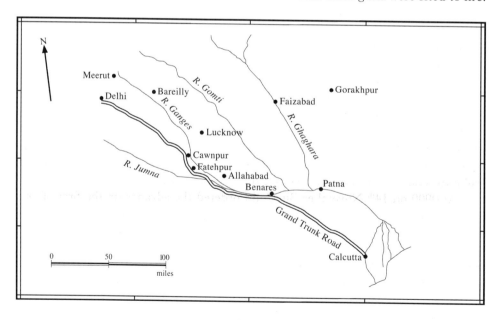

The route along the Grand Trunk Road taken by the crew of Peel's Brigade

two well up and the third further back covering a bridge. Colonel Pownell extended his force to the right and attacked, Pownell himself leading the charge at the two forward guns, to die as they were taken. Captain Peel succeeded to the command, having led a successful attack on the enemy positions in front of the Naval Brigade. Leaving them to hold the ground they had won and to secure that flank, Captain Peel collected all the fresh men he could. He led an attack, which, breaking the enemy line, wheeled and drove them successively from their positions. The rebels broke and ran, leaving Captain Peel's force to occupy their camp. The exhaustion of the force precluded pursuit so, after collecting his dead and wounded and destroying the enemy camp Captain Peel marched back towards Fatehpur and bivouacked for the night. For the loss of 95 men killed and wounded two guns had been captured, 300 out of the 4000 rebels killed and the remainder dispersed. To make the victory complete the third enemy gun was found abandoned and brought in the next day.

Captain Peel's force, with raised morale, marched on to Cawnpur, where with the arrival of Sir Colin Campbell on 3ʳᵈ November the final dispositions for the relief of Lucknow were made. Sir Colin found that a large force of rebels from Gwalior were threatening Cawnpur but decided that Lucknow must be relieved. He left General Windham with 500 men, including two guns of the Naval Brigade to defend that city and the essential Bridge of Boats over the Ganges, the capture or destruction of which would cut the lines of communication and trap Sir Colin between Cawnpur and Lucknow.

With the remainder of his force, Sir Colin advanced on Lucknow and on 12ᵗʰ November reached the Alambagh on the outskirts of the city. Here he was met by Mr Kavanagh, a civilian, who earned a VC by making his way in disguise from the Residency through the rebel lines with a despatch from General Outram. In it he suggested, in the light of his own and General Havelock's experiences, that the best line of approach to the Residency was to avoid the narrow streets of the city, instead circling in from the southeast through a series of palaces and large buildings interlinked by parks and open ground. This suggestion was adopted and Sir Colin issued his orders accordingly. On 13ᵗʰ November Sir Colin held an inspection of his forces, his first chance to see his assembled army and, for most of the men he was to lead into action, their first chance to see their new commander-in-chief.

At 0900 on 14ᵗʰ November Sir Colin ordered the advance on the first of the palaces with a forward wave of his arm and the order "There is your bed — take and lie in it". As the troops approached the walls of the Dilkusha they came under fire from a battery of six guns and from matchlock and musketry fire. The guns of the Naval Brigade were brought into action and quickly the enemy retreated to the next large building, the Martinière. The attack was carried forward but again when the rebels opened fire the artillery, including the guns of the Naval Brigade, were rushed into action and when the infantry resumed their advance the rebels evacuated their positions and retreated to the next stronghold, the Sikanderbagh, a stronger building than either that had so far fallen. Sir Colin called a halt to the advance and spent the day securing his position. November 15th was spent bringing up the heavy baggage of the Army from the Alambagh while the poachers and butchers in the Army were kept busy for the camp in a park swarming with deer — dinner that night was venison or peacock or even parrot!

The night of the 15th/16th was noisy with the Naval Brigade, as a deception, firing off to the left along an approach that the rebels expected to be used. At daybreak, after a canteen of tea and carrying three pounds of salt beef and twelve biscuits a man as three days rations, the Army moved off towards the Sikanderbagh. Helped by an early morning mist and the success of the deception, the Army passed over two natural defensive positions unopposed and marched on until fired upon from the outer works of the Sikanderbagh. The artillery, including the Naval Brigade, were brought up to breach the walls while some of the infantry moved round to seal off the escape routes. After about an hour and a half, a small breach in the wall was made and in a bloody assault this was forced. The Sikanderbagh was taken in even bloodier hand to hand fighting. Over 1800 dead rebels were found within the walls.

The next objective, about half a mile further on, was the Shah Nujeef, a mosque surrounded by a garden and enclosed within a very strong wall, the whole most artfully prepared for defence. Although it was now early afternoon Sir Colin determined that it must be taken that day and moved against it.

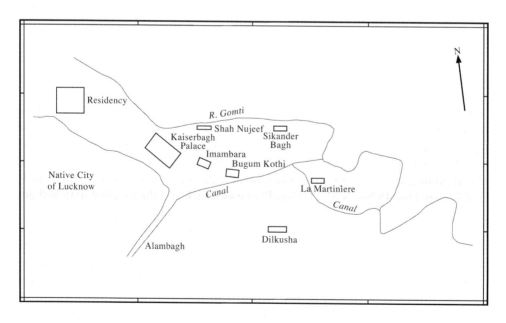

Lucknow, the city relieved in November 1857 during the Indian Mutiny

At first the artillery could make little impression on the walls. Captain Peel therefore ordered the Naval Brigade forward, and manning drag ropes the guns were moved up to within about twenty yards of the walls, according to Sir Colin's despatch "very much as if he had been laying the *Shannon* alongside an enemy's frigate". Here the Naval Brigade remained for three hours, covered by musketry fire from the 93rd Regiment, and at this close range maintained a steady and accurate fire. At this range the shot pierced the walls too cleanly and no practicable breach was made. At dusk, when all assaults on the walls had been beaten off, Sir Colin was about to abandon the assault for the day. To provide cover for the withdrawal Captain Peel brought his two rocket tubes into action. At this moment a Sergeant of the 93rd Regiment discovered a small, concealed and undefended breach. Led by a small party of the 93rd, infantry rushed the breach to find that the rebels, terrified by the rockets, were fleeing the defences. The Shah Nujeef was taken and the Army bivouacked for the night where they stood. Captain Peel was knighted and two officers and two ratings of the Naval Brigade were awarded the Victoria Cross for their work that afternoon.

Only two fortified positions now remained between Sir Colin's forces and the defences of the Residency. On 17th November the guns of the Naval brigade were brought forward and at about 1500, after a long bombardment had silenced the fire of the defenders, the first objective was rushed and the attacking troops, having taken their objective, charged on to the second building where they were stopped by the walls. The engineers were brought forward to blow a breach, the rebels fled and the Residency was relieved.

Sir Colin held a very narrow corridor between the Alambagh and the Residency, threatened on both sides by superior numbers of rebels and knew that his communications with Cawnpur were also threatened. There could be no question of holding the Residency and clearing Lucknow of rebels with the forces at his disposal. He determined to evacuate, leave an advanced force encamped at the Alambagh to hold this invaluable springboard for the final clearance of Lucknow and to contain the rebel forces there. After a day of preparation, the evacuation began on 19th November when the women and children were brought out and continued until the night of the 22nd, when under cover of diversionary fire from the Naval Brigade which lasted for 48 hours, the Union Flag was struck and the garrison marched out unopposed.

Leaving General Outram with a force of 4000 men, 25 guns and 10 mortars to hold the Alambagh, Sir Colin with some 3000 to guard the 2000 women, children, sick and wounded set out for Cawnpur on 27th November. That night Sir Colin learnt that heavy firing had been heard from Cawnpur and ordered a forced march next day. On the march, at about 1200, a message was received that all was not well at Cawnpur. Leaving the infantry with the convoy, the cavalry and artillery pushed on and Sir Colin with his escort galloped on to find that though the bridge of boats over the Ganges was intact, the city of Cawnpur had fallen to a rebel force and General Windham was holding an entrenched position covering the end of the bridge.

Windham had been defeated by the Gwalior contingent of 25 000 rebels. During the battle the Cawnpur detachment of the Naval Brigade had been heavily engaged and came close to disaster. Their two guns had been brought into the firing line to engage the advancing rebels at close range. There was considerable confusion, the guns were left without infantry support and, there being insufficient time to harness up the bullock teams, the guns were overrun by rebels. The gun teams and the infantry rallied, charged back and retook the guns. With the help of the infantry who improvised traces from their rifle slings the guns were hurried away. Later, during the general retreat through the city to the entrenchment, one gun overturned at the corner of a narrow street and had to be abandoned. However in the early hours of the morning the gun team set out, found the gun, demolished the obstruction, righted the gun and brought it safely back without a shot being fired.

Sir Colin now faced the problem of passing his force, together with the women, children, sick and wounded from Lucknow over the bridge of boats to the entrenchment at Cawnpur. He placed the guns and rockets of the Naval Brigade under Captain Peel in position on the river bank with orders to dominate the rebel artillery and, supported by the cross fire from the entrenchment, to protect the crossing. The rebel guns were silenced by the accurate fire brought upon them, and their infantry much distracted by the rockets. The column made its way across the bridge without loss, concentrated in a position based on Windham's entrenchment.

It took four days to arrange for the evacuation of the women and children to Allahabad *en route* for Calcutta, and it was a great relief both to the evacuees and to the commander-in-chief when the column marched out. During these four days reinforcements (including a further contingent of the Naval Brigade brought up from Allahabad) reached Cawnpur. Sir Colin, by 6th December when he attacked the rebels in Cawnpur, had a force of about 10 000 as against 25 000 rebels.

The rebel position was centred on the city of Cawnpur, their left flank resting on the Ganges with their right, though covered by a canal, stretched out into the plain. If the right wing could be broken, one of the two available lines of retreat might be cut. Having examined the rebel positions, Sir Colin planned to attack the right in force after bombarding the centre and left in an attempt to convince the rebels that this would be the point of his attack.

After a two hour cannonade the attack was launched. Captain Peel brought forward his 24 pdr guns into the skirmishing line at the canal bridge, rushed one across and opened fire to cover the infantry crossing. With the infantry across and redeployed, the advance continued and the rebels broke and fled. In his despatch Sir Colin reported,

> "The canal bridge was quickly passed, Captain Peel leading over it with a heavy gun...I must here draw attention to the manner in which the heavy

24 pdr guns were impelled and managed by Captain Peel and his gallant sailors. Through the extraordinary energy with which the latter have been worked, their guns have been constantly in advance throughout our late operations, from the relief of Lucknow until now, as if they were light field pieces, and the service rendered by them in clearing our front has been incalculable. On this occasion there was the sight beheld of 24 pdr guns advancing with the first line of skirmishers."

The broken rebel force was pursued for about ten miles, their camp was taken intact and 17 guns and the ammunition train were captured.

That night the British troops bivouacked where they were, and having outrun the commissariat had no provisions. Fortunately the battalion lying next to the Naval Brigade had had the forethought to carry with them a supply of rum which, next morning, they shared with the sailors. Not to be outdone the sailors cut out and slaughtered oxen from their gun teams. Crudely butchered, the beef was roasted over campfires and shared so that, at least, the friendly battalion and the Naval Brigade breakfasted well.

Sir Colin's next move, made on 24th December, was to march on Fatehgarh, the only town between Cawnpur and Delhi still held by the rebels and through which a large convoy of ammunition and stores must come. The rebels concentrated to meet him at the bridge at Kali Nadi which they attempted to destroy but only damaged. On 1st January 1858 a small force was thrown across the river to secure a bridgehead. Working through the night the bridge was repaired ready for a further advance. On the morning of 2nd January the rebels attacked the bridgehead and were held on its perimeter by rifle fire supported by the guns of the Naval Brigade. A rebel gun was making very good practice on the bridge. Peel ordered forward one gun and requested his First Lieutenant to destroy it. Laying his gun himself Lieutenant Vaughan hit his target with his third shot and destroyed the gun's limber with his fifth. Sir Colin brought the main body of troops over the bridge. The infantry quickly broke the rebel forces who were pursued for about seven miles towards Fatehgarh. At nightfall the pursuit was called off and the victors enjoyed another cold and supperless bivouac.

Fatehgarh was occupied without opposition the next day. This town had been the principle site of artillery gun carriage manufacture in India, and the factory and its stock of seasoned timber was found intact. Captain Peel, knowing that there would be a pause in the campaign, turned a part of the Naval Brigade to the construction of field carriages for the six 8 inch guns left at Allahabad. The dismounted guns were to be floated up-river from Allahabad to Cawnpur, where they would be married to the carriages brought there from Fatehgarh.

The rebels were concentrated at Ramgunga, about eight miles from Fatehgarh, where they had destroyed the bridge. With the twin objectives of pinning this rebel force in position and threatening an advance towards Bareilly (a rebel stronghold),

Sir Colin sent a force, including a detachment of the Naval Brigade, to face them and to see whether the bridge could be repaired. This confrontation continued for a month, broken by occasional artillery duels.

The bridge was found to be beyond repair with the resources available. Captain Peel's restless activity drove on the detachment of the Naval Brigade. Using a boat they found, they rigged an endless whip from bank to bank and built a raft large enough to carry 50 men or a field gun across the river. Though their activity may have helped deceive the rebels, it was otherwise wasted for neither were used.

At the beginning of February Sir Colin moved his forces back to Cawnpur, concentrating for the final retaking of Lucknow. By 11th February all detachments of the Naval Brigade were together at Cawnpur and next day moved into camp at Onao, about fifteen miles towards Lucknow. Daily they drilled with their 'new' 8 inch guns and on Sunday 15th February held an athletics meeting for their own, and the Army's amusement. There were horse, pony, foot and sack races, and the finale was a team buffalo race with two sailors mounted and six pushing, pulling, encouraging and steering their beast to the finishing line. Captain Peel took a leading part and was roundly cheered when he fell from his horse.

Lucknow was now the major centre of the revolt and was defended by a force of rebels conservatively estimated at 100 000. Sir Colin's army numbered 20 000 and a force of 9000 Gurkhas of the Royal Nepalese Army was moving down from Nepal to join, as allies, in the taking of Lucknow. The British army moved slowly towards Lucknow and halted to wait for the Gurkhas when a days march short of General Outram's position at the Alambagh. It was here that Captain Peel heard of his KCB.

Sir Colin planned a partial encirclement of Lucknow, passing a division, under General Outram, to the northern bank of the Gomati to cut the rebels' main line of retreat and to provide a diversionary attack. He would lead the main attack through a line of defended palaces and houses, which he had skirted during his relief of the Residency, heading for the Kaiser Bagh, the rebels' main citadel. These two attacks would be mutually supporting. The Naval Brigade with its heavy guns and rockets formed a part of Sir Colin's force. By 8th March the dispositions of the force were complete and next day the operations began.

Early in the morning the guns opened fire to breach the walls of the Martinière, the first of the fortified and defended buildings. Although the guns of the Naval Brigade were extremely effective as usual, the rockets because of age and prolonged exposure to the heat were so inaccurate as to be useless. While the bombardment was in progress Peel was ordered to open a further breach. He sited two of the guns well within musket shot of the walls. When satisfied with the position, Peel moved to an exposed spot on a small knoll about fifty yards to the left to observe the fire. Here he remained, oblivious to the musket fire aimed at him, until he was hit and seriously wounded in the thigh. He was carried from the field and the command of the Naval Brigade passed to Vaughan (recently promoted Commander).

At about 1400 the breaches were ready and an assault was ordered. The Martinière was captured with only slight resistance, the bulk of the rebels having retired in the face of the bombardment. They occupied a line of earthworks to the rear but, under the flanking fire from General Outram's batteries, retired to the next fortified buildings, Bank's House and the Begum Kothi, which commanded the line of advance.

On the morning of 10th March the Naval Brigade guns were sited to breach the walls of Bank's House and when this task was accomplished and a successful assault mounted the guns were brought forward and sited for the attack on the Begum Kothi. The field of fire was obstructed by a large tree. Commander Vaughan and a carpenter from *Shannon* went forward and, under heavy fire from the walls, felled it. When the breaches in the outer wall were nearly practicable Commander Vaughan was ordered forward to breach two inner defence walls and then the wall of an adjacent *serai*. He brought forward two guns and a party of picked rifle shots. The riflemen kept the breach clear and kept down the fire from the loopholed walls of the *serai*. It was thought that it would take some time to breach three walls in succession, but the first two or three shots showed that at 100-yards range the 8 inch balls penetrated all three. One gun became unserviceable with trunnion trouble, but the other made excellent practice and all three walls were quickly breached. As the 93rd Highlanders and the 4th Punjab Rifles assaulted the Begum Kothi and the Gurkhas the *serai*, the Naval Brigade rushed a gun forward on to the road between the two buildings to engage and silence a rebel battery firing on the advancing troops.

Sir Colin now halted the main advance while he consolidated his position and re-organised his forces consequent to the arrival of the Maharajah Jung Bahadur with his Ghurkha Army. By the evening of 13th March he was ready to attack the Imambara, the last building before the Kaiser Bagh. The Naval Brigade guns were positioned within 30 yards of its walls and began a destructive bombardment which lasted all night, the thick masonry walls, two or three in succession, being pierced by every shot. At 1900 on 14th the Imambara quickly fell to the assault, the rebel garrison, hotly pursued, fleeing to shelter in the Kaiser Bagh. Well up the pursuit was Lieutenant Hay with a party of sailors. They took a rebel gun, turned it on its previous owners and opened a rapid and destructive fire.

It had been Sir Colin's intention to halt his advance after securing the Imambara, expecting that the Kaiser Bagh would be the most difficult fortification to take. However the rapidity of the pursuit from the Imambara carried the British forces into its outworks. Sir Colin pushed on and the elan of his men carried them into the Kaiser Bagh. This was a rectangular enclosure containing a number of interlinked courtyards and gardens in which were small buildings and pavilions. The clearing of these was difficult and dangerous. Lieutenant Stirling, of the Royal Marine Light

Infantry (RMLI), and *Shannon*'s Marine Detachment earned the praise of the army for their part in this work.

Fighting in and around Lucknow was to continue for another five days, though the Naval Brigade was not seriously engaged. In fact their active part in the campaign was finished. On 1st April, having handed over their guns to the Army, they began their march back to Calcutta. When about half way back they were halted and, in the face of a rebel threat went into garrison to dominate the area. They remained in this employment until August when they were released once more and continued their march to Calcutta. After a rapturous reception here the Naval Brigade rejoined HMS *Shannon* and sailed for England on 15th September. But not commanded by Captain Sir William Peel VC, KCB. Whilst recovering from his wound he had contracted smallpox, from which, on 27th April he died at Cawnpur.

One of his officers wrote, "We do not consider ourselves as the Naval Brigade nor as *Shannon*'s Brigade but as Peel's Brigade". If that was so then this posthumous tribute written by a fellow Captain who served as a volunteer with the Naval Brigade seems aptly to describe the leader and honours him and his men.

> "Brave but humane, daring but forethoughtful, he so perfected the means at his disposal that when they were brought into the field they were irresistible and did as much as men and material could do."

HMS *PEARL'S* NAVAL BRIGADE

On 7th November 1857 the first and second contingents of *Pearl*'s Brigade were united at Siwan, a village in the middle of the district of Saran, the triangular area formed by the junction of the Rivers Ghaghara and Gandak. On 10th November, leaving a small force of six officers and 44 ratings at Siwan, Captain Sotheby moved to Myrwah and encamped there, to be joined by the Ramdal Regiment of Gurkhas of the Royal Nepalese Army.

The Brigade remained in camp at Myrwah for about a month, carrying out daily drills and exercises in preparation for a future campaign: as yet the force was not strong enough to take offensive action. Indeed intelligence indicated that the scattered rebel forces were concentrating and it was thought wise to entrench the camp. No attack came, though there were a series of spy scares, arrests and summary executions — arrest, trial, sentence, execution and interment usually following each other within a few hours. On 27th November Colonel Rowcroft, who had commanded the 8th Native Infantry that had mutinied at Dinajpur, arrived to command the 'Saran Field Force' that now consisted of the Naval Brigade, the Ramdal Regiment of Gurkhas and a detachment of 50 Sikhs.

On the evening of 12th December news arrived of a rebel raid on the magazine at Guthnee, on the north bank of the Ghaghara. Half the force marched towards the enemy who, however, retreated across the river before contact could be made.

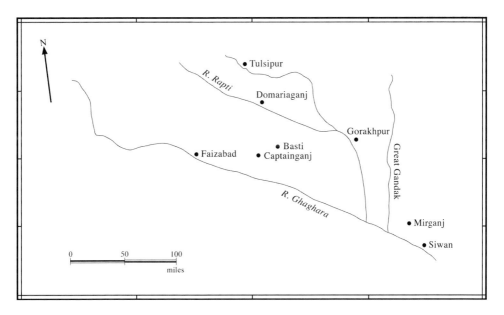

*The area of north India in which the 1st and 2nd contingent
of HMS Pearl campaigned in 1857*

Meanwhile the camp had been struck and everything prepared for a rapid move. Eventually the tents were re-pitched and for a week the force settled back into a routine of daily drills and exercises.

Intelligence was received on 19th December that a rebel force was advancing from the northeast. Leaving only four officers and 21 men in his camp at Myrwah, Colonel Rowcroft moved towards the enemy line of advance and camped in a defensible position on higher ground. Here, until Christmas Eve, the force was busy entrenching the encampment. To deceive the enemy, dummy guns were sited. These and the four guns of the Naval Brigade were kept covered. On 24th December the enemy were reported to be approaching the camp and the force stood to under arms eagerly awaiting the attack. To everyone's disappointment, apart from reconnoitring cavalry patrols, there was no sign of the enemy and the force stood down. Next morning the Goruknath Regiment of the Royal Nepalese Army joined the force, but needed a day of rest after their march. The enemy made no move so Christmas Day passed peacefully.

At 0800 on 26th December Colonel Rowcroft marched out to attack. The enemy were found, at about 1000, positioned across the road about six miles from the camp. The force deployed into line behind a screen of skirmishers of Royal Marines and sailors, and halted when their guns were within range. For about two hours the guns kept up a steady fire on the enemy positions, making excellent practice. One shot (lucky or aimed?) was acclaimed as knocking a Rajah off his elephant. An attempt to outflank the force was broken up by shrapnel as was a cavalry attack on the skirmishing line. Then the general advance was sounded and the force moved on, pushing the rebels before them until the enemy camp, partially entrenched, was reached. An immediate charge drove the enemy out of his defences and into retreat abandoning his tented camp, two guns and all his provisions and stores. Rowcroft halted whilst the booty was secured and the tents burnt, then set out in pursuit. At about 1600 the force came up with the enemy rear guard at a river crossing near Mujhowlee. Rifle fire from the Royal Marine detachment hastened the retreat and secured the capture of another gun, its limber and two tumbrils full of ammunition. The enemy was estimated at 6000, including 1200 regular sepoys and 150 cavalry.

That night the force bivouacked on the outskirts of Mujhowlee. Next day half of the force with two guns crossed the river to burn the nearby houses of two prominent rebels. Meanwhile the tents and baggage were brought forward from Myrwah and the whole force went into camp at Mujhowlee. Next day, 28th December, was a grizzly and perhaps unique occasion for the Royal Navy. A sepoy of the 10th Regiment of Native Infantry, captured after the engagement was executed, was blown from the muzzle of one of the guns.

After this engagement the rebels evacuated the area and life for the force became a routine of marching, resting in camp and minor punitive actions of burning the property of known rebels. Despite the fatigue of marching and daily training, the Naval Brigade enjoyed the interlude and they enjoyed sport of a kind. Musket bullets were melted down into lead shot with which, using their muskets as shotguns, they hunted snipe and peafowl. The junior officers also risked their necks practising 'pig sticking' with pariah dogs as the quarry.

On 6th February 1858 the Naval Brigade exchanged their muskets for Enfield rifles. Daily thereafter they practised in the new loading drill and judging distance as they now had a weapon with adjustable sights, accurate to nine hundred yards.

Jung Bahadur had marched 9000 Ghurkhas of the Royal Nepalese Army into India as an allied force to assist Sir Colin Campbell in the retaking of Lucknow, now the major centre of rebel resistance. To rendezvous with Sir Colin the Ghurkha army had to cross the River Ghaghara. Colonel Rowcroft was ordered to build a bridge of boats for the crossing at Gai Ghat, about fifty miles upstream, where the Ghurkhas were encamped. About 150 river craft were collected and the river steamer *Jumna* was requisitioned, armed and readied for the passage upriver which, since the south bank was in rebel hands with strong forts in dominating positions, was likely to be opposed. There was also a rebel force of 5000 encamped opposite Gai Ghat which would threaten the bridge building.

Captain Sotheby with 160 officers and men of the Naval Brigade embarked in the *Jumna* and the river craft and, with the remainder of the force marching on the north bank, proceeded up river. It was a difficult trip – without a pilot, into the current and a strong head wind and through a sandstorm – but, averaging twelve miles daily, they were close to the first fort on 17th February. Captain Sotheby landed the Naval Brigade, Gurkhas were brought over the river and the fort was attacked. The initial attack failed but when the *Jumna* bombarded the fort and the Gurkhas were seen to be working round to surround the fort the rebels panicked and bolted. The force pushed on and two days later were within four miles of Gai Ghat. That evening the second fort was found to be abandoned and was burnt. Next day the force marched out to attack the rebels in the open nearby. In a sharp engagement during which the Royal Marines captured and turned a gun, which they used to great effect, the rebel force of 2500 was driven off. Two more guns were captured and the area was cleared of rebels. The bridge of boats was quickly constructed without opposition.

Leaving Jung Bahadur to cross the Ghaghara for Lucknow, taking with him the Ramdal Regiment, Colonel Rowcroft moved the remainder of his force forward towards Faizabad on the north bank, reaching the town of Amorah on 2nd March. They were joined by the Bengal Yeomanry Cavalry: 250 mounted European volunteers drawn from planters and unemployed officers from disbanded or mutinous sepoy regiments. The Naval Brigade cheered them into camp, more delighted perhaps after four months to greet fellow Europeans than at the accretion of strength, important though this was.

The road to Faizabad was dominated by a strong fort at Belwah and on the afternoon of 2nd March Colonel Rowcroft attempted to surprise and seize it. The guns of the Naval Brigade were not heavy enough to breach the walls, even when brought up to 'grape shot range' and after two hours, as darkness fell, the force withdrew and bivouacked for the night. Next day they returned to camp at Amorah. Aware that the rebels from Faizabad were advancing in strength they began to dig an entrenchment.

Throughout the 4th March, Colonel Rowcroft received reports that an attack was imminent. At 0100 the following day, he got his force under arms, struck camp, and at 0730 marched out. He disposed his forces about a mile from the camp. The infantry were drawn up in a line, one deep, across the road with cavalry on each flank and the guns in a battery in the centre of the line.

The rebels advanced down the road and at 0900 opened fire with an 18 pdr gun which outranged the guns of the Naval Brigade. The whole force, therefore, advanced until their guns were within range of the enemy. For about an hour the rival artillery fought a duel and the skirmishers disputed the ground between the forces. The rebels now attempted to outflank the force on the right. Colonel Rowcroft changed front, two of the Naval Brigade guns limbered up and galloped to the support of the right hand squadron of the Bengal Yeomanry Cavalry who charged, took the rebels in flank and forced them to retreat. Colonel Rowcroft now reformed his infantry two deep, advanced on the rebels and when within range engaged them with volley fire from the prone position. The rebels countered with an outflanking movement on the left, aimed at the camp. The left hand squadron of the Bengal Yeomanry Cavalry supported by the other two guns of the Naval Brigade and the Royal Marines broke up this attack. The rebels began to retire, a bayonet charge turned the retirement into a rout and the whole force pursued the rebels for about five miles, capturing seven guns. By 1400 simple exhaustion brought the pursuit to an end and the rebels drew off under desultory fire from the Naval Brigade guns. Colonel Rowcroft with 1700 infantry, 250 cavalry and four guns had defeated a rebel force of 10 000, about half being trained sepoys with ten guns. One officer of the Naval Brigade had been killed and nine men wounded.

The force returned to the campsite at Amorah and pitched camp. Here they were to remain until 26th April, busy training and strengthening the entrenchments. False alarms of rebel advances were frequent, each alarm meaning 'an excursion without'. On 26th March a further reinforcement of three companies of the 13th Regiment commanded by Major Cox arrived. On 17th April there was a sharp engagement with a party of rebels that had ventured too close to Amorah and a gun was captured. The temperature at noon now reached 110 degrees Fahrenheit and Colonel Rowcroft made preparations to pass the hot weather at Amorah. Huts were being built and the daily drills and exercises were relaxed and took place in the evenings only. But in six days everything changed.

On 25th April intelligence came in that rebels were advancing, in three columns, to attack the camp. Colonel Rowcroft, as always, moved out to meet these attacks. He split his force in two, the left wing under Captain Sotheby and Major Cox, commanding the right wing himself. The left wing was first in action against the centre column of rebels that were pushed back after a sharp engagement and followed for about two miles. Captain Sotheby then retired and swinging left engaged the left hand column of rebels, being joined by Brigadier Rowcroft (news of whose promotion had just been received), but only for a short while. The right hand column of rebels was moving to attack the camp and Brigadier Rowcroft moved off to attack them. Having driven off the left hand column Captain Sotheby marched towards the sound of firing on his right. The intervention of the Naval Brigade's rockets assisted in routing the rebels.

Next morning, 26th April, intelligence was received that a rebel force had attacked and been beaten off by the small garrison at the town of Basti some 22 miles in the rear of the force, that considerable numbers of rebels were moving towards that town and that the garrison, in the face of this threat, was retiring towards Brigadier Rowcroft's position. The force spent that day destroying the entrenchments, burst all their captured guns, struck camp and at 2200 started on a night march to join, at Captainganj, the troops retiring from Basti. After a nine-hour march the forces met and went into camp. On 28th April a report was received that 1000 rebels had occupied the fort of Nuggar some seven miles away. Brigadier Rowcroft sent Major

Cox with a mixed detachment of 500 men, including 90 of the Naval Brigade with two guns and rockets to deal with them. After some sharp fighting the rebels were defeated and bundled out of the fort.

Until 6th May the force remained in camp at Captainganj, then, to prevent a rebel occupation of Basti, marched on that town. The rebels withdrew and the force settled their headquarters there for the hot weather and monsoon seasons, building a hutted camp as a base from which flying columns marched out to attack rebel forces reported in Gorakhpur and Faizabad districts and from which the detachments scattered to dominate the area were relieved in rotation. Two days after the arrival at Basti, Jung Bahadar with his Gurkha army passed through on their return from the taking of Lucknow. The Goruknath Regiment now returned to Nepalese command and marched home.

Apart from the alarms and excursions of the flying columns with which detachments of the Naval Brigade played a distinguished part in seven engagements, the depleted force settled into an easy routine. The Naval Brigade expected to be recalled to their ship but made the best of the opportunities for rest and relaxation. The Chaplain organised and established a library and reading room and the other officers organised cricket matches, athletic competitions and race meetings. In the evenings there were 'theatricals'.

As the monsoon season ended hard training for field service was resumed. The force had been reinforced by a further wing of the 13th Light Infantry under Lord Mark Kerr and the Ferozepore Regiment of Sikhs under the redoubtable Lt Colonel Brasyer VC, whose name was to be, in time, incorporated in the title of the Regiment. The force was readied for the final campaign of the Indian Mutiny.

The one remaining rebel army, commanded by Bala Rao, the Nana Sahib's brother, occupied the country to the north and east of Lucknow in the Himalayan foothills. The broken and disorganised remains of the other rebel armies were slowly making attempts to join him. The commander-in-chief, Sir Colin Campbell, planned a three-pronged attack to clear the area and destroy the rebels. With his main force he would march in from the west, General Sir Hope Grant would advance from the south with a large cavalry force and from the southeast would come Brigadier Rowcroft with his field force. To shorten operations the scattered forts and strongholds in rebel hands would have to be subdued quickly and to this end a part of the seige train was to be brought up from Lucknow to be worked by the Naval Brigade.

On 16th November the force left its quarters at Basti and advanced to Captainganj where it halted and waited for the scattered detachments to rejoin. On 23rd November, the force marched off, heading for Domariaganj where they intended to cross the River Rapti. Whilst on the march the force was joined by a light field battery of Madras Artillery that brought the first instalment of the siege train, two 5½-inch mortars.

On 25th November, the advance guard came upon enemy pickets at about 0900. The 13th Light Infantry, a squadron of the Bengal Yeomanry Cavalry and two of the light field pieces made an immediate attack. This developed into a running fight that drove the enemy back for four miles into and over the Rapti. There was no ford so a great many of the rebels were drowned. That evening two of the Naval Brigade guns were sited on the riverbank to cover the building of a bridge of boats.

On 2nd December an enemy force of some 3000 men and 6 guns was reported in camp about nine miles away and about to attempt to cross the river to join Bala Rao. On 3rd December a detachment of 350 men of the 13th, 200 Sikhs, 70 Bengal Yeomanry and four guns (two from the Naval Brigade) attacked. The rebels stood their ground in their trenches in the face of the artillery for nearly two hours while the infantry worked round the flanks. Under this threat the rebels broke, ran into the protection of the surrounding forest and dispersed. By 1500 the action was over and the detachment rejoined the main force.

Next day the work on the bridge was finished. The whole force crossed the river and marched on to Intwa where it pitched camp to await the arrival of the siege train. This arrived on 18th December. The Naval Brigade was immediately reorganised into an artillery unit. Besides the four 12 pdr guns with which they had started the seamen manned one 8-inch mortar, two 18 pdr guns and their two rocket tubes. The Royal Marine detachment manned two 8-inch mortars and two 5½-inch mortars.

There was little time to exercise with the new weapons. The force was held in camp by heavy rain and waterlogged ground on 19th December but marched out next day. Two days of marching and it was in touch with the other two columns and in contact with a rebel army of 20 000 with 20 guns drawn up in a position based on the strong fort at Tulsipur, with its flanks resting on fortified villages.

At 0300 on 23rd December the 53rd Regiment, 700 strong, joined the force from Sir Hope Grant. At 0900 the whole force struck camp, crossed the River Rapti and formed up in line, field artillery in the centre, cavalry on the flanks and the siege train in the rear. With a strong force of skirmishers to the front the advance began at 1200 and at 1230 the first shot was fired. Despite the difficulties of the ground, Captain Sotheby with the four 12 pdrs and the rockets managed to keep close up with the skirmishers and for the next two hours maintained a heavy fire on the enemy line. This drove the rebels back into a line of trenches. Brigadier Rowcroft ordered his cavalry, with infantry support, to turn the flanks and brought forward the siege train, drawn by elephants, to fire upon the fort and the fortified villages. By 1600 these had been taken by assault and the rebels broke and ran. A three-hour pursuit ended at nightfall and the force bivouacked near the fort.

Heavy rain fell during the night, the countryside was swamped and the whole force spent Christmas Eve in the bivouac. On Christmas Day they marched back to camp and settled in, expecting to enjoy the Christmas dinner that, by noon, was prepared and cooking. Sir Hope Grant was no Father Christmas. At noon he galloped into camp and incontinently despatched the force in pursuit of the rebels, believed to be escaping eastward.

Having great difficulty moving the siege train across roadless country cut up by dykes and *nullahs* Brigadier Rowcroft led a forced march, sleeping rough in the open each night. His route circled back to Intra where he joined Hope Grant on 27th December. The siege train had proved to be a hindrance and was ordered back to Domariaganj. On 29th December, having rested men and animals for a day, Hope Grant began the mad chase after the fugitive sepoys who were scattering and hiding in the forest. For three days the exhausting marches continued — quite fruitlessly — and were called off on 31st December.

On 1st January 1859 hostilities were officially brought to an end, but the Naval Brigade was allowed no rest. On 2nd January it received its orders to return to HMS *Pearl*. The guns were hastily transferred to units in Hope Grant's force and on 3rd January, marching light, they set off. Allahabad was reached after ten days marching (with Sunday rests) with the proud claim that on one day they covered twenty-six miles and on another eighteen. At Allahabad the Viceroy, Lord Canning, welcomed them with a laudatory General Order.

At last the Naval Brigade was able to enjoy a well-earned rest. They embarked on a river steamer and flats and sailed down river to reach Calcutta on 2nd February. Eleven days later, after the feting and banqueting, HMS *Pearl* sailed for home where, just ten days after arrival she paid off.

Bibliography

Collier, R. (1966) *The Indian Mutiny*. Fontana

Edwards, M. (1963) *Battles of the Indian Mutiny*. Batsford

Edwards, M. (1973) *Red Year*. B T Batsford Ltd.

Edwards, M. (1973) *A Season in Hell*. Hamish Hamilton

Fraser, E. (1926) The Pearl's Brigade in India. *Mariners Mirror*, **12**(1)

Hibbert, C. (1978) *The Great Mutiny, India 1857*. Allen Lane

Jones, O. (1859) *Recollections of a Winter Campaign in India*. Saunders and Otley

Naval Records Society (1947) The Naval Brigades in the Indian Mutiny

Montague, V. (1898) *A Middy's Recollections*. (Publisher unknown)

Roberts, Field Marshall Lord, VC (1897) *Fortyone Years in India*. Macmillan

Roberts, Field Marshall Lord, VC (1924) *Letters written during the Indian Mutiny*. Macmillan

Russell, W. H. (1957) *My Indian Mutiny Diary*. Cassell

Tuker, F. (1953) *The Chronicle of Private Henry Metcalfe*. Cassell

Verney, E. H. (1862) *Shannon's Brigade in India, being some account of Sir William Peel's Naval Brigade in the Indian Campaign of 1857–1858*. Naval and Military Press

Verney, G. L. (1956) *The Devil's Wind*. Hutchison

CHAPTER 3

THE ABYSSINIAN RESCUE

1867–1868

In the 1860s Abyssinia was a landlocked state, a shrunken remnant of a once large Empire that had stretched across the Red Sea into Arabia. Inhabited by four large and mutually antagonistic tribes it was ruled by an Emperor whose claim to the title depended upon descent from King Soloman through his child by the Queen of Sheba; an absolute despotism wholly dependent on the might of the Emperor.

At this time the Emperor was Theodore, a man of considerable force of character and military ability, but of obscure origins whose mother had at one time supported her family by selling the local laxative worm medicine. Theodore had risen from a position as a postulant in the Coptic Church, a vocation abandoned for a career as a soldier of fortune, firstly to a position of dominance in his tribe, then as their chief, and with their support had claimed and obtained the Emperorship.

This was not the summit of Theodore's ambition. He intended to modernise his country, though his idea for this was the limited one of creating an up-to-date armaments industry, to re-establish the mediaeval Abyssinian Empire and then, as the Coptic Christian king to lead a crusade to free Jerusalem from Islam.

Theodore's knowledge of Europe was slight though he had for a time an English adventurer as his Grand Chamberlain and was on guardedly friendly terms with the British Consul at Massawa. Under their influence Theodore had admitted into Abyssinia, under the aegis of the English Missionary Societies, two groups of missionaries, one to convert the indigenous tribe of Jews and the other (a group of German and Swiss artisans) to teach their skills but forbidden to proselytise.

In the spring of 1860 the British Consul was killed by dissident Abyssinian tribesmen and the Grand Chamberlain was killed leading, under Theodore's orders, a punitive expedition against the tribe concerned. As a gesture of thanks for his actions against the murderers of her representative Queen Victoria sent a pair of engraved pistols to Theodore. But it was two and a half years before a newly appointed British Consul was received in audience by the Emperor.

At this audience Theodore handed to Mr Cameron, the new consul, a letter to Queen Victoria soliciting her assistance against the Turks and the sum of one thousand Maria Theresa silver dollars (the only acceptable currency in Abyssinia) to cover his expenses in delivering the letter. Cameron merely enclosed the letter with a routine despatch to the Foreign Office and sent them by messenger to his unofficial locum tenens in Massawa for onward transmission to London. Cameron lingered in Abyssinia and by his activities gave Theodore reason to doubt his diplomatic integrity.

After a year had passed and Theodore had received no reply to his letter he summoned Cameron to his presence and made it plain that he was displeased. In an earlier incident, the French consul was placed in chains and subsequently deported for having angered Theodore by the tone and content of the French reply to a similar letter. The members of the Mission to the Jews, one of who's published writings had denigrated Theodore, were treated with greater barbarity. The offending missionary was beaten unconscious and then fettered, his companion was fettered and two of their servants were beaten to death. Cameron lodged his official protests that were brushed aside. In January 1864 he then sought permission to return to Massawa. Instead, he was also placed in chains and, along with the other captives, removed to the mountain fortress of Magdala. This was built by Theodore to dominate the Galla tribe and was used by him as a place of confinement for prisoners and hostages.

The news of Cameron's arrest startled the Foreign Office into action. By the end of June 1864, Queen Victoria had signed 'her' reply that was sent to the resident agent at Aden for onward carriage by the hand of his First Assistant Secretary (Hormuzd Rassam, of mixed Armenian/Parsee descent). Rassam reached Massawa at the end of July and sought permission to travel through Abyssinia. This was not forthcoming for many months and when it was finally received it was couched in terms that raised doubts as to Theodore's real intentions. It was not until 15th October 1865 that Rassam and his party set off on a leisurely journey. Finally on 28th January 1866 Rassam handed Queen Victoria's letter to Theodore. It was over three years since Cameron had been given Theodore's letter and for two of them Cameron had been in chains.

Theodore agreed to release his captives and had them brought from Magdala to his camp at Lake Tana, a journey that took nearly a month. On 13th April 1866 Rassam despatched the released captives on their way to Massawa and went to take a formal farewell of Theodore. Rassam and his party were placed under restraint and the next day Cameron and the Missionaries were brought back in chains. Ten days later one of the Missionaries was sent to London by Theodore with what amounted to a demand for ransom — not money but skilled artisans and a selection of artefacts, nearly all of which would add to Abyssinian military strength. The remainder of the captives (including the wife and three children of the missionary messenger) were sent to Magdala.

The Foreign Office continued their efforts to reach a peaceful conclusion, recruited the artisans, collected the artefacts and despatched them to Massawa. But when further news of the captives revealed that they were prisoners in chains rather than hostages, the missionary messenger returned to Theodore with a stiff note demanding the release of the captives before either the artisans or the artefacts would be handed over to him. In April 1867 a final, strongly worded letter was sent to Theodore requiring him, within three months, to release his captives. At the same time initial steps for sending a military force to rescue the captives were taken.

Lieutenant General Sir Robert Napier was the commander-in-chief of the Bombay Presidency Army. Little known in England, he had served as an Engineer Officer with the East India Company's Army. During the Indian Mutiny he had shown himself to be a brave and forceful leader in action and an excellent staff officer. He had commanded a Division with distinction during the China war and had served on the Viceroy's Council before being appointed to his present command. He was now asked to prepare an appreciation of the situation for the British Government. His appreciation was accepted and, in August 1867, he was given the command and instructed to implement his proposed solution.

The force to be employed was made up of: half a regiment of British Cavalry; four regiments of Indian Cavalry; one battery of 9 pdr Armstrong guns; three batteries of mountain guns; two heavy 8 inch mortars; one company of Royal Engineers; seven companies of Indian sappers and miners; four British Infantry battalions; ten Indian Infantry battalions, including a battalion of Sikh Pioneers.

The Armstrong guns were horse drawn but Sikh Pioneers could be broken down for carriage on the backs of elephants. The British Infantry were re-armed for the expedition with the new Snider breach loading rifle, and the Cavalry carried the new Snider carbine. The Indian infantry were still armed with smooth bore percussion muskets.

Napier had to transport his army from India to some still to be determined place on the Red Sea coast of Africa, establish a firm base and then march some four hundred miles across unmapped, roadless, mountainless country to Magdala to release the captives. He might meet Theodore's army in the field or find his opponent ensconced behind the defences of the mountain stronghold into which, in any case, he would have to force an entry. The extent to which supplies and forage would be available for purchase was quite unknown. Consequently, the expedition was planned to be completely self-sufficient though the Austrian Government was requested to mint two million Maria Theresa dollars that were delivered to provide coin for local use.

The essence of Napier's plan was to advance a small well-equipped force to Magdala, establishing as he went a series of well-guarded depots of supplies upon which to draw. His striking force was to consist of 5000 combatants to secure his line of communication and his base. The baggage train and camp followers for an Indian army at this time usually numbered about three times as many as the army it supported. Napier was ruthless and allowed only 8000 to accompany his force. But still some 35 000 chargers, draught and pack animals, mules, oxen and camels were required and there were 44 elephants in the artillery train.

The resident agent at Aden, Colonel Merewether, had moved forward to Massawa and had established a line of communication with the captives whom he kept supplied with money for the purchase of provisions and to bribe messengers. Napier co-opted him to head a reconnaissance party made up of Colonel Phayre (Napier's Quarter Master General), a Colonel of the Royal Engineers, and junior specialist officers, escorted by a company of infantry and 40 sabres of Indian cavalry. They were charged to select a site for a landing place and main base, to begin work on the site, and to reconnoitre the line of advance into the hinterland. The advice of the Senior Naval Officer was to be sought if required.

The best of a number of poor alternatives was at Annesley Bay, about 50 miles south of Massawa. Here there was ample room for the transports to anchor, a little fresh water was available and there were only 14 miles of the burningly hot and waterless coastal plain to a pass, which could be made suitable for wheeled traffic. Then came the ascent of the steep escarpment to the Abyssinia plateau, 7000 ft above sea level. This was the site selected for the base camp of the advance brigade, some 60 miles from Massawa. The transports would have to anchor three quarters of a mile offshore and two piers, each three hundred feet long, would have to be built. Until they were constructed men had to wade, carrying stores as necessary, while horses and mules were swum ashore.

The reconnaissance complete, the party began to prepare Annesley Bay to receive the army. Local labour was hired and a start was made on the building of the first jetty. At the end of October the advance brigade arrived, but only a few were left to work at the base. The bulk of the brigade moved forward, where they were employed on road making and in establishing the advance base at the head of the pass at Senefe. The number of men left at Annesley Bay was totally insufficient to adequately cope with the flood of animals and stores that were arriving. There was no one to co-ordinate the efforts of the individual departments and confusion was inevitable. The biggest problem was the large number of mules that had arrived. There was insufficient water and the arrangement for the issue of fodder was lamentable. The beasts, maddened by thirst and hunger, gnawed through their rope

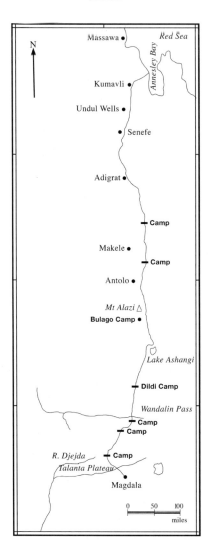

N

Red Sea

Massawa

Annesley Bay

Kumavli

Undul Wells

Senefe

Adigrat

Camp

Makele

Camp

Antolo

Mt Alazi △
Bulago Camp

Lake Ashangi

Dildi Camp

Wandalin Pass

Camp
Camp

R. Djejda   Camp
Talanta Plateau

Magdala

0   50   100

miles

The route taken by Lieutenant General Sir Robert Napier from Annesley Bay
to Magdala to rescue the British Consul

tethers, wandered about the camp, fouled any provisions they found and died in large numbers.

Fortunately, before the situation became disastrous, Major General Staveley arrived with the second brigade. He surveyed the scene and set the brigade to work. Loose mules were rounded up, all mules were tethered with chain, arrangements were made for feed and water and the dead mules that surrounded the camp were buried. When this work was complete Staveley turned his attention to organising the base. Stores and provisions dropped higgledy-piggledy on the beach were sorted into proper dumps, tents, horse and mule lines were laid out, and order introduced.

Work on the first jetty, a substantial stone structure (the remains of which could still be seen in 1960) continued and work on the second, of wooden piles and planks, begun. Three steam transports were retained in the bay as distilling ships and when the stone jetty was complete another distilling plant was built on its seaward end. Concurrently the advance brigade at Senefe, working on the road up the pass, was kept supplied and a start was made on the stockpiling of provisions at the advanced base.

The Royal Navy had its own part to play. The anchorage was surveyed, a channel buoyed and individual anchor berths designated. There was a constant requirement for boatwork in the landing of men, material and animals, with some interesting problems in seamanship to be solved. How do you land an elephant? How do you land an engine? Fortunately someone in Bombay had had the foresight to provide lighters large enough for the task. One of the disadvantages of Annesley Bay was that the pattern of wind and currents was such that mail transports had to be towed out for between one and two hundred miles before they could catch a wind and make headway. All of Her Majesty's Ships at Annesley were steamers and all were employed as tugs when required.

Theodore was aware of the British intentions and reacted to them. He enslaved the missionary artisans; the men were set to work making small guns and repairing muskets, their women folk to sewing and darning the clothing of the army. Theodore's rule was simple — "No work, no food!" Theodore had a naïve belief in the invincibility of artillery. To him the possessor of the biggest gun must win the battle. To ensure the success of his, so far, undefeated army he commanded the missionary artisans to make him a piece " to fire a ball of 1000 lbs." The artisans cast a gigantic mortar weighing some seven tons. When this was complete at the end of October, Theodore abandoned his camp city of Debra Tabor, burning it behind him, and marched for Magdala with his 5000 fighting men and 40 000 camp followers. The speed of his advance was limited by the movement of his great mortar that was towed by teams of never less than 100 men at a time and for which a roadway had to be cut. His march to Magdala was to last nearly six months and an average day's progress was a scant mile and a half.

Napier, embarked in HMS *Octavia*, arrived in Annesley Bay on 2nd January 1868 and with the full ceremony of gun salutes, guards and bands. He remained here for twelve days inspecting and generally approving, though he was dissatisfied with the supply position to, and the stockpile of, provisions at Senefe. The muleteers, he found, were riding one and leading two loaded mules. In short order the muleteers walked, leading three loaded mules. The elephants were waiting in idleness so they too were pressed into use to carry supplies. Finally the road was made passable for wheeled traffic and, after the horse drawn artillery had moved up, a train of bullock carts came into use. On 25th January Napier moved on to the advance base, inspecting the road and the roadside camps on his way, arriving there on 29th January.

During his stay at Annesley Bay Napier had, in recognition of the work of the Royal Navy, invited the Senior Naval Officer to form a small Naval Brigade to accompany the force advancing into Abyssinia. A Naval Brigade of 90 men, drawn from HMS *Dryad*, HMS *Octavia* and HMS *Satellite*, commanded by Commander Fellowes of HMS *Dryad*, was quickly formed. It was armed with twelve 6 pdr Hales Rocket Tubes and 1000 rockets. The sailors were armed with Snider Carbines and cutlasses.

For transport the Naval Brigade was given its own mule train, of which it became very proud. The pack saddles, as provided, were not designed for transporting rocket tubes and rockets. They were in fact poorly designed for carrying anything and were very likely to gall the mules. With ingenuity, skill with palm and needle and loving care, those saddles were worked upon until they were the best fitting saddles in the whole force and were ideally suited to their particular purpose. Though in the early days, while the sailors became accustomed to their mules and the mules accustomed to the sailors, there must have been some interesting moments, mutual understanding was quickly reached and the Naval Brigade earned a reputation as being amongst the best muleteers in the force, leading the most docile and enduring animals.

The Naval brigade was outstanding in other ways. They were always particularly well turned out, cheerful and with excellent discipline. They were recognised as the fittest members of the force and their efficiency was never in doubt. But they were considered eccentric. Their close companions on the line of march happened to be two companies of the Sikh Pioneer Battalion and despite language difficulties on either side the sailors and Sikhs became the greatest friends. After a day's march the Sikh band would play for the Naval Brigade and the sailors would set to partners and dance, not only the hornpipe but waltzes and polkas as well.

On 31st January Napier began his carefully controlled advance on Magdala. Colonel Phayre (The Quarter Master General) and his staff set off escorted by 150 sabres, two companies of Indian Infantry, a company of Sikh Pioneers and a company of Bombay sappers. They selected, surveyed and marked the route for the rest of the force, making rough maps and topographical sketches that were sent back to Napier, reproduced by a photographic section of Royal Engineers and issued to the main force. Two days behind them came the advance Brigade of Infantry and another day behind came the second Infantry Brigade, the Artillery (which included the Naval Brigade) and a baggage train. As each part of the force moved on so another part came up and occupied the vacated camps. Communication between the separate parts of the force and between Napier and his base was maintained by one of the Indian Cavalry Regiments, which established a 'pony express' the length of the route to Senefe. From Senefe to Annesley Bay a telegraph line was run and, once the natives had been discouraged from removing lengths of wire, this worked well.

Napier found that cattle could be bought from the tribesmen, who were eager to acquire Maria Theresa dollars, and that along his route there were areas of grass large enough to graze his animals. The need to carry meat and fodder was reduced. The daily ration for the British troops was established as one and a quarter pounds of fresh beef, compressed vegetables, biscuit or flour, tea and sugar (but no milk), a tot of rum and tobacco. There was no favouritism; Napier and his staff ate as well, or as badly, as any private soldier. The Indian troops were fed to the same scale, but with rice, pulse or other grain instead of beef. For them there were no local supplies and all their rations had to be brought forward.

After advancing for four days Napier halted for twelve. He was busy establishing diplomatic relations with the Abyssinian chieftains through whose lands he must march (and so successful was he that his march was unopposed and he was able, at Magdala, to obtain the active assistance of the Gallas). He reorganised his transport arrangements, rested and re-supplied his force. He also slimmed the tail of the force and increased its mobility. The baggage allowances were reduced to 75lbs per officer and 25lbs per soldier, and the camp followers, officers' native servants, grooms, grass cutters and the like were sent back to base.

On 25th February Napier moved on and until 21st March the advance continued in a steady rhythm of seven to ten days march, a rest to replenish and then on again, climbing steadily through country which was becoming more broken and difficult. At times the column was reduced to single file and the battery of Armstrong guns had to be transferred to the elephants' backs.

On 21st March Napier received unwelcome intelligence both from the captives in Magdala and from native sources. Theodore was much closer to Magdala than was expected and might well enter the fortress before Napier could arrive. Napier's reaction was bold. He loaded his mules with fifteen days basic rations to a scale of 1lb of meat, biscuit and tea per man with rice or grain instead of meat for his Indian troops, reduced tentage to a bell tent for every twelve officers and one for every twenty men, restricted baggage to what each person could carry (this was, in practice, a greatcoat, a blanket and a groundsheet; everyone, from Napier downwards was required to sleep on the ground) and pushed on, increasing his daily mileage from about 10 to 15 miles a day.

The country through which the force now had to march was the worst of the whole journey. There were three major gorges cutting the tableland that had to be crossed and, to add to the difficulties, high winds and thunderstorms of rain or hail caused discomfort and delay. After marching for a week, with one day's break, the first gorge had been passed and Napier, being informed that Theodore had reached Magdala, paused to concentrate his force. Four further days marching brought the force to the edge of the next gorge, 3500 ft deep and eight miles wide. It had taken Theodore six weeks to cross. Napier feared an attack on his force and ordered a forced march of 18 miles across the gorge onto the plateau beyond and using the road so painfully hacked out by Theodore. This was the longest and worst march of all; it was 24 hours after the advance guard had made camp when the rear guard came in.

From the plateau, with one more 3000 ft-deep gorge to cross, it was 12 miles as the crow flies to Magdala although the fortress itself was hidden from view by the spurs of Selassie and Fala. Napier wrote

> "I was able with a good telescope to appreciate the formidable character of the whole position and became aware that I should require all the infantry I could possibly collect to make the attack effective, and that every cavalry soldier that I could bring forward would be necessary for the investment."

For five days Napier halted his force while he treated with the Queen of the Gallas to bring every man she could muster to seal off the southern approach to Magdala, and made tentative plans to move forward and assault the northern gate of the fortress. He intended to cross the gorge, establish himself on the next portion of the plateau and mount an attack to clear the Fala spur to open the final short, but very steep, section of the road into Magdala. Once at the bottom of the gorge he could follow either the route pioneered by Theodore (known as the King's Road) that followed a pass on the left side of the plateau and debouched close to the feet of the Selassie and Fala spurs, or force his way up a very steep spur onto the northern edge of the plateau.

At dawn on 10th April Napier's first brigade, with which marched Colonel Phayre, moved off with orders to climb up the spur to the plateau and select a campsite for the whole force. At 1000 the second brigade which included the Naval Brigade, followed. At 1200 they reached the river crossing at the bottom of the gorge where they caught up with the tail of the first brigade resting; the remainder of the brigade was strung out and struggling up the spur where the going was very much worse than expected.

Colonel Phayre, with his party of sappers and miners, disobeyed Napier's orders and marched up the King's Road for about half a mile then turned and climbed up to the plateau. He had seen that the pass was undefended and reported back that this was so, adding that the head of the ravine had been secured. When he received this information Napier changed his plans and ordered the Naval Brigade, the guns and the baggage train up the King's Road. He, himself, made his way up the spur to the plateau, finding the 4th (King's Own) Regiment and the Baluchi Regiment fallen out, without water and apparently exhausted, on the edge of the plateau. On the plateau, well advanced were the Sikh Pioneers. Such were the relative speeds of advance of the column up the King's Road, and Napier up the spur, that he found that a mountain battery was emerging from the mouth of the pass which had not, in fact, been secured.

Theodore had massed his artillery, some thirty guns of assorted calibres, on the Fala spur to dominate the field. On Selassie he had massed some 5000 fighting men. Napier appreciated the dangers of his position and took immediate steps to improve it. The Sikh Pioneers were despatched to cover the mouth of the pass and the 4th (King's Own) and the Baluchis were called forward. While these movements were in progress the Abyssinian artillery opened fire using stone shot and, surprisingly, chain shot. At extreme range and firing from the height of Fala, the fall of shot was near vertical, there was no ricochet effect, and there were no casualties. As the artillery opened fire the Abyssinian horse and foot began the 3000-yard advance on the British positions.

The Abyssinian force split when it reached the foot of the Selassie spur. One body advanced straight at Napier's position where the infantry were beginning to arrive, a second advanced towards the mouth of the pass where the Sikhs had taken up position and where the mountain battery was rapidly assembling its guns, and a third headed for the baggage train halted in the mouth of the pass.

Suddenly, about midway between Napier's position and the mouth of the pass, Commander Fellowes and the Naval Brigade appeared over the edge of the plateau. The rockets came into action (the first shots to be fired by Napier's force) as quickly as the rocket tubes could be lifted from the mules. The unexpectedness of this intervention, surprise at this new weapon and its effectiveness caused the Abyssinians temporarily to check their advance and allowed the infantry to complete their deployment into line. Recovering from the shock, the Abyssinians continued their advance until at a range of 250 yards the 4th (King's Own) opened rapid independent fire (with a Snider six or seven rounds a minute). The attack wavered, the Abyssinians fell back a short way and went to ground. An unequal fire-fight followed with the Abyssinians double barrel muskets outranged by the rifles. When the Abyssinians started to fall back, the British and Indian infantry began a slow inexorable advance, continuing until halted by Napier who was careful not to over-extend his position.

The second Abyssinian attack fell on the mountain guns and the Sikh Pioneers to the left of the Naval Brigade, who shifted target to this second column that went to ground. Both the mountain guns and the rockets caused casualties but were not themselves sufficient to stop the attack that rolled steadily forward. The Sikh Pioneers fired two volleys, all that the limited range and slow reloading of their muskets would allow, and then charged home with fixed bayonets. In half an hour of fierce hand-to-hand fighting this Abyssinian force was cut to pieces.

The third party of Abyssinians worked further round the flank to attack the baggage column in the pass. The baggage guard had moved up to the front of the column and met the onslaught with rapid fire from their Sniders. Retreating up the pass, unable to face the rifle fire, the Abyssinians passed under the positions held by the Sikh Pioneers, who had by now been wheeled round to line the side of the King's

Road. The Sikh Pioneers charged the fleeing Abyssinians and turned retreat into rout. The mountain guns engaged any groups of Abyssinians that had managed to break back onto the plateau and were fleeing towards Selassie.

The Naval Brigade, when there were no more targets on the plateau, had shifted position and were engaging, at their extreme range of 3000 yards, the Abyssinians grouped round Theodore himself, on the top of the Selassie spur. The rockets caused few casualties but their effect on morale was significant. One rocket exploded close to Theodore, killing a horse. Theodore was reported to have said "a terrible weapon against which no man can fight". For a brief period the rockets joined the mountain guns in engaging fleeing groups of Abyssinians, taking over as the groups passed out of gun range. Having fired the first shot in the engagement at about 1600 they fired the last at about 1900. In these three hours the Naval Brigade had fired 219 rockets, the artillery 102 shells while the infantry used 20 rounds per Snider and 8 rounds per musket. The Abyssinian casualties were estimated at 700 dead and 1400 wounded. British casualties were 20 wounded, of whom 2 died.

The British forces on the plateau, standing to arms, held their positions throughout the night and were relieved at dawn when the remainder of the force came up with much needed water and provisions. Having cooked a meal and drunk their milkless and sugarless tea they attended to the business of clearing up the battlefield. Napier was engaged in the negotiations begun by Theodore and in planning his assault on Magdala.

Theodore was vacillating between defiance and despondency. At about 0400 on 11th April he sent, under a flag of truce, two of the hostages to treat with Napier on his behalf. Napier returned them with the message that unless all the hostages were released and Theodore surrendered himself into his custody hostilities would continue. Theodore returned a defiant message to Napier and then had to be forcibly restrained from committing suicide. Persuaded by his Chiefs, Theodore then made a conciliatory gesture and ordered the major captives, Rassam and his associates, Cameron and his party and the two 'Jewish' missionaries to make their way to Napier's camp. Next day, in a further effort to make peace, Theodore released the 'enslaved' artisans – a party of 50 Europeans who brought with them 187 Abyssinian servants and over 300 domestic animals.

On 12th April Napier began his preparations for the assault of Magdala, pushing forward and occupying the heights of Fala and Selassie without opposition. The bulk of Theodore's cannons, which had been abandoned after the battle, were captured when a sortie by Theodore, during which he challenged Napier or his champion to single combat, was driven off. In despair Theodore offered his army the choice of remaining to fight with him in Magdala or release from his service. Unable to escape to the south where the Gallas gave short shrift to any who tried to escape that way (Theodore tried himself and fled for his life back to Magdala) the defecting warriors, with their wives, families and dependants, poured out of Magdala by the northern gate to surrender to Napier's force.

It was not until 1500 on 13th April that the route into Magdala was clear and Napier could order the attack begun. He had positioned his artillery and the Naval Brigade to concentrate their fire, at ranges from 3000 yards down to 1300 yards on the main gate, and to cover the assaulting column that had to climb 300 ft up a narrow and very steep path open to the defensive fire from the walls. When the artillery and rockets ceased fire two companies of the 33rd (Duke of Wellington's) were to provide covering fire from their Sniders whilst Royal Engineers and sappers and miners forced the gate. This proved difficult and the Commanding Officer of the 33rd ordered his men to attempt to scale the walls, a feat that was finally accomplished by a drummer and a private (who were both awarded the VC) who opened the way for their fellows. With the main gate cleared there was little further resistance and the Abyssinians quickly laid down their arms. Theodore's body was found close to an inner gateway — he had shot himself with one of the pistols presented to him by Queen Victoria!

Napier wasted no time at Magdala. He was anxious to get back to Annesley Bay before the summer rains could cut him off from his base. Theodore was buried in a suicide's grave, Magdala burnt, the gates blown up and the guns destroyed. Then the march back began. It was as hard, if not harder, than the march to Magdala.

The destruction of Magdala (Illustrated London News, June 13, 1868)

Rations could not at first be increased; there was an alarming increase in minor sickness and some of the troops showed the early symptoms of scurvy. But when rum, tobacco and sugar became available the spirits and health of the men improved. As the column neared its base so supplies improved in quantity and variety until the day came when Napier authorised the disposal of the hospital comforts. Each man received an issue of bottles of porter.

By 10th June the re-embarkation of the whole force was complete. The successful, but very expensive, rescue operation was over.

Bibliography

Bates, D. (1979) *The Abyssinian Difficulty: Emporor Theodore and the Magdala Campaign, 1867–68*. Oxford University Press

Hoolan and Hosier (1870) *Record of the Expedition to Abyssinia*. HMSO

Myatt, F. (1970) *The March to Magdala: The Abyssinian War, 1868*. L Cooper

Napier, H. D. (1927) *Field Marshall Lord Napier of Magdala*. Edward Arnold

MacMunn, G. (1952) *Always into Battle*. Gale and Polden

Stanley, H. M. (1874) *Coomassie and Magdala*. Ayer Co.

CHAPTER 4

THE SECOND ASHANTI WAR

1873–1874

British interest in the Gold Coast of Africa began with our participation in the
slave trade and was maintained because of our efforts to abolish it. It increased
with the development of an alternative trade in palm oil. By 1870 there was an ill-
defined Protectorate (with a small Dutch enclave at Elmina) over the unwarlike
tribes, including the Fantee, who lived in the coastal strip some seventy miles wide,
separating the Ashanti from the sea. The centre of British influence was at the fort at
Cape Coast Castle. This was garrisoned by the West Indian Regiment (West Indian
Negroes commanded by British officers) along with other minor forts. There was
also a small Hausa Gendarmerie recruited from Nigeria. A squadron of ships of the
Cape of Good Hope and West Africa Squadron patrolled the coast.

The Ashanti were a powerful, warlike and bloodthirsty people. Their capital
was at Kumasi, about 170 miles inland from Cape Coast Castle from which it was
separated by thick forest and thicker bush penetrated only by narrow native paths
running from village to village. Brutal slavemasters themselves, the Ashanti had
been the chief purveyors to the trade.

Their addiction to human sacrifice required a steady supply of victims, satisfied
by incessant warring on their neighbours. Their large army was, consequently, well
disciplined, well equipped and well practised. Each man was armed with a flintlock
musket which, loaded with slugs, nails and scrap metal, had an effective range of
something less than fifty yards. They also carried a heavy knife, not for combat but
for beheading the enemy dead.

The Ashanti had long been turbulent neighbours of the British Protectorate. They had a low opinion of Britain's warlike prowess founded on their undoubted successes in the first Ashanti War in 1824–26. They had invaded Fantee territory and defeated a force of Fantee tribesmen supported by a detachment drawn from a penal battalion of the British Army. The British Governor in command was killed. His skull became a drinking cup for the Ashanti King and his skin the batterhead of a ceremonial drum.

In 1872 the Dutch decided to withdraw from the Gold Coast and, in a deal of dubious legality, sold the fort at Elmina, about eight miles westward along the coast from Cape Coast Castle, to the British. The Dutch had annually paid money to the King of Ashanti. They represented this to the British as a subvention. The Ashanti considered it a rent. They took exception to the deal, which ignored their interest in the fort and became furious when they learnt that any further payments of the subvention were conditional on the immediate surrender of two German missionaries and their families held as hostages. The King of Ashanti, King Kofi Kalkelli, threatened war.

The British Government was reluctant, for financial reasons, to act in the face of Ashanti threats. Eventually they ordered the despatch of a force of 100 Royal Marines under Colonel Festing from the United Kingdom and the 1ˢᵗ Battalion of the West India Regiment to join the 2ⁿᵈ Battalion on the Gold Coast. The Royal Marine detachment arrived off Cape Coast Castle on 7ᵗʰ June 1873 in HMS *Barracouta*

The castle of Elmina (Illustrated London News, December 6, 1873)

Colonel F W Festing, Royal Marine Artillery (Illustrated London News, April 25, 1874)

commanded by Captain Freemantle of the RN. Captain Freemantle, new to the coast, found himself the Senior Officer of the Squadron and with a crisis on his hands. An Ashanti army, estimated at 30 000 men, had errupted into Fantee territory and was threatening Cape Coast Castle and Elmina. Two days before it had defeated the Fantee tribal levy, stiffened though it was with 200 Hausa gendarmerie, only 20 miles from Cape Coast Castle.

Within the castle and its outworks were detachments of the 2nd Battalion, West India Regt and 150 Hausas, all commanded by Colonel Hartley, the Commanding Officer of the 2nd West Indians, who was also the Civil Administrator of the Protectorate. Afloat, under his command, Freemantle had at Cape Coast Castle a corvette, HMS *Druid*, a sloop, HMS *Seagull* and a gunboat. At Elmina were HMS *Argus*, a paddle steamer like *Barracouta* and two gunboats.

Freemantle's orders were to land the Royal Marines only if he found it necessary after consulting with the Administrator. The necessity for any operation was to be decided between the Administrator, Colonel Festing and himself. There was a final caveat — the Marines were to defend the forts but were to take no part in field operations.

On 8th June Freemantle conferred with the Administrator and it was decided to land the Royal Marines. This was done on 9th June and the Administrator immediately put forward a plan for a prompt attack on the Ashanti. Freemantle judged Hartley a weak and vacillating character who acted as his momentary optimism or pessimism dictated. He appreciated that the plan was based on unreliable information and determined to visit Elmina and establish the position there before deciding on a course of action.

Freemantle and Festing spent 10ᵗʰ June on a detailed reconnaissance in and around Elmina. They found that the Ashanti army, split into detachments, was quartered on villages in the surrounding country and drawing arms, ammunition and food from the native inhabitants who considered themselves Ashanti subjects.

On their return to Cape Coast Castle Freemantle and Festing called on Colonel Hartley and pressed on him a plan to disarm the Elminas and cut them off from the Ashanti. The Administrator's mood had changed overnight; he demurred, and considering that such action would precipitate an undesirable collision with the Ashanti, called upon his colonial secretary, magistrate and other prominent citizens to support his view. Freemantle's forceful presentation of his plan finally, on 12ᵗʰ June, won him permission to proceed.

No time was lost. Festing, with 50 of his Royal Marines, made a night march to Elmina to reinforce the fort. Freemantle, with the remainder of the Royal Marines embarked in ships of the flotilla, sailed up to Elmina where, manning and arming his boats, he landed at 0530 on 13ᵗʰ June. Having, they believed, sealed off the native town Freemantle and Festing demanded the surrender of all arms and ammunition. Although armed men could be seen in the town no arms had been surrendered. At 1030 a further proclamation was made giving an hour's grace for the removal of women, children and unarmed men from the town. After that time, unless arms were surrendered, the town would be bombarded.

At about 1200, no arms having been surrendered, fire was opened from the fort and rockets launched from the boats. The incendiary effect of the rockets was marked. Within twenty minutes parts of the native town were ablaze and a stream of armed men were escaping through the cordon of Royal Marines, 2ⁿᵈ West Indians and Hausas, and heading for the bush. The Royal Marines and Hausas were ordered in pursuit and a running skirmish began. Then a body of about 2000 Ashantis were seen advancing to the aid of the Elminas. Men from the boats were landed and the Ashantis withdrew in the face of long range Snider fire. They were followed up for about three miles. Nothing decisive was being achieved and the men were nearing exhaustion so they were recalled to the boats that they reached at about 1430. Here they dined and awaited developments.

Nothing had happened by 1630 and re-embarkation was ordered. When this was almost complete information was received that the Ashantis were advancing in force to attack the town. All available men were landed, the *Barracoutas* were sent off to the right while the remainder marched to join Colonel Festing who had taken up a position on the edge of an open salt plain across which the Ashantis advanced, overlapping and outflanking Festing's line. The *Barracoutas* came up, unobserved in the bush, and outflanked the Ashantis who reeled under the unexpected enfilading fire. Festing ordered a general advance and in a running fight across the salt plain the Ashantis were dispersed and driven into the bush. At dusk the force marched back to Elmina and the seamen re-embarked.

The official result of this action was reported as 200 of the 3000 Ashanti killed. One Royal Marine and one soldier of the West India Regiment were killed and one officer and six men wounded. This little action left a profound impression on the Ashanti — "They had never seen so many men killed so quickly". During the rest of the war they eschewed fighting in the open though their ingrained belief that "White man no fight in bush" remained unshaken.

This small success was followed by a period of consolidation on the coast. Freemantle busied himself with the security of the string of forts and Festing enlarged the 'safe' area, setting up redoubts a few miles inland and dominating the area by aggressive patrolling. Early in July Commodore Commerell arrived from the Cape in HMS *Rattlesnake* and the 1st West India Regiment arrived from the West Indies. Heavy rains were also an inhibiting factor, making field operations almost impossible. During this lull in action a reinforcement of two hundred Royal Marines arrived in HMS *Simoon,* which also brought a quantity of stores and was under orders to remain on the coast as a hospital ship.

The commodore was anxious for action and on 16th August he led an attack, in ships' boats, past the village of Chamah at the mouth of the Prah river, to attack a force of Ashanti established on an island about eight miles upstream. Under cover of this operation he ordered a small force of ten native police installed in the fort at Chamah that up until then had been unarmed and unmanned.

Commodore Commerell at Chamah asked the local chief to provide men to assist in this enterprise. There was an angry scene when the chief refused to cooperate and the commodore set off upstream in his gig and a galley under tow from a steam cutter. On the advice of the local natives he kept close to the right hand bank of the river. After travelling about a mile the string of boats was ambushed and brought under musket fire at about ten yards range. The commodore and Commander Luxmore of HMS *Argus* were both wounded, as were about half of the gig's crew and all but two of the men in the galley. Fortunately the steam cutter escaped lightly and was able to tow the other boats out of range and then back to HMS *Rattlesnake*.

On board the flagship the wounded commodore found that the operation to install the police at Chamah fort had also gone disastrously wrong. Having landed the policemen on the beach to occupy the fort, *Rattlesnake*'s cutter capsized in the surf. While the boat's crew were struggling ashore and preparing to right their boat a large body of armed men approached from the village. The sub-lieutenant formed the police into line to cover, as best they could, the righting operation. This bold face was sufficient to halt the approaching natives and there developed an uneasy lull during which the boat was righted and anchored off the beach. The lull was broken by the arrival of a party straight from the successful ambush that led to an immediate charge. The police fired one volley, then broke and ran. Those members of the unarmed boat's crew left on the beach entered the water and with the police began to struggle out to the boat. Of the sailors one, who could not swim, was caught and beheaded, one, seriously wounded, was captured but bribed his captor with all his clothes and ten shillings and regained the boat. Two of the police were caught and killed. Every man who had been on the beach was wounded. The commodore ordered Chamah to be bombarded. When the village was ablaze in several places *Rattlesnake* returned to Cape Coast Castle.

On 18th August the commodore ordered Freemantle to take *Argus* under his orders and cruise up the coast to reassure the friendly forts: to shell Chamah, Apoassi, Aboaddi and Tacoraddi, all hostile, and to burn their canoes. Freemantle was under strict orders not to land. Freemantle did not agree with the prohibition on landing but, anchored as he was at Elmina, had no chance to discuss his orders with the commodore. Rather tongue in cheek he interpreted his orders liberally. All that day *Barracouta* and *Argus* moved up the coast landing stores at the forts on the way whilst Freemantle wrote his orders for the operations the next day.

At daybreak *Barracouta* and *Argus* began the bombardment of Tacoraddi and Apoassi. At Apoassi, against slight opposition, boats from both ships landed and burnt 100 canoes, a large quantity of palm oil and the village. The bombardment at Tacoraddi was not very effective and Lieutenant Young (temporarily in command of *Argus* in place of the wounded Commander Luxmore) asked permission to land and burn the village. Freemantle told him to leave the village alone but gave him permission to land and burn a group of canoes abreast his ship, while he, Freemantle, dealt with a group further on. Young landed and having burnt the canoes as directed, marched his men along the beach and so close to the bush that his party could be ambushed. When Freemantle saw Young's movements he ordered *Barracouta* to fire into the bush to give the marching men some protection and rushed ashore to take personal charge. He found the whole party in retreat, having been ambushed. Lieutenant Young and one other officer were wounded as were twelve ratings. The boats, which should have been placed to give close covering fire, were in no position to support the party. Freemantle repositioned the boats, a few rounds of case shot cleared the bush and the canoes were burnt. Freemantle returned to *Barracouta* and took her to renew the bombardment of Tacoraddi. Just to round off the day's events, *Barracouta* struck an uncharted rock and sprang a small leak!

On 22nd August the wounded commodore left for the Cape. Before leaving he gave Freemantle very restrictive orders that cramped his initiative. Not that this mattered for little could have been done. It was a sickly season and with more than half the European officers and Royal Marines out of action with fever, operations on land, except for some desultory road making by the Hausas, were impossible.

In any case on 29th August the Administrator informed Freemantle that the supply of arms and powder to the Ashanti must be stopped. Freemantle declared a blockade of the whole of the Gold Coast and deployed his vessels to enforce the order. The legality of his action was doubtful but there were no official objections, though ships were arrested and sent into Cape Coast Castle with arms and ammunition on board. This was hardly surprising since trade guns and powder were one of the major media of exchange on the coast.

In London the Cabinet was divided on how best to solve the Ashanti problem. One faction supported the 'cheap' solution propounded by the Admiralty that the Naval squadron and the Royal Marines would ensure the safety of the forts (and therefore British interests) until climate and disease drove the Ashanti army home and control could be re-established. This solution was strongly opposed by the Minister for War, Cardwell, briefed by the Adjutant General Sir Garnet Wolseley, who maintained that a lasting peace would only be obtained through a military victory and an occupation, however brief, of the Ashanti capital.

Wolseley had been promised the command of the expedition if the Cabinet could be persuaded to adopt his proposal. He seems to have believed that the Admiralty opposition to his plan was intended to frustrate his personal ambitions and deprive him of his chance of glory. He developed a paranoic dislike for the Admiralty that was later, perhaps, to lead to his failure to relieve General Gordon in Khartoum.

After two plans had been rejected Wolseley tabled his third. In this he undertook, at a cost of not more than £150 000 using two (later raised to three) battalions from the UK, and only in the good season between December and February, to defeat the Ashanti, occupy Kumasi and ensure a lasting peace. At a stormy meeting of the Cabinet on 13th August 1873 Cardwell forced his colleagues to accept this plan.

Taking full advantage of his position in the War Office and his influence over Cardwell, Wolseley began his preparations. He selected 36 officers for his staff or for 'special service' (the famous Ashanti Ring). He designed a special uniform for the British regiments: the Wolseley Helmet and a loose fitting uniform of light, hodden grey serge. He also introduced special weapons, namely cut down Snider rifles for convenient use in the bush and sword bayonets with one edge sharpened for cutting, with the back of the blade toothed to act as a saw. He planned to raise two Battalions of native levies to fight alongside his British battalions. A part of his plan was to cut a road from Cape Coast Castle to facilitate the approach march of his force.

On 12th September Wolseley and his 36 officers sailed for the Gold Coast, taking with them a comprehensive library of books on the Ashanti and their country. Under their General's direction the days were spent in study and after dinner each evening two officers, previously detailed, lectured their companions on what they had read that day.

On 2nd October Wolseley and his staff disembarked at Cape Coast Castle. Wolseley insisted upon the fullest ceremonial for his landing. Once this was over he startled everyone by his decision and phenomenal energy. Within a week the

Sir Garnet Wolseley's attempt to land at Port Durnford
(Illustrated London News, August 23, 1879)

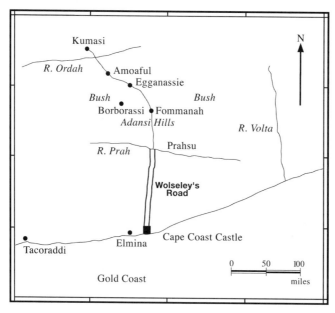

The route taken by Adjutant General Sir Garnet Wolseley
to Kumasi to defeat the Ashanti

preparations for the recruiting and training of two battalions of native levies were made. The Hausa Gendarmerie began training as gunners with 7 pdr pack guns that were made man-portable, and work on the road to Prahsu began. Wolseley also found time to study the local intelligence and determined on taking some action against the detachments of the Ashanti army quartered in the villages adjacent to and surrounding Elmina.

On 11th October Wolseley and a part of his staff visited Elmina and returned to Cape Coast Castle that night. Next morning Wolseley began to weave an elaborate deception plan, telling his staff that he must move west to the Volta and making sure that this news spread through Cape Coast Castle (presumably therefore also to the Ashanti). On 12th October he took Captain Freemantle into his confidence but forbade him to issue any orders or take any action that could not be construed as furthering the cover plan. So, on 13th October, a detachment of seamen was landed to relieve the 90 strong detachment of the 2nd West India Regiment in Cape Coast Castle that embarked in *Decoy*. 160 Royal Marines from *Simoon* transshipped to *Barracouta* where, at 2100 Wolseley and his staff joined them. At last Freemantle could issue his orders and the force sailed for Elmina, arriving at 0230 to begin disembarkation.

The disembarkation did not go smoothly. The loaded boats encountered heavy surf at dead low water and had to return to their parent ships to be lightened before they could beach. Unfortunately, because of the surf breaking into the boats, some of the biscuit for the day's ration was spoilt, of which Freemantle said, "The want was felt during the trying day which followed". Wolseley laid all the blame for this on Freemantle, believing that the Navy had miscalculated the tides. Freemantle blamed the excessive secrecy because of which he had been unable to check the tidal conditions with his navigators or with anyone who knew the state of the surf at dead low water.

However the delay was only for about an hour and by 0500 a column made up of 160 Royal Marines, 90 West India Regiment soldiers and 30 sailors supported by 200 native porters, led by a party of skirmishing Hausas, started the five mile march to the village of Essamen. They had with them with a 7 pdr gun and a rocket trough, both carried by Kroomen (Liberian tribesmen employed on ships). The way to Essamen was a bush track over a range of hills, across a swamp and through thickening bush, which, from time to time, forced the column to advance in single file. By 0645 the head of the column was about a mile short of Essamen where the Ashanti sprang an ambush on it. The Hausa skirmishers fell back on the main body and there was a heavy, if generally wild, exchange of fire (in which, though, both Wolseley's chief of staff and Captain Freemantle were wounded) before the column could push on. At about 0800 the gun and rocket trough were established in a firing position about 200 yards from the village. Though themselves under fire from the bush they began to bombard the village covering the advance of the Royal Marines. By 0830 the village was secured.

The column rested in Essamen for about an hour and a half while they searched out and destroyed the Ashanti camps around the village. Then it marched on, unopposed, through thick bush for six miles to the coastal village of Amguana and then down the coast to Akimfoo and on to Ampini. From Akimfoo Freemantle sent orders to *Argus* and *Decoy*, which had bombarded Ampini that morning, to land armed parties to join with the column in an assault upon the village, which was taken and burnt. Wolseley and Freemantle embarked in *Decoy* and sailed first to Cape Coast Castle to drop Wolseley and then back to Elmina where Freemantle rejoined *Barracouta* and welcomed the returning column. They had completed a circular march of twenty miles, fought one small pitched battle, taken two villages from the Ashanti and destroyed a number of enemy camps and supply bases.

On Sunday 26th October Wolseley received news that the Ashanti were threatening outposts of Cape Coast Castle at Dunquah and Abrakampa. He requested Captain Freemantle to land all available men. By 1230 Freemantle was landing a Naval Brigade of fifteen officers and 250 seamen supported by 50 Kroomen as water carriers. Tents, provisions and ammunition were to be carried by native porters, but 400 of these deserted as the first sailors landed. Only women could be recruited to replace the deserters and only enough of these to carry the absolute minimum requirement. By 1430 the march began and at 1530 Freemantle, despite his wound, and Wolseley, who because of an old wound was carried in a hammock (as he was throughout the campaign) set off with the rearguard. The heat, bad march discipline and bad water discipline took a heavy toll on the marching sailors. On the ten-mile march to Assayboo, the campsite at the end of the first stage, men were constantly falling out. Nearly all recovered under the rudimentary treatment of water, shade and loosened clothing and staggered on into camp. The main body arrived at the campsite well before the tents and baggage. They cleared and prepared the site so that with the arrival of the tents the camp was quickly set up.

Next morning the force was ready to march at 0600. Colonel Festing, with a detachment of the 2nd West India Regiment under command, was detached to Dunquah while the Naval Brigade, screened by a detachment of native levies, made a four and a half mile march to Abrakampa. Although the march was unopposed the going was so bad, necessitating movement in single file, that it took over three and a half hours to cover the distance. For the rest of the day and overnight the Naval Brigade remained in the village. On 28th October they marched to a village six miles north of Abrakampa and after a number of false alarms marched back again, spending one more night there before returning, by easy stages, to Cape Coast Castle to re-embark. Garrisons of Royal Marines and native levies were left at Abrakampa and Assayboo.

Colonel Festing at Dunquah had made contact with the Ashanti. He was daily engaged in heavy skirmishing and had succeeded in destroying one of their camps. Perhaps as a result of this the Ashanti concentrated a part of their army and on 5th November launched an attack on the small garrison of Royal Marines and native levies in Abrakampa. News of this attack reached Wolseley early on 6th November and his request to Freemantle to land all available men was received at 0445. The first boatload of the 300 seamen and marines detailed to land were ashore by 0630 and the column marched off at 0825. The march was a repetition of that on 26th October and the Naval Brigade marched into Assayboo at 1440 only 200 strong, a third of their number having fallen out.

Here Wolseley received a message that Abrakampa was still under attack, nearly surrounded and in need of assistance. With the 50 Royal Marines from Assayboo, who were fresh, and the fittest 140 men of the Naval Brigade (60 sailors were left to garrison the village and collect the stragglers as they came up) he moved off at 1600. As he was shepherding a string of native porters carrying "an ample supply of rockets, ammunition and food", he chose to follow a circuitous route so as to enter Abrakampa through a gap in the Ashanti line. This must have been a remarkable march for at 1730, in half the time that it had taken on 27th October, the sailors were entering Abrakampa. In the latter stages of the march they could hear the sounds of heavy firing and as they entered the village they were led straight into position to open fire on the Ashanti. The fire-fight slowly petered out after sunset and by 2100 the relieved garrison were asleep after nearly 48 hours of continuous action.

Firing began again at dawn but slowly died away until by 1000 it ceased. By 1400 Colonel Evelyn Wood VC, one of the special service officers, brought up a heterogeneous collection of native auxiliaries, the Cape Coast Chieftains with their tribal warriors. Wolseley deployed them to attack the Ashanti positions, and led by their Chieftains they 'advanced' rapidly to the rear until they were met by a 'beating' line of staff officers (armed with canes and umbrellas) and the native levies who had defended Abrakampa. The direction of the 'advance' was reversed but progress was so slow that Wolseley passed the Hausas and some more bellicose native levies through the line of reluctant heroes. This more rapid advance surprised the Ashanti rearguard, overran the Ashanti camp and came near to capturing the Ashanti War Chief. Wolseley's efforts to organise further pursuit were frustrated as Hausas, native levies and native auxiliaries (led by their Chieftains) were far too busy looting the Ashanti camp.

Wolseley ordered fresh dispositions; he left a garrison of 50 Royal Marines at Abrakampa and ordered 110 sailors and marines of the Naval Brigade to join Colonel Festing at Dunquah. He then rushed back to Cape Coast Castle where he arrived delirious from a severe, almost fatal, attack of fever that for twelve days rendered him unfit to exercise command.

When he recovered he found that the situation had changed. The Ashanti army, in sickly condition and short of ammunition, was withdrawing towards the Prah. Wolseley considered concentrating all his troops and with them, a Naval Brigade and the Hausas, striking at the retreating Ashanti. Deciding that he could probably not inflict a decisive defeat on them and fearing the ravages of fever on his small force he took no major action.

Instead, using his native levies, Wolseley shepherded the Ashanti army back to and across the Prah. Under cover of these operations he continued the preparations for the attack on Kumasi, particularly the cutting of a track from Cape Coast Castle to Prahsu on the bank of the River Prah. Working under the direction of officers of the Royal Engineers, hired native labour hacked a track of between eight and ten feet wide through the bush, built bridges over 237 creeks and rivers and corduroyed the road through the swamps. Staging camps were built at suitable points along the way. Each camp was built to accommodate 400 British officers and men in wattle, palm thatched huts into which were built bamboo sleeping platforms two feet off the ground. A mess hut and cooking facilities were built, all within a perimeter fence outside which the ground had been cleared to a range of a hundred yards to give a field of fire.

Commodore Hewett VC, who had relieved the wounded Commodore Commerell in command of the station, arrived off Cape Coast Castle on 14th November. Almost

Naval Brigade men breakfasting in the courtyard of an Ashanti house
(Illustrated London News, March 7, 1874)

his first action was to recall all the seamen to their ships. Then he set about restoring the health of his command. Ships were sent to Fernando Po, Ascension or St Helena to spend time in a more salubrious climate. The worst cases of fever were transferred to the hospital ship *Simoon* that also sailed for St Helena. *Barracouta* alone sent five officers and 21 ratings on board her, retaining 36 sick on board herself. When Captain Freemantle himself fell sick *Barracouta* was ordered away.

By 25th December the road was ready for use and the advance base at Prahsu, with accommodation for 2000 British troops, two battalions of native levies, the Hausa artillery, the Engineer's native labourers and the native porters, was near completion. Cruising off Cape Coast Castle in their transports were three British battalions, the 23rd (Royal Welsh Fusiliers), the 42nd (Black Watch) and the 95th (Rifle Brigade) and a British artillery battery, awaiting orders to disembark.

On 26th December, having given his orders for the disembarkation of his troops, Wolseley inspected the Naval Brigade of 19 officers and 250 ratings and Royal Marines which Commodore Hewett had formed from HM Ships *Active*, *Tamar*, *Argus*, *Encounter*, *Amethyst*, *Druid* and *Decoy*. The inspection complete Wolseley began his personal journey to Prahsu.

On 27th December the Naval Brigade marched out for Prahsu where it arrived on 3rd January, able to boast that it had completed the march of 73 miles without a single man straggling or falling out on the way. Unlike the rest of the army which relied on locally recruited porters, the Naval Brigade used the Kroomen landed with them from their ships. They were reliable, less trouble on the march and did not desert.

Wolseley had been met at Prahsu on 2nd January by a delegation from King Kofi sent to discuss matters with him. This was probably an attempt to temporise while he, Kofi, assembled his army. The arrival of the Naval Brigade was made a spectacle to impress the delegation which was brought out to view a march past of the Brigade on its arrival. Then on 6th January the Brigade crossed the Prah and marched towards Kumasi. It was contrived that the Ashanti envoys passed the sailors on the march. As soon as the envoys were out of sight the Naval Brigade returned to camp and settled to the mundane task of clearing bush on the far bank of the Prah while waiting for the rest of the army to arrive.

Back at Cape Coast Castle disembarkation began at 0045 on 1st January 1874 and the first half battalion of the Rifles moved off at 0245. Disembarking half a battalion a day, everything was running smoothly until the 5th January. With the Rifles and the Black Watch ashore and away, and with the first half battalion of the Royal Welsh Fusiliers ashore and about to march, the whole movement was brought to a halt by an acute shortage of porters. This was brought about by wholesale desertions all along the line, which, besides stopping the forward movement of the troops, threatened the provisioning of supplies to an extent that jeopardised the whole expedition.

Artillery park in the camp at Prah-su (Illustrated London News, February 28, 1874)

Sharpening cutlasses in the camp at Prah-Su
(Illustrated London News, February 28, 1874)

As an emergency measure the 1st and 2nd Battalions of the West Indian Regiment and Colonel Wood's battalion of native levies became porters, carrying forward to Prahsu the food and ammunition that was required there. Colonel Colley, in charge of transport, began to recruit local replacements. His measures were draconian and more resembled slave taking than recruiting. Whole villages were surrounded and all available man and womanpower impressed. (It was found, in practice, that the women were in every way better porters than the men). This display of force ensured that an adequate number of porters were available in the future.

Wolseley had planned to begin his advance on Kumasi on 15th January but the breakdown of the transport arrangements had prevented the stockpiling of food and ammunition, and left the main body of his troops halted, strung out in the camps along the road. Accepting the inevitable he set about improving his position. Lord Gifford (a special service officer) with his body of native scouts reconnoitred forward, followed by the Native Regiments commanded by Colonels Russell and Wood, and then by a strong detachment of the West India Regiment and by Rait's Hausa Artillery. This force advanced some 20 miles, seized a commanding position on the Adansi hills and improved the road back to Prahsu. The Naval Brigade continued its work on the north bank of the Prah improving the bridgehead.

When Wolseley was informed that the transport arrangements were working again he called forward his disembarked troops, leaving a half of the Royal Welsh Fusiliers and all his Royal Artillery still on board their transports where they remained. On 20th January, escorted by the Naval Brigade, Wolseley set off for the Adansi hills. Unexpectedly, he was joined by Commodore Hewett who marched in from the rear on 22nd January. Unopposed, the advance was so rapid that Wolseley reached the Adansi hills on the original planned date and, having made up the lost five days, he halted in the village of Fommanah where he paused to concentrate his force and establish the advanced base from which to launch his final advance to Kumasi.

The route to Kumasi lay through the villages of Egginassie and Amoaful, both of which were expected to be defended. On the left lay the village of Borborassi from which the Ashanti threatened the flank or rear of any advance. On 29th January Wolseley sent the Naval Brigade, a company of the Royal Welsh Fusiliers, two rocket tubes of the Hausa Artillery and a company of native levies to clear Borborassi whilst he, with the main body, advanced towards Egginassie.

After a three-hour march through the bush towards Borborassi the force broke into a clearing around the village. The Royal Welsh Fusiliers rushed the village, completely surprising the Ashanti, who broke from the village into the bush where they reformed to work round and attack the left flank. Met by steady volleys from the Naval Brigade firing at the puffs of powder smoke in the bush, the attack petered out. Borborassi was occupied for about an hour while the force rested. Then the village was burnt and the return march begun with the Naval Brigade forming

A detachment of the Royal Artillery leaving Woolwich for the Gold Coast (Illustrated London News, November 29, 1873)

the rearguard. Shortly after the Ashanti launched a heavy attack on the rearguard coming straight down the path from the village and through the bush on either side of the track. The Naval Brigade halted, assumed the 'kneeling fire' position and beat them off. So roughly were the Ashanti handled in these few minutes that they broke off the action. That evening the force from Borborassi rejoined the main body on the road to Egginassie. All the intelligence, confirmed aurally by loud and persistent drumming, indicated that the Ashanti were massed between Egginassie and Amoaful.

On 30th January the force advanced slowly towards Egginassie cutting a road as they went. Lord Gifford and his scouts made contact with the Ashanti army, finding them encamped in force close to and just the other side of the village. The Ashanti drums again beat all night.

*Lord Gifford and advance scouts on the Adansi Hills warned by an Ashanti priest
not to go forward (Illustrated London News, February 28, 1874)*

After an early breakfast Wolseley launched his men to attack the Ashanti army.
At 0730 Lord Gifford and his scouts seized Egginassie in a pell-mell rush and the
column behind marched through and began to shake out into the hollow square
formation in which Wolseley intended to fight. The face of the square was made up
of the Black Watch extended 300 yards on either side of the path on which, and level
with them, moved the two guns of the Hausas. The sides of the square were to be
formed by the native Regiments of Colonels Baker Russell and Evelyn Wood, each
stiffened by a half of the Naval Brigade and a Hausa rocket team. When clear of
Egginassie each 'side' was to strike out diagonally through the bush to make contact
with their flank of the Black Watch. Wolseley, with his staff and half a company of
the Royal Welsh Fusiliers, marched in the centre of the square. The Rifles covered
the rear and also provided the reserve.

By about 0830 the Black Watch were in line and beginning their advance,
making slow progress against hot opposition. Colonel Baker Russell's command was
the next to pass through the village and advanced in a column on the left diagonal.
They quickly came under heavy fire at close quarters but struggled slowly on.
Colonel Wood's column was the next through and moved off to the right. They were
faced with very thick bush, met the strongest Ashanti opposition and were quickly
brought to a halt. Under cover of the volleys of the half Naval Brigade the native
levies cut a clearing in the bush in which they took up a defensive position.

By 0930 Wolseley and his staff were ensconced in the village, protected by the company of the Royal Welsh Fusiliers and the Rifles. The Black Watch were advancing steadily in concert with the Hausa Artillery, guns and rifles firing volleys into the bush. When opposition fire was beaten down, they advanced about 50 yards and then repeated the action. (One veteran of both the Crimea and Indian Mutiny claimed that the Ashanti fire was heavier than anything he had endured in either war!) The left hand column was also making progress but the right hand column was pinned down and a gap had opened between it and the Black Watch.

The Ashanti now launched a series of attacks on the village and the right hand column. All were beaten off, though not without difficulty. The last attack, just after noon, reached to within 100 yards of Wolseley himself and was only beaten back by the combined fire of the Fusiliers, the Rifles, the staff and the civilian war correspondents. Commodore Hewett drew his sword and led the charge that drove the Ashanti back into the bush.

During the three hours that these attacks had lasted the Black Watch had fought their way into and occupied Amoaful. The left hand column had made contact with them, cleared the left flank and held the road from Egginassie to Amoaful. There was, however, still heavy fighting on the right. Wolseley therefore ordered the Rifles to extend in that direction and sweep through the bush toward Amoaful. This attack was strengthened when it picked up the half Naval Brigade on that flank and gained momentum as Ashanti resistance was overcome. By 1345 all firing had ceased.

Headquarters at the Battle of Amoaful (Illustrated London News, March 29, 1874)

Wolseley concentrated his force on Amoaful to prepare for the final advance on Kumasi. Colonel Colley was sent back to Fommanah with the wounded under escort and to bring up the Regimental baggage, supplies and ammunition. He was to find that the Ashanti were attacking the lines of communication all the way back to Fommanah and had occupied the village of Quarman through which he must pass. Colley fought his way back, cleared Quarman of Ashanti and pressed on to Fommanah, where he arrived in time to help beat off another determined attack. Next morning, leaving the wounded (including the Commanding Officer of the Naval Brigade, five of his officers and 26 ratings) Colley loaded the porters with the stores and other items and set off on the return journey. Again he had to fight his way through Quarman before he rejoined Wolseley.

On 1st February Wolseley disposed his force to cover the return of Colley with the baggage and ammunition. When the convoy arrived he detached a contingent led by Lord Gifford and his scouts and the Naval Brigade as advance guard to clear the village of Becquah, a mile and a half away, where an Ashanti contingent threatened the left rear. Gifford and his scouts rushed the defences and suffered 50% casualties in securing a foothold in the village. The Naval Brigade, close behind, burst through them into the village and hunted the Ashanti from street to street and hut to hut until Bequah was clear. Particularly successful was No. 2 company, drawn from HMS *Druid* that trapped a large party of Ashanti in the central square on which they inflicted heavy casualties. Leaving the place burning, the Naval Brigade withdrew, closely followed by the Ashanti who were drawn into a most successful ambush.

At dawn on 2nd February Wolseley marched from Amoaful. Physical opposition was slight but spiritual opposition was strong — the column marched past a series of mutilated human sacrifices, ju-ju, to prevent the advance. These added to the terror of the native porters, who finally refused to move. The Naval Brigade, acting as rearguard, were left to shepherd the porters along. It was after midnight before they completed the six-mile march and entered camp.

Wolseley's position was precarious. Whilst he was within twelve miles of Kumasi there were 10 000 Ashanti between him and his objective. Another 10 000 were attacking his line of communication back to the Prah. He had rations for four days and could not expect a resupply to reach him for six days. Wolseley made the bold decision to press on and, telling his troops that they would have to do six days work on four days food, entrenched the village in which he dumped all tentage and baggage under guard of his invalids. At dawn on 3rd February he marched for Kumasi.

The River Ordah (sacred to the Ashanti) was reached at about 1500. Baker's native regiment was passed over to form a bridgehead to cover the Royal Engineers who worked through the night to bridge the twenty-yard wide river. All night there were thunderstorms and heavy rain. Wolseley commented, "I never spent a more

Ju-ju house (Illustrated London News, November 29, 1873)

wretched time in any bivouac. No fire would burn and the ground was a soaking mass of mud where few could find any sleep at all".

At dawn on 4th February the column marched over the bridge and within a quarter of an hour came under very heavy fire. Wood's native regiment went to ground and the column halted. Wolseley ordered the Rifles, supported by one gun, to take the lead and continue the advance. It took three hours to fight forward a mile but eventually the Rifles charged into the small village of Ordahsu and secured it. While they held the village Wolesley with his HQ moved in. The remainder of the column formed a lane, firing into the bush on either side, and up this the Naval Brigade, 'an iron shield', drove the terrified porters forward while beating off the Ashanti to the rear. The Ashanti pressed hard and at one time came so close that the staff were firing their revolvers. Wolseley was struck on the helmet by a slug, knocked to the ground and suffered a severe headache.

As soon as the porters with their loads of rations and ammunition were safe in Ordahsu Wolseley ordered the Black Watch, now only 340 strong but the freshest of his troops, to advance to Kumasi. The Black Watch formed into a column of double files and doubled, pipes playing, towards the Ashanti. The leading company halted, turned outwards, and fired steady volleys into the bush. The succeeding companies marched through them, and as each in turn reached the front it too halted and turned to fire. The rear company moved through to take its turn in the vanguard and then the manoeuvre was repeated. In this way the Black Watch cut through the

Ashanti army and vanished towards Kumasi. The Ashanti closed behind them and continued to attack Ordahsu.

After three hours under attack, at about 1400, Wolseley received a message from Brigadier Alison who was with the Black Watch, "Their army is flying…if you will support me vigorously I will be in Kumasi tonight". The troops at Ordahsu, on hearing the content of the message broke into spontaneous cheers. As though this was a signal the Ashanti fusillade ceased. Wolseley, having detailed a garrison for Ordahsu marched off to Kumasi, which he reached at about 1815 to find the Black Watch paraded to greet him with a general salute and to give three cheers for the Queen. The last body of men to enter Kumasi was the Naval Brigade, still acting as the rearguard.

Wolseley was in Kumasi, but in the town his men were outnumbered by armed Ashanti. After 48 hours with very little sleep and having marched for more than 12 hours his men were bone weary. Wolseley decided that all that he could do that night was to keep his troops concentrated. He ordered them to camp along the main avenue and in the main square. Wolseley did not believe in alcohol on active service and throughout the campaign there had been no rum ration (though the Naval Brigade, with its own band of porters, found ways to keep themselves supplied most of the time) but now he authorised an issue of gin, found in King Kofi's palace and pronounced 'excellent Hollands' by the medical staff.

In the morning, after a night disturbed by a series of alarms as large fires broke out in all quarters of the town, the troops woke in a deserted city. They found that the Ashanti had taken their valuables and stolen away. Wolseley hastily mounted a guard over King Kofi's palace where a party of Ashanti loaded with treasure had been caught. He immediately sent in a team of four 'Prize Agents' who worked for the next 24 hours seeking the most valuable items as prize. (Their selection, when sold later at Cape Coast Castle, raised £5500). Then the wounded were sent back and the officers and men spent the day sightseeing. The evidence of human sacrifice and the smell of putrefaction spreading from the sacred grove nauseated almost all.

On 6th February the march back to the coast began. The column simply turned about so that the Naval Brigade became the advance guard. As the Naval Brigade marched out the Royal Engineers began the systematic destruction of the capital by firing the houses and finally exploding all 300 pounds of powder captured in the palace.

The spring rains had set in and the return march, though unopposed by the Ashanti, became a nightmare struggle through viscous mud and across swollen streams and rivers. The bridge over the Ordah was found submerged and breaking up. Here the Naval Brigade rendered their final service.

Together with the Royal Engineers they struggled to repair the damage and keep the bridge usable. Before the rear guard could pass the bridge was finally washed away. Miraculously no one was drowned as the rear guard and those of the

Naval Brigade caught on the wrong side struggled safely through chin high water to the other side.

With the rain came a dramatic increase in the cases of fever. Sickness, increasing weakness and the bad condition of the track reduced the force to chaos. At one time all cohesion was lost and the troops struggled on in groups of ten or twenty, helping to carry or support their sick comrades.

Once back at Prahsu order was re-established. The men were rested and then, detachment by detachment, marched back by the road with all its facilities, to enter Cape Coast Castle through a triumphal arch to re-embark: the soldiers to return to England and a Royal Review in Windsor Great Park, the Naval Brigade to return to their respective ships and their duties on the Cape Station.

Bibliography

Arthur, G. (1922) *The letters of Lord and Lady Wolseley*. Weineman
Brackenbury, H. (1968) *The Ashanti War*. Frank Cass
Howard, P. (1968) *The Black Watch*. Hamish Hamilton
Lehman, J. (1964) *All Sir Garnet*. Jonathon Cape
Lloyd, A. (1964) *The Drums of Kumasi*. Longman
Maxwell, L. (1985) *The Ashanti Ring*. Secker and Warburg
Myatt, F. (1966) *The Golden Stool*. Kimber
Moulton, J. L. (1973) *The Royal Marines*. Sphere
Wolsley, G. (1903) *The Story of a Soldier's Life*. Westminster
Wood, E. (1906) *From Midshipman to Field Marshal*. Methuen

CHAPTER 5

THE ZULU WAR

1878

The Zulu War is one of the more bizarre episodes in the nineteenth century. It
was brought about, against the wishes of Parliament, by the policies of the High
Commissioner for South Africa. It was marked by the great military debacle at
Isandhlwana, by the great heroism at Rorke's Drift, and by the death in a futile
skirmish of the Prince Imperial. It was brought to a successful conclusion by a
disgraced general whose tactical doctrine, ignored by his subordinates who died at
Isandhlwana as a result, was vindicated.

Bizarre, too, were some of the results of the participation of the Royal Naval
Brigades. The first casualty of the war was a sailor, eaten by a crocodile. Details of
the battle at Isandhlwana were to be reported to the Army Commander by a Naval
Officer viewing the fight, through a telescope from a tree. The same Naval Officer
was to be the only member of Army Commander's Staff wounded in the final battle,
and a part of the Naval Brigade was to be besieged for three months thirty miles
from the sea.

In 1878 Cetawayo had ruled the Zulus for five years and had, under his hand,
a large, disciplined and formidable army which posed a considerable threat to the
Boers encroaching from the south and to the developing colony of Natal to the east.
Sir Bartle Frere, the High Commissioner, a Pro-Consul trained in the atmosphere of
India at the time of the Indian Mutiny, was apprehensive of the power and pretention
of the Zulu King. After repeated requests to the Home government, it finally and
reluctantly provided military reinforcements, under the proviso that they were not
to be used aggressively. When the reinforcements arrived, Frere used two minor

border incidents as a reason to provoke a confrontation. An ultimatum was then delivered to Cetawayo, couched in terms which were unthinkable could be accepted, and if not met within thirty days would be enforced by invasion.

The Army Commander was Lieutenant General Lord Chelmsford. He began his career in the Rifle Brigade, transferred to the Guards and saw active service in the Crimea and then in the Indian Mutiny. After commanding the 95th Regiment in India he became Adjutant General on Lord Napier's staff for the Abyssinian campaign. Chelmsford had been in command in South Africa for about a year and had brought an end to the Gaika rebellion, a scrappy bush war from which he could have learnt little that would have been of use in the more open country of Zululand and against the extremely mobile, highly organised Impis of the Zulus. What he had learnt were the general logistic difficulties of operating in South Africa. Bullock-drawn transport, water supplies and firewood for cooking were the factors that limited freedom of movement and the numbers that could reasonably be moved in a formed body.

The logistical difficulties precluded the operation of the army as a united force. It was organised into three columns of approximately equal force to make a concentric advance upon the Zulu capital of Ulundi. This was where Chelmsford expected to bring the Zulu army to battle. Chelmsford himself commanded the centre. To the right hand column, to be commanded by Colonel Pearson, was attached a Naval Brigade of nine officers, 121 seamen and 42 Royal Marines equipped individually with rifles and bayonets with two Armstrong 12 pdr guns, two 7 pdr guns, two rocket tubes and a Gatling gun.

This Naval Brigade was landed from HMS *Active*, the Flagship of the Cape Station in November 1878. It had relieved a company of the Buffs on guard at the Lower Tugela Drift that was to be the river crossing used by the right hand column in its advance into Zululand. A detachment with two Armstrong guns occupied Fort Pearson, an earthen redoubt controlling the Drift, the remainder settled in under canvas. The majority of the men had gained experience of land fighting during the Gaika rebellion just ended, and quickly settled into camp life growing lettuce, radish and keeping poultry.

The first task was to construct a ferry across the Tugela to facilitate the crossing when the time came, and to provide a safe easy route for the onward transport of stores from Natal to the advancing columns. By 4th January 1879 the work on the ferry was complete. The bower anchor had been landed from HMS *Tenedos* and placed on the Zulu shore. From this ran a steel hawser, stretched taut across the 300 yard river. Secured to this and towed back and forth, first by native manpower and latterly by oxen, was a pontoon capable of holding up to 100 men or a heavily laden wagon with its span of oxen. It was the launching of this pontoon that caused the first casualty of the war. As the pontoon was floated, an officer and an able seaman were thrown into the river and the strong current swept them under its bottom. The officer, on the point of collapse, was rescued but the able seaman, reported as taken by a crocodile, was never seen again.

On this day the second battalion of the Buffs marched into camp, followed two days later by another Naval contingent landed from HMS *Tenedos* to take over the garrison duties in Fort Pearson and free the more experienced (in land warfare) members of *Active's* contingent to form a part of the column for the advance into Zululand.

By 11th January the column was complete and ready to advance. The Naval Brigade was accorded the honour of being the first formation to cross, taking up defensive positions to guard the passage of the rest of the force, which was completed on 15th January. By this time the pontoon had carried 2000 soldiers, over 2000 native irregulars, 384 ox wagons and 3500 transport animals. Colonel Pearson was now ready to advance but before doing so he secured his crossing point by constructing an earthwork, christened Fort Tenedos and garrisoned by the Naval contingent from that ship.

Pearson's plan was to advance to an abandoned Mission Station at Eshowe 30 miles into Zululand, to establish an advanced base there and then to co-ordinate his further movements with Lord Chelmsford's central column. His route passed through a rolling stretch of grassland, up steep foothills onto the plateau on which stood Eshowe. The road was bad and the going made worse by the mud resulting from the steady rain which had fallen for days and which had poached the river crossings. Pearson split his force into two columns, and on 18th January set out with the first column of which the Naval Brigade formed a part, followed the next day by the remainder of his command. He advanced steadily, scouting his route systematically and having, on 21st January, burned the deserted military *kraal* of Gingindhlovu (nicknamed by his troops Gin Gin I love you) camped, ready next day to climb up onto the plateau.

The column broke camp at 0500 and after a three-hour march halted for breakfast at the foot of the central of three spurs, up which ran the track to the plateau. Down each of the valleys between the spurs of land ran small streams, and these valleys and the flanks of the spurs were covered in thick bush. At the top of the central spur was a small *kraal*. Concealed behind the right hand spur and waiting to attack the column lay a Zulu Impi of 6000.

Whilst the column was halted for breakfast and the first of the wagon train was coming into the area, a party of Zulu scouts appeared halfway up the central spur. Colonel Pearson sent a company of his native levies to clear the road. The Zulu scouts fell back through the valley onto the right hand spur closely followed by the native levies who, in turn, climbed onto the right hand spur. They were immediately attacked by a large body of Zulus and thrown back. The left wing of the Zulu Impi advanced onto the centre spur while the remainder swept down the right hand spur in an attempt to surround the troops and cut them off from the wagons and rear guard that were still moving up. Colonel Pearson rushed forward his guns and rocket tubes and brought a concentration of fire onto the right hand spur with devastating results. The attack was broken in half, those ahead of the zone of fire vanished into the bush. The main force of Zulus recoiled, to reform at the top of the centre spur under cover of their left wing that had occupied the *kraal*. Zulus started to move down the left hand spur and the British force was engaged from the front and both flanks. The guns and rockets were re-directed onto the *kraal* and the remainder of the Naval Brigade and a company of the Buffs were ordered to advance up the path. The rear guard had come up and began to work through the bush on the right, slowly driving the Zulus before them.

It was then that the Naval Brigade really distinguished themselves. A well-aimed rocket demolished a hut in the *kraal*. The Naval Brigade led the advance up the track and after a short check charged the Zulus with fixed bayonets, driving them back behind the *kraal*, onto the plateau and isolating the Zulus on the left spur. Behind the advance came the Gatling gun, commanded by Midshipman Lewis Coker who had rushed forward from the rear (earning his small niche in history for that was to be the first time that a Gatling was used in battle). Coker's gun was brought into action against the left hand ridge that was quickly cleared of Zulus.

The Impi had now been beaten back at all points and withdrew. The battle had lasted just an hour and a half, the British casualties were ten killed (eight in the first rush) and 16 wounded, of whom seven were sailors: the Zulus withdrew with their dead, estimated at 350.

Pearson did not linger, he had his force, their morale high, well in hand and he pushed on to the plateau to camp in a defensible position a short march from the mission at Eshowe, which he reached without further opposition the next day at noon. Here he decided to stay, consolidate his position and co-ordinate his further advance with the centre column. His empty wagons, under escort, were sent to reload at base and return, whilst the remainder of the force (including the Naval Brigade) began to construct a defensive earthwork round the buildings of the deserted mission station. This earthwork, a rectangle 200 by 500 yards when complete consisted of a trench seven feet deep and an earthen wall six feet high.

Three days after reaching Eshowe, Pearson received the first indications that all was not as well as it might seem. Two messages reached him, the first conveyed the information that a part of Lord Chelmsford's centre column had been destroyed, the second was a report that Fort Tenedos had been attacked the night before. Despite heavy fire from the Fort that had no casualties, no dead or wounded Zulus had been found. After two days of uncertainty and a night stand to for a false alarm, a despatch from Lord Chelmsford arrived. This gave no details of the disaster at Isandhlwana but cancelled his previous instructions and ordered Pearson either to hold Eshowe or to retreat to and hold the Tugela crossing as seemed most appropriate.

Pearson called a council of war. The first decision was to retreat even though — due to a lack of transport — tents, wagons, stores and ammunition (other than the three days rations and ammunition that could be carried) would have to be destroyed. Then it became known that the first of the convoys bringing up provisions was only a few miles away and the orders for the retreat were rescinded. Instead it was decided to hold Eshowe as long as provisions made this possible and to reduce the garrison to the minimum required. The Natal Native Regiment, The Natal Volunteer Horse and the Mounted Infantry were sent back by a forced march.

This left 1397 Europeans and 462 natives within the, by now, well entrenched encampment. There seemed no reason to expect a long siege. Nevertheless work continued on the defences. A field of fire was cut out to a distance of 800 yards and range markers for both artillery and small arms positioned. This cleared area also provided space in which by day the diminishing asset of ration cattle and trek ox could be grazed in safety. The church building was taken over by surgeon Norbury of the Naval Brigade and became the hospital.

The last written communication was received on 11th February, brought in by native runners who had made their way up from Lord Chelmsford through the surrounding Zulus. They brought the unpalatable news that relief could not arrive for a considerable time and ordering the return of the surplus garrison. Colonel Pearson called another council of war and after deliberation it was proposed that the Naval Brigade with one gun, three companies of the 99th Regiment, the Royal Engineers and their native Pioneers should break out and make a night march to Tugela. This decision was quickly reconsidered and the whole force settled down to endure a long siege.

The Zulus made no attempt to attack the defences. They were content to cover the Fort and to try and ambush small parties out scouting, herding cattle and cutting wood. These ambushes took the form of volleys of rifle fire from concealed positions in the long grass, often from long range. Eventually it became necessary to guard the grazing cattle and their herdsmen with a force of three companies of infantry. This was regarded as a dull chore, though the daily sighting of bodies of three of four hundred Zulus circling the defences at about 1500 yards justified this daily activity.

Colonel Pearson was not content to remain inactive. At the end of February he led a force of about half his command and one gun on a sortie to destroy a large military *kraal* some seven miles away. This force included the Royal Marine contingent of the Naval Brigade. After a night march starting at 0200, the force was within half a mile of the *kraal* when it was detected and the alarm raised. One shell was fired into the *kraal* that was then rushed and within a few minutes it was in flames. Another *kraal* about a mile away seemed too difficult to attack and the force commenced its return.

A running fight then developed as the Zulus attacked the flanks of the column with rifle fire. The small Royal Marine detachment was ordered to clear a hill of

Zulus. At the summit they were greeted with a volley fired from concealment. Their return fire aimed at the muzzle smoke brought down two Zulus and the remainder fled. Later the Marines were in the rear, guarding the one gun, and halted whilst the gun was brought into action to clear another hill, giving another successful little action. Later Colonel Pearson led another sortie, but without the Naval Brigade, to capture cattle to augment the stock of beef on the hoof. This sortie brought in 35 head of cattle.

Conditions within the perimeter were not good. The season was unusually wet and the temperature fluctuated wildly. The garrison slept in the open or, at best, under a parked wagon in full uniform and ready to man their defensive position within three minutes. Snakes were a constant cause of alarm. Rations were monotonous: one and a half pounds of fresh meat (slaughtered cattle or trek ox) with a third of an ounce of salt and three quarters of a pound of biscuit or meal daily, with a third of an ounce of coffee and one and a quarter ounces of sugar. One sixth of an ounce of tea was issued on three days of the week only. For a short period, half an ounce of limejuice and half an ounce of compressed vegetables were available to supplement the ration. When these were exhausted there were rare occasions when pumpkins from the abandoned mission garden could be gathered or sufficient leaves of the white arum lily found and served boiled (described as an excellent dish, resembling spinach). For entertainment the bands of the Buffs and of the 99th Regiment gave evening concerts. The chaplain (an Anglican missionary who had volunteered his services to the column) held Bible classes three times a week. There was a church parade each Sunday.

By the end of February the health of the garrison deteriorated. Remittent fever and dysentery appeared. Medicines became exhausted. Surgeon Norbury was reduced to treating the sick with horse medicines and a concoction from the bark of the water-boom tree that was used for its powerful astringent qualities. Five of the Naval Brigade, including Midshipman Coker, died during the siege.

After 11th February there was no communication possible until the Naval Brigade constructed a heliograph. The greatest problem had been to direct the reflected ray of sunlight accurately over a distance of some 30 miles. Directing the ray down a fixed tube from a stationary mirror and using a simple shutter to make the signal solved this. The tube was bore sighted at the receiving station and when the sun shone there was a signal link with Fort Pearson on the Tugela. After 35 days of complete isolation communication was sometimes possible.

Three days after communication had been established the garrison was cheered by a message that an attempt to relieve them would be made in the middle of March and giving orders that they were to sally out to meet the relieving force. This they prepared to do, cutting in the face of Zulu resistance a new road through the trees and bush to facilitate the rapid movement of men and guns when the time came. But relief was delayed. Lord Chelmsford decided to command a larger force himself and set the date of 1st April.

Lord Chelmsford had been forced, with the remnant of the centre column, to retreat to Natal after the defeat at Isandhlwana and required time to re-organise and re-equip and for reinforcements to arrive. The first of these were due to the initiative of the Captain of HMS *Shah* which, returning to England to pay off, was anchored at St Helena when the news of Isandhlwana reached the island. On his own responsibility he embarked a company of the 88th Regiment and a battery of Royal Artillery from the island garrison and took them to Durban. Here he landed 16 officers and 378 men who, together with ten officers and 218 men from HMS *Boadicea* and the three officers and 58 men from HMS *Tenedos* formed a Naval Brigade under the command of Commodore Richards (the commander-in-chief of the Cape Station) as a part of the force that marched to the relief of Eshowe.

By 25th March Lord Chelmsford had assembled a force of well over 4000 of which less than 1000 were natives with a minimum number of ox carts and oxen. The first task of the Naval Brigade was to ferry the force and its transport across the Tugela using the pont constructed by the crew of *Active* five months before. This took three full days; over 100 trips were required for the transport alone.

On 29th March the advance to Eshowe began. Hampered by wet and foggy weather, the column pushed slowly forward until on 1st April, after making good

Life on board a troopship: Heaving the log
(Illustrated London News, November 29, 1873)

Life on board a troopship: Washing the decks
(Illustrated London News, November 29, 1873)

only five miles, it camped close to the burnt *kraal* of Gingindhlovu. The state of the ground after the very heavy rain made it impossible to move the wagons next day and reconnaissance during the march had revealed that an Impi was nearby.

The camp was laid out as a square of 130 yards with 30 wagons or carts to a side and with a shelter trench holding 2000 men in close order 15 yards in front of the wagons. The four corners of the square and the adjacent parts of each front were manned by the Naval Brigade with their guns, rockets and Gatlings. The remainder of the faces were filled with the infantry. The mounted infantry, volunteer cavalry and the native contingent camped within the wagon wall. A screen of pickets was thrown out round the laager. With these dispositions made Lord Chelmsford planned an early morning sortie by his native irregulars to make contact with the Impi, engage it and then fall back on the laager, enticing the Zulus within range of the fixed defences.

The 2nd April dawned fine but with an early morning mist. At 0600, as the natives were setting out, firing was heard from the pickets. As they fell back and the mist lifted, an estimated 10 000 Impi could be seen. They were armed with guns, *assagai* and small shields, facing the front and left faces of the laager, advancing in their usual formation with the horns moving out to encircle the British position. The whole force stood to and were ordered not to fire until the Zulus had closed to 300 yards.

A part of the Zulu Impi was formed in full view about half a mile from the left front angle of the laager. To the petty officer in charge of the Gatling gun in this position this seemed a perfect target and possibly a golden opportunity about to be lost. His demands to open fire were heard by Lord Chelmsford who approved the firing of a short burst to try the range. The petty officer promptly fired a long burst which cut a swathe through the massed Impi. (This petty officer, by his conduct during the battle, greatly impressed a senior army officer who commented that during the fight his exhortations to his crew would have made, when carefully expurgated, an admirable essay on behaviour under fire.)

The Zulus continued their advance and encircling movements. When 300 yards away, they were met by controlled volley fire from the infantry and by bursts of fire from the Gatling guns. Under cover from the long grass the Zulus were able to press forward, in places to within 30 yards of the British positions, and made repeated, uncoordinated but unsuccessful attempts to reach the British lines. In the intervals between these attacks the Zulus fired with very little effect upon the British lines, whilst the British infantry remained at the kneeling alert position, ready when ordered to open fire.

After about an hour and a half the Zulus were wavering and those in the right horn, facing the rear of the laager, began to pull back. The infantry were ordered to stand fast. A final volley was fired while the mounted troops and native contingent were released to attack the retreating Zulus who fired once more and broke into flight. About a mile from the laager a large party rallied but before this rally became general the body of Zulus were brought under accurate shellfire by the Naval Brigade guns and dispersed. Apart from the cavalry pursuit this sharp action was over. The rest of the day was spent in burying the dead, scavenging the battlefield and preparing for the relief of Eshowe the next day. British casualties were nine killed and six officers and 46 men wounded, including two officers and six men of the Naval Brigade. The Zulu losses were estimated at 1200, some 700 of which were buried on the field. 400 guns and rifles (many of which were Martinis lost at Isandhlwana) were picked up.

On 3rd April Lord Chelmsford, leaving half his force in camp, made a forced march to Eshowe with the remainder (including one company of the Naval Brigade and the Royal Marines). The route took them along the path followed by the fleeing Zulus and was littered by the detritus of the broken Impi. More loot from Isandhlwana was recovered. With a touch of typical Victorian panache the final junction of the two forces was made to the sound of the pipes of the Argylls.

The 4th April was spent in the systematic destruction of Eshowe and any of its contents that could not be carried away. Next morning Colonel Pearson marched out his garrison, followed after another four hours of demolition by the relieving force. By 7th April the combined force was back on the banks of the River Tugela and there went into camp where the Naval Brigade, now including the crew of the *Active* from Eshowe, remained whilst Lord Chelmsford, awaiting further reinforcements, reformed his army for another invasion of Zululand.

Chelmsford reformed his army into two Divisions and a flying column, both under his direct command, to march on Ulundi from the hinterland of Natal, the other Division commanded by Major General Crealock, to advance on Ulundi from the coast. The whole Naval Brigade was attached to this division. Their base was moved up the coast from the mouth of the Tugela to an open beach, misnamed Port Durnford, where it was possible, when surf was not running, to land supplies over the beach. It was on beach duties that the Naval Brigade was to be employed for the rest of the war. Crealock was beset by supply difficulties and could make no advance — his division earned the nickname of 'Crealock's crawlers' and was to see no further action.

When ready, Chelmsford set off for Ulundi, aware that Sir Garnet Wolseley had been appointed in overall command. He was determined, if possible, to win the war before Sir Garnet could arrive, claim all the glory and, by inference if nothing else, denigrate his efforts. On 28th June Wolseley arrived in Durban. He appreciated that Chelmsford was probably approaching Ulundi but could not establish his whereabouts and knew that it would take days to find him. He determined to take command of Crealock's Division, advance by forced marches to Ulundi and pre-empt Chelmsford by fighting and winning the final battle. He embarked in HMS *Shah* for Port Durnford where his efforts to land were confounded by heavy surf. Wet and seasick he returned on board and arrived back in Durban on 3rd July, setting out the same day to ride to Port Durnford.

Whilst Wolseley was riding north Chelmsford brought the Zulu army to battle near Ulundi, smashed them with volley fire from his square and, finally seeing his tactical doctrine vindicated, brought the war to a victorious conclusion. Chelmsford then resigned his command and returned to England, leaving to Wolseley the problem of capturing Cetewayo and pacifying the country. In this battle, the only Naval representative, Lieutenant Milne the Naval Liaison Officer on Chelmsford's staff (the same officer who, with his telescope, had climbed a tree and reported something of the scene at Isandhlwana) was one of the few wounded.

It is the final irony that it was Sir Garnet Wolseley, under whom the Naval Brigade had not fought, who issued the general order that marked the dissolution of this Naval Brigade:

"It is the Naval Brigade is now about to embark, General Sir Garnet Wolseley wishes to place on record his very high appreciation of the services it has rendered while acting on shore. The conduct of the men has been admirable and their bearing in action in every way worthy of the service to which they belong, while they have worked hard and cheerfully in these laborious duties which constitute a part of all military operations. In returning to their ships, they will have the satisfaction of knowing that all recollection of the Zulu war will be associated with the Naval Brigade, which has borne so distinguished a part in it. "

Bibliography

Fletcher-Campbell, J. H. (year unknown) *Naval Brigades*. RUSI

Clammer, D. (1973) *The Zulu War*. David and Charles

Emery, F. (1977) *The Red Soldier*. Wodder and Stoughton

Lloyd, A. (1973) *The Zulu War — 1879*. Longmans

Molyneaux, W. C. F. (1896) *Campaigning in South Africa and Egypt*. London

Morris, D. R. (1965) *The Washing of the Spears*. Konecky and Konecky

Norbury, (1880) *The Naval Brigades in South Africa during the years 1877/78/79*. London

CHAPTER 6

THE FIRST BOER WAR

1880–1881

The Great Trek of the Boers from British rule in the Cape Province resulted in the establishment of the two autonomous republics of the Orange Free State and the Transvaal. The citizens of the Transvaal, having left British rule behind, were unwilling to accept another authority, even that of their own legislature. Their contempt for government, evinced by a general refusal to pay taxes, produced a chaotic situation and near bankruptcy with, by 1877, a national debt of £15 000 and only 55 pence in the Treasury.

The growing military power of the Zulu nation was a threat to the Transvaal and to its neighbour, the growing British colony of Natal. Therefore in 1877 the British Government stepped in, and with the consent of the President and the agreement of a fair number of the most prominent citizens, annexed the Transvaal giving vague promises to grant representative government in the future.

The British efforts to impose orderly government and, in particular, an insistence upon the payment of taxes was resented. There was no progress toward self-government. Slowly the Boers accepted the leadership of their former Vice President, Paul Kruger, who campaigned for complete independence. Whilst the Zulu nation threatened, he advocated for a peaceful settlement with Britain. Based on Prime Minister Gladstone's earlier fulminations in opposition and during the election campaign of 1880 Kruger believed that a Liberal government in London would restore independence to the Transvaal.

The Zulu war removed many of the Boers inhibitions against covert action. Whilst the debacle at Isandlwana left them with contempt for the fighting ability of the British army, the victory at Uluni destroyed the threat of Zulu power. The Boers found that Mr Gladstone, as Prime Minister, had no intention of granting them independence. The British government, misled by complacent reports from the administrator in Pretoria and the assurances from Sir Garnet Wolseley that the Boers were overawed and would not fight, reduced the garrison in the Transvaal and in Natal to only three battalions. The one battalion in the Transvaal was split into seven detachments dotted in towns throughout the country. The Boers had arranged a mass meeting at Paardekraal for January 1881, and on 25th October the administrator in Pretoria assured General Colley in Pietermaritzburg that he had no anxiety about this. Indeed, on 7th November a force of 285 mounted volunteers were sent out of the country to assist in the suppression of an armed rising in Basutoland.

On 11th November there was a riot at Potchesfstroom where a party of armed Boers, led by Piet Cronjie, broke up the auction of a farmer's wagon which had been distrained for tax arrears. The administrator sent infantrymen to arrest the ringleaders but sent far too small a force to take any effective action. Meanwhile Boers brought forward their mass meeting to 6th November when 4000 Boers assembled, declared the independence of the Transvaal, elected to power, pending a meeting of a representative Volksraad, a triumvirate in which political power rested with Paul Kruger. Joubert was appointed as Commandant General and three Commandos were formed. One of these moved toward Pretoria, one occupied Heidelburg as a temporary capital, and the third moved on Potchesfstroom where on 16th December the first shots of the war were to be fired and the small British garrison came under siege.

General Colley had two bodies of troops moving towards Pretoria, one company of the 58th routed through Standerton and the headquarters and two companies of the 94th moving through Lydenburg. Colley ordered the company of the 58th to halt in Standerton to reinforce the small garrison there; and there they remained, under siege, until the end of the war. The 94th were allowed to continue their march; Colley believing that they were moving as a flying column. This was the first of the mistakes that Colley was to make for the C O of the 94th thought of the march as a leisurely journey between stations under peacetime conditions and was making good no more than ten miles a day with a column of nine officers, 254 rank and file, three women and two children, twenty eight ox wagons and five mule carts all straggling over a mile of road.

On 20th December, after the midday halt, the column, led by the Band, was moving down towards the Bronkhorst Spruit when, on a ridge to their left, a party of mounted Boers appeared and sent down a message under a flag of truce. It stated that the Transvaal was now a republic and that the advance of the troops beyond the Spruit would be regarded as a hostile act. The Colonel was allowed two minutes to reply to this ultimatum and answered, predictably, that he had no wish to fight the Boers but he was ordered to Pretoria and to Pretoria he must go. The Boer messenger rode off and vanished into the cover at the side of the road. Colonel Anstruther rode back and ordered his men to collect ammunition and move into skirmishing order. While the ammunition boxes were being broken open the Boers, from cover on each side of the road and at about 200 yards range, opened rapid fire. The Colonel and all his officers were shot down and the other ranks were decimated. Within 15 minutes the seriously wounded Colonel ordered his men to surrender. British casualties were 57 dead and over 100 wounded of whom 20, including Colonel Anstruther, died later. The volume and intensity of the Boer fire can be judged from the fact that the average number of wounds per man was five.

The Boers had by now brought all the scattered British garrisons in the Reansvaal under siege and moved a force to Laing's Nek inside Natal. There they effectively cut the direct road from Natal into the Transvaal in the pass where it ran through the Drakensburg Mountains. Their position was a naturally strong one. Laing's Nek is a high ridge, running from the dominating height of Majuba Hill to the lower height of Table Hill, where the flank was anchored on a deep gorge through which ran the Buffalo River. The approach from the British side was over a four-mile stretch of open ground cut by ravines and with a steep climb to the ridge. The reverse slope was gentler and the Boers, laagered behind the Nek could gallop from the laager to their positions, or from point to point to reinforce a threatened strongpoint.

General Colley set about collecting his forces and on 3rd January 1881 he reviewed the army that he had scraped together. It consisted of the 21st (100 men), the 58th (480 men), the 3rd/60th Rifles (350 men), a regular battery of four 9 pdr guns and a makeshift battery of 7 pdr guns drawn by mules and nicknamed the Royal Ass Battery, and 120 irregular cavalry. In addition there was a Naval Brigade of five officers and 124 ratings with two Gatling guns and three rocket tubes which had been raised by Commodore Richards, the naval commander-in-chief of the Cape Station at the request of General Colley.

Colley had been promised reinforcements from home but he decided that he should advance to relieve the besieged garrisons, believing that the Boers could not stand in the face of artillery and, therefore, that his six guns and three naval rocket launchers gave him a decisive advantage. On 24th January, in heavy rain, the force marched out of Newcastle. The weather and road conditions reduced progress to a crawl such that it took three days to march a mere twelve miles. At the end of the third day the force went into camp at a farm named Mount Prospect, four miles from the ridge at Laing's Nek. Here they dug an earthwork and settled in to wait for better weather.

On 28th January there was a break in the weather and Colley moved to attack the Boer positions on the Nek. Leaving the 100 men of the 21st and 30 sailors with the two Gatling guns to protect the camp he marched out at 0700. At 0915 the column had reached the foot of the rise to the Nek and, in full view of the Boers,

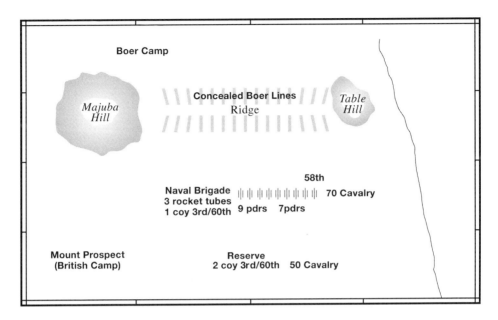

Boer Camp

Concealed Boer Lines

Majuba Hill

Ridge

Table Hill

58th

Naval Brigade
3 rocket tubes
1 coy 3rd/60th

9 pdrs   7pdrs

70 Cavalry

Mount Prospect
(British Camp)

Reserve
2 coy 3rd/60th   50 Cavalry

Laing's Nek, where Colley launched an attack on Boers positioned along the ridge

took up their positions for the attack. Colley planned to attack the Boer positions on Table Hill on the right of his line and placed the 58th, supported by 70 of his horse, to make the attack. In his centre he placed his guns and on the left a company of the 3rd/60th and the Naval Brigade with its rockets. Three companies of the 3rd/60th and the remainder of the horse he held in reserve.

Colley began the action with searching fire from his guns and the Naval rockets directed at the Boer positions on the skyline. This bombardment caused few casualties but affected Boer morale, and the sight of some burghers galloping from their positions and of horses bolting gave Colley a false impression of the strength of the opposition. After only 20 minutes Colley ordered the 58th to advance, supported by the cavalry. With their colours in the centre (the last time that Regimental Colours were carried into action) and with the cavalry in two lines on their left the 58th doubled up the hill towards the enemy. The steepness of the slope slowed the advance of the infantry and the cavalry's charge was launched prematurely. With only 70 men the charge lacked weight and withered under the Boer fire with half the men unhorsed and 17 killed, wounded or missing.

The 58th struggled on up towards the summit. When they were so close that the artillery ceased fire, the Boer riflemen hit them with a punishing volley. Their officers suffered heavy casualties and with control lost, the 58th went to ground and fired wildly towards the Boers. Officer after officer, including some of Colley's staff, tried to organise a charge and at one time, to quote Joubert (the Boer Commander), "came so close that the dead of each side fell in amongst each other". But the Boers were being reinforced quickly and after half an hour Colley sounded the retreat. The men of the 58th ran back down the hill and reformed at its foot, followed by the Boers who broke cover in pursuit. The artillery and Naval rockets gave covering fire to the retreating infantry, which when it had reformed drove off the Boers. Over on the left a party of Boers moved to attack the Naval Brigade, still in action with its rockets. The Boers were checked by fire from 3rd/60th Rifles and withdrew. Colley allowed the action to peter out and the last shot was fired at 1200.

Under a flag of truce Colley buried his 83 dead and collected his 111 wounded and then marched back to his camp at Mount Prospect. Here he settled down in his entrenchments hoping that Joubert would attack the camp. Joubert was too wise to do this but instead sent bodies of mounted men to operate on the lines of communication between Mount Prospect and Newcastle. Such was the effect that on 8th February the commanding officer in Newcastle delayed the despatch of a convoy of 40 bullock wagons loaded with stores and ammunition until, with the arrival of reinforcements from Pietermaritzburg, there would be an adequate escort. Colley determined upon a demonstration in force to clear his communications and early on 9th February he set off with 38 mounted infantry, 237 men of the 3rd/60th and four guns. Expecting to be back in camp by 1530, at which time he had ordered his men's dinners to be ready, he took no water cart. Having dropped off a company of the 3rd/60th and two guns to guard the ford he crossed the Ingogo River and climbed onto a small plateau of about four acres. It offered little cover, was surrounded by slopes covered with grass four feet high, rocky, and split by shallow *dongas*, making it ideally suited to the Boers' tactic of firing from cover. Colley met the Boers taking up a position with his infantry disposed round the rim, apart from a small reserve that with the two guns were placed in the middle of the plateau. Nearly surrounded, Colley was pinned down and suffered heavy casualties but at dusk managed to drive off a large Boer attack delivered under cover of the incessant rain that had been falling since 1700.

In the increasing darkness the Boers disengaged and returned to their camp. Believing that the Ingogo River was now impassable because it was swollen by rain, and that Colley must surrender in the morning, they failed to keep him under observation and neglected to keep any force at the ford. At 2100 Colley began his preparations for retreat and at 2300, leaving his wounded under the care of a surgeon, the chaplain and a non-combatant volunteer, began a remarkable night march. He brought his men across the Ingogo, missed the force he had left to secure the ford and which had been reinforced by all the remaining infantry from Mount Prospect, and finally reached camp where he was greeted by the Naval Brigade which had been left in charge. Next morning the Boers were so surprised to find only the wounded on the plateau that they made no attempt to follow up their success, so Colley was able to withdraw the remainder of his troops unopposed to within the camp from the ford.

After these two battles Colley had lost, in killed and wounded, a quarter of his force and had no choice but to wait for the reinforcements that were on the way to him. Ironically, it is probable that it was the beleaguered forces, pinning down the Commandos inside the Transvaal, preventing a Boer concentration and attack in overwhelming strength before the reinforcements arrived.

Meanwhile Colley, in his capacity as High Commissioner, was, at the direction of the Westminster government and with the President of the Orange Free State, acting as a mediator, negotiating with the Boers. These negotiations led, on 21st February, to the offer of an armistice.

Brigadier Evelyn Wood VC arrived in Newcastle on 17th February, bringing with him two veteran battalions from India (2nd/60th and 92nd), a part of the 17th Hussars, and a reinforcement of 60 men from HMS *Dido* and *Boadicea* for the Naval Brigade. Wood's arrival was an embarrassment to Colley. Wood was his senior, with an outstanding record as a successful fighting leader of men, and though Wood had agreed to subordinate himself to Colley he began to impose his own ideas. He took a party of the 17th Hussars and made a 60-mile reconnaissance round the Boer left flank. On his return he agreed with Colley that there should be no advance until reinforcements arrived. He then returned to Newcastle to hasten forward the three battalions of infantry, the regiment of cavalry and the guns that were on their way.

Colley had written to Sir Garnet Wolseley at the War Office, "My failure at Laing's Nek will inflict a deep and permanent injury on the British name and power in South Africa which it is not pleasant to contemplate". He had told Wood, "You will understand that I want to take the Nek myself." Back at Mount Prospect, and having sent off the offer of an armistice to Kruger, Colley began to study Majuba hill.

Majuba hill is an extinct volcano about 2000 feet high with a saucer shaped summit between 300 and 400 feet in diameter, edged with boulders and rocky outcrops. It dominated the Boer laager. The face above this was the easiest to climb and offered much dead ground and ample cover on the slopes. The remaining faces of the hill appeared unclimable. Colley knew that the Boers mounted a daily picket on the summit but left the hill unoccupied at night.

On 24th February Colley made a reconnaissance round the reverse slopes of Majuba. From natives encountered and questioned he learnt of the existence of a goat track to the summit where he would find plenty of water. He spent the whole of 26th February sitting at the door of his tent examining, through binoculars, the nearest face of the hill and conferring with his chief of staff. At dusk he saw the Boer picket leave the summit.

At 2030, to everyone's surprise, Colley issued a verbal order for two companies of the 58th, two companies of the 3rd/60th, three companies of the 92nd and a part of

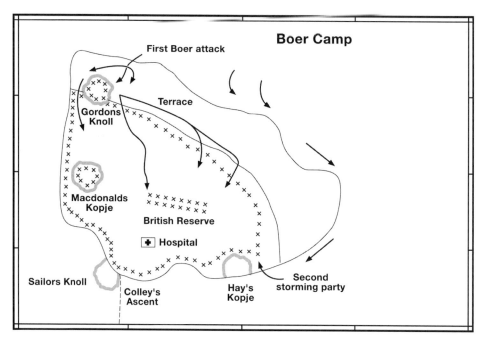

Colley led a column up to the summit of Majuba Hill before forming defensive positions

the Naval Brigade to prepare for a march carrying three days provisions, 70 rounds of ammunition, a blanket, waterproof sheet and a greatcoat. Each company was to carry four shovels and six picks. At 2200, led by Colley himself, the march began, the destination unannounced. After an hour Colley dropped off the two companies of the 3rd/60th to occupy the low hill between Mount Prospect and Majuba and then moved on. There was an hour's delay when the Naval Brigade at the rear of the column lost touch and had to be found and led back to its proper place.

At the foot of Majuba, Colley dropped off a company of the 92nd and sent back all horses. Then, at 0130 on 27th February the column, in single file, began to climb the goat track leading to the summit. Sometimes on hands and knees, hauling themselves up by any available handhold, the straggling, single file column struggled upwards. At 0340 the first man slipped over the lip of the saucer and found the summit unoccupied. Each man, at the end of his climb, was allowed a five minute rest with loosened equipment and was then directed to his position, either a defensive one at the line of the saucer's lip or in reserve in the hollow in the centre, where a well was dug and a tented hospital erected.

Colley made his defensive dispositions in the dark, splitting each component in his force in half, one half on the perimeter, one half in a central reserve. The 92nd were placed to cover the north and west sides with pickets on two forward spurs, the eastern face was the responsibility of the 58th. The Naval Brigade covered the line of ascent. No instructions to dig in were given, and when the 92nd asked if they might entrench themselves, Colley replied, "No – the men are tired and there is no necessity for it". He then commented to his chief of staff, "We could stay here for ever". So the force settled in with some complacency.

As dawn broke and the light improved the main Boer laager could be seen. When an officer of the 58th borrowed a rifle and fired a random shot into the laager to be followed by a spattering of other random shots the Boers were taken completely by surprise. There was a period of confusion in the Boer camp and in the expectation of an artillery bombardment and/or an attack on the Nek, the Boers began some panicky preparations for retreat. When nothing happened Joubert stopped the preparations for retreat and ordered an attempt to retake Majuba before riding off to resist the attack on the Nek that never came.

By about 0700 the Boers had made their dispositions and began the assault. About 150 of the older men were posted to keep the rim of the summit swept with rifle fire. The remainder of the Boers, about another 150 men, were split into two bodies, about 100 yards apart. They employed fire and movement tactics, covering each other as they advanced alternately up the northern and western faces where the going was comparatively easy and there was, near the summit, a natural terrace which provided dead ground in which to shelter. When more men arrived, a third party was formed to climb the eastern face so that the British position could be attacked from three sides.

Colley cannot have believed that the Boers would actually come to close quarters. He made no attempt to check his dispositions, made in darkness, to see if they could be improved. The reserve, in the centre of the saucer, breakfasted, smoked and relaxed with all equipment off — many fell asleep. At 0930 Colley, now in touch with Mount Prospect by heliograph, signalled, "All very comfortable. Boers wasting ammunition. One man wounded in foot." Colley later announced his intention to return to Mount Prospect himself, leaving Commander Romilly of the Naval Brigade in command of all troops on the summit. Just before 1100 he was discussing the arrangements with his staff and Commander Romilly when Romilly was hit by a bullet that passed through his body and out of his back. Romilly was taken to the hospital by the naval surgeon, who happened to be nearby. Colley made another signal: "Boers still firing heavily on the hill but have broken up laager and begun to move away. I regret to say Commander Romilly dangerously wounded, other casualties three men slightly wounded."

The Naval Brigade was disposed with a picket of six men on a knoll about 20 feet below the lip of the summit. Guarding the approach to it were 28 men in positions covering a stretch of about 200 yards of the lip of the summit and 29 men with the reserve. Lieutenant Trower, now in command of the Naval Brigade and his only other officer, Sub Lieutenant Scott, were with the men on the lip. Surgeon

Mahon and his sick berth attendant were with the army surgeons and their orderlies at the hospital

Just before he was wounded Commander Romilly had ordered Lieutenant Trower to take twelve of his seamen across the plateau, but for what reason is now unknown. The reserve was still left untouched. When Trower returned to his position, he ordered Sub Lieutenant Scott to take charge of the picket below the lip.

At about 1100 the Boer fire increased in severity. The pickets of the 92nd, on which the Boer attack was closing, requested reinforcement. Colley's only reply was, "Hold the place for three days". Then he calmly lay down and slept. While he was asleep the Boers closed up on the positions held by the 92nd and 58th and came so close that their voices could be heard. Lieutenant (later General Sir) Ian Hamilton of the 92nd sought Colley to obtain approval for a bayonet charge to clear his front. Colley's chief of staff intercepted him and told him that the General (who was still asleep) knew what was going on and that there was no reason for concern. In the next half hour there was a lull in the firing as the Boers worked round the hill, in the shelter of the dead ground, and established two firing lines.

At 1330 Colley was awake and, oblivious to the true position, was discussing the siting of and construction of redoubts. Lieutenant Hamilton of the 92nd appeared and again requested orders for a bayonet charge. Colley replied, "Wait till the Boers come across the open and we will give them a volley first and charge afterwards".

At about this time a party of Boers slipped over the lip unobserved. Their first volley into the rear of a picket of the 92nd destroyed it. Then shooting obliquely into the rear of the positions held by the 92nd and 58th they inflicted heavy casualties and covered further Boer penetrations of the saucer. Sub Lieutenant Scott, alarmed by the sudden increase in the volume of fire and by some men who passed his position shouting that the Boers were on the top of the hill and driving the British back, used his initiative and led his six men towards the sound of the firing. He saw nothing of the rest of the Naval Brigade but observed "a great number of wounded men" in the hollow before receiving an order from Colley, passed to him by the correspondent of the *Daily News*, to return to his original position.

Colley suddenly found that his perimeter had been broken and called on the reserve that had not been alerted and was still resting, some indeed still asleep. There was considerable confusion because time to form up properly was not allowed. Inextricably mixed and not knowing to whom to look for orders, they were pushed into line and marched towards the rim. Suddenly they were halted facing a line of Boers who immediately fired a volley that dropped a quarter of them. Already disorganised and confused, the shock of this proved too much and the reserve line broke and ran. Some of the men bolted over the lip of the saucer in panic, but most were rallied in the centre and were joined by men falling back from the lip. In the centre of the line was Colley trying to steady them.

Under fire from three sides the British line wavered and broke in confusion. Colley advanced towards the Boers and was shot. He was not supported, instead, in panic and rout the remnants of the British force made a wild rush down the slopes of Majuba hill hastened by the Boers firing down from the lip. Sub Lieutenant Scott, seeing the rout, led his six men down to safety at Mount Prospect, although two were wounded. Lieutenant Trower and two men of the Naval Brigade were among the last killed on the summit, still guarding the path down. One sailor said, "It took me five bleedin' hours to get up that hill but I only touched it three times coming down".

The company of the 92nd at the foot of Majuba had, during the forenoon, been reinforced by a company of the 60th, who had brought forward a stock of provisions and a reserve of ammunition. The position had been entrenched. The commander of this little force acted with determination and initiative. The infantry manned the entrenchment while the Hussars, of who 50 had also come forward, rode out collecting stragglers and aiding the wounded. Eventually the Hussars were driven off by a larger body of mounted Boers that had ridden round the foot of Majuba to break up the British line of communication with Mount Prospect. The entrenchment was brought under "really heavy and sustained fire" and it was possible that the men there might be cut off. At the last minute, orders to fall back to Mount Prospect came through, and in a skilful fighting retreat the companies of the 60th and 92nd made their way back. They suffered casualties from Boer rifle fire and from 'friendly' gunfire, losing an officer and 22 men cut off and captured, but bringing in the reserve ammunition. The end of the retreat was covered by infantry, Hussars, artillery and by the remainder of the Naval Brigade with the two Gatlings.

Mount Prospect had been hastily prepared to withstand an assault, and as the men came in the wounded were sent to hospital and the fit to their posts on the defences. But there was to be no assault. Towards 1700, when the last shot was fired, a thick mist rose and Joubert called off further operations saying, "Look at the mist, the Lord won't allow us to go on."

On the top of the hill remained the victorious Boers and the British dead, wounded and prisoners with surgeon Mahon, his sick berth attendant and the two surviving army medical orderlies. Both army surgeons and the other two orderlies had all been killed while tending the wounded. Mahon had some difficulty in persuading the Boers that he was a doctor and even more in preventing the summary execution of the wounded Commander Romilly who was taken for either Sir Garnet Wolseley or Sir Evelyn Wood. Mahon obtained an interview with the Boer Commander on the spot who promised every assistance with the treatment of the wounded, but who did not prevent the looting of the dead, the wounded and the medical stores. All the medical brandy was quickly drunk.

By about 1430 Mahon was able to set to work. The unwounded prisoners were sent to search for and bring into the hospital the seriously wounded, and with the

Boers consent the walking wounded were sent down the hill to find their way into camp. Mahon also tried to send down Commander Romilly on a stretcher, carried by four unwounded sailors. Half way down they were intercepted by a party of Boers who removed three of the sailors and left Commander Romilly, with one to care for him, to spend the night under a bush. Found next morning, he was taken into Mount Prospect where he later died.

Thirty-six seriously wounded were collected into one spot and luckily there were just enough blankets and waterproof sheets to cover them. At about 1800 the Boers withdrew the unwounded prisoners just as a thick mist reached the summit. Mahon and Davis, his sick berth attendant, carried on searching as long as they could do so in safety, and then settled down to care for the wounded through the night. Not that they could do much, for they were without any form of artificial light, had only a little opium and it began to rain heavily with a severe temperature drop near morning.

At about 0600 on 29th February a party of two doctors with stretcher bearers carrying medical comforts arrived on the summit and relieved Mahon who brought down the hill as many wounded as could be moved, arriving in camp at about 1700.

The cost of the battle was six officers and 93 men dead, seven officers and 125 men wounded and 49 nine captured. The Naval Brigade lost 36, more than half the number who set out.

The morale of the garrison at Mount Prospect sank to a very low level, and there was much inter-unit bickering about who was to blame. Then Sir Evelyn Wood rode into camp and assumed command. His personality and leadership and the news of reinforcements to come quickly brought a change for the better, and defeatism gave way to bellicosity. But until reinforcements arrived, who were stuck in the mud on their way up from Pietersmaritzberg, Wood was happy to play for time. He negotiated a temporary armistice with Joubert, pending receipt of Kruger's reply to Colley's letter. This arrived on March 7th and led to further negotiations, conducted by Wood at the order of the Government, but against his personal inclinations (and those of the Queen, the Duke of Cambridge and the whole hierarchy of the War Office). But Gladstone would have no more war.

So, finally, a provisional peace treaty was signed and the way was opened for the Transvaal to regain its independence. Kruger was their leader, and Kruger had learnt all the wrong lessons from Colley's ineptitude that he applied to Great Britain as a whole. The seeds of the Second Boer War had been sown.

Bibliography

Butler, W. (1899) *The Life of Sir George Pomeroy Colley*. Murray

Emery, F. (1986) *Marching over Africa*. Hodder and Stoughton

Hamilton, I. (1966) *The Happy Warrior*. Cassell

Hamilton, I. (1944) *Listening for the Drums*. Faber and Faber

Lehmann, J. (1972) *The First Boer War*. Cape

Marling, P. VC (1931) *Rifleman and Hussar*. John Murray

Preston, A. (1976) *Send a Gunboat*. Longmans

Ransford, O. (1967) *The Battle of Majuba Hill*. Murray

CHAPTER 7

THE BATTLE OF TEL EL KEBIR

1882

Egypt, though nominally a province of the Turkish Empire, had become a hereditary dictatorship and was under the arbitrary rule of the Khidive Ismael by 1675. Ismael was a spendthrift and had borrowed such sums on the international money market that Egypt was on the verge of bankruptcy. In this year Ismael sold his personal shares in the Suez Canal Company. These were snapped up by Benjamin Disraeli and this purchase began the uneasy relationship between Great Britain and Egypt which lasted until 1956. In 1876 it was found that Egypt could not even pay the interest on her borrowings and under international pressure she handed over her financial affairs to Anglo-French control. Khedive Ismael quickly sought ways to circumvent this control. Pressure was therefore brought to bear on the Sultan of Turkey who deposed Ismael and appointed his son, Twefik, in his place.

Tewfik was more complaisant. He accepted foreign guidance while other parties, objecting to foreign control, coalesced into an active opposition, with a rallying cry of "Egypt for the Egyptians". By 1881 the opposition was led by Colonel Ahmed Arabi who had the backing of the Egyptian officers and the rank and file of the Egyptian army. (The Egyptian officers felt that promotion and career prospects were blocked by foreign mercenary officers, and Arabi was an Egyptian whose promotion to Lieutenant Colonel was a 'reward' from the Khedive Ismael when he ordered Arabi's betrothed wife into the Khedivial hareem.)

In 1881 Arabi began to make demands on the Egyptian government. As each was granted, his demands escalated. Finally in January 1882 he had the Prime Minister dismissed and himself made Minister for War, a Pasha and became the de

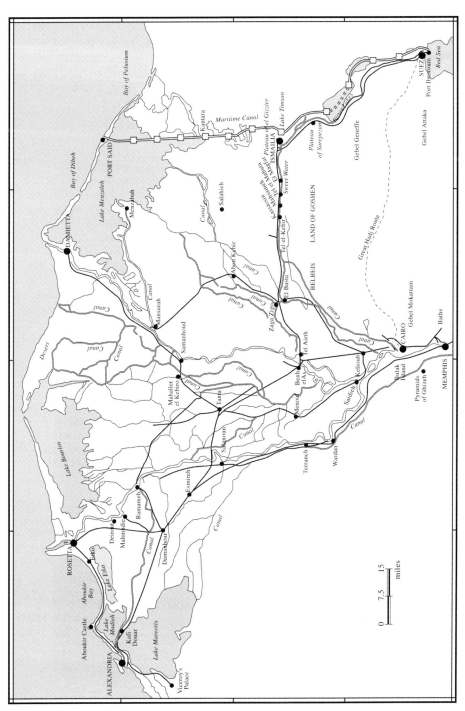

Isthmus of Suez and Lower Egypt, 1882

facto ruler of Egypt. His actions soon created international alarm for the safety of the 90 000 foreign nationals in Egypt and as a first reaction the British and French Mediterranean fleets were ordered to Alexandria, arriving there in May.

There followed a period of rising tension. Arabi Pasha began to fortify the waterfront and the mood of the Alexandrian mob became increasingly ugly. On the night of 11/12th June the mob erupted into violence and about 50 Europeans were killed. The remainder of the European community fled for their lives. On 24th June

Naval Brigades in Alexandria (Illustrated London News, June 29, 1882)

Arabi Pasha announced that the landing of sailors from the fleets to restore order in Alexandria would be opposed by force, and speeded up the arming of the forts until they posed a real threat to the British and French fleets.

At this point the French fleet was ordered home as the French Government, reoccupied with affairs in Europe, abandoned their interest in Egypt. The mood in London was very different. The Admiralty, sensitive to the threat to free passage through the Suez Canal had begun to position ships ready to seize the canal by a coup de main. General Sir Garnet Wolseley, again the Adjutant General at the War Office, was tasked with making an appreciation of the problem of defending the canal once seized and the preparation of a plan to implement his chosen course of action.

Wolseley concluded that only by defeating the Egyptian army and occupying Cairo could the defence of the canal and its availability for free navigation be assured. This being so there were two possible lines of advance on Cairo, from Alexandria or from Ismailia. The route from Ismailia was shorter and the going was better, giving the prospect of a speedy advance. It also led through Tel El Kebir, a major military station where it seemed certain the Egyptian army would stand and fight, so offering an early opportunity for its destruction. Wolseley, relying on the Royal Navy to secure the canal, decided to use this route. He planned to use two divisions of infantry (using Ismailia one of these could come from India) and a Brigade of Cavalry, all units to land self-sufficient in horse and transport. Units in the United Kingdom were 'as preparation for autumn manoeuvres' brought to short notice to move, and Battalions in the Mediterranean garrisons were shipped to Cyprus and placed under the command of Major General Sir Archibald Alison.

By 10th July Admiral Sir Beauchamp Seymour, the commander-in-chief, Mediterranean Fleet, having received instructions to order the Egyptians to disarm the threatening forts and being satisfied that the European fugitives were safe, delivered an ultimatum to the Egyptian commander in Alexandria. He demanded that the forts be surrendered to him within 24 hours, failing which he would destroy them by bombardment. There was no surrender and at 0700 on 11th July the bombardment of Alexandria began.

The bombardment lasted for ten and a half hours and was by no means one sided, for the Egyptian guns were fought with some skill and bravery and caused damage and casualties to the British ships. By nightfall the forts ceased fire and during the night, under orders from Arabi Pasha, were abandoned as a start to the general evacuation of Alexandria by Egyptian troops. These were withdrawn to positions at Kafr el Dauwar, between Lakes Mareotis and Madieh, 14 miles from Alexandria covering the railway line from Alexandria to Cairo. As it withdrew the Egyptian rearguard, assisted by the Alexandrian mob, pillaged and then burnt the European quarter of the city. Then the mob fell to looting the bazaars and native quarters.

On 13th July, therefore, Sir Beauchamp Seymour landed all available seamen and Royal Marines from the fleet both to enforce law and order in the city and to watch Arabi's men at Kafr el Dauwar. On 17th July General Alison arrived from Cyprus with two battalions of infantry (3rd/60th Rifles and the South Staffs). The infantry disembarked next day and Alison busied himself in preparation for the defence of Alexandria, establishing a strong position facing the Egyptians backed by the field guns and Gatlings landed from the fleet and manned by their seaman crews. There was also an armoured train, the brainchild of Captain (later Admiral of the fleet) Jackie Fisher, carrying a 40 pdr gun, a 9 pdr gun and Gatlings, manned by 200 sailors. This enjoyed daily skirmishes with the Egyptians, in one of which a midshipman was captured by an Egyptian cavalry patrol. After interrogation by Arabi Pasha himself he was kept prisoner in Cairo.

Khedive Tewfik sought safety with the British forces, and on 26th July he officially dismissed Arabi Pasha who ignored this and so placed himself in the position of a rebel. Khedive Tewfik appealed to Great Britain for help in suppressing the insurrection and gave express authority for the canal to be occupied by British forces. Gladstone authorised armed intervention and the movement of ships and men began.

While the troops were concentrating, the Royal Navy positioned ships at strategic points ready to seize the canal when required to do so. A squadron under Admiral Hoskins lay off Port Said. HMS *Orion* was anchored in Lake Timsah off Ismailia and Admiral Hewett brought the East Indies fleet to anchor off Suez.

Wolseley arrived in Alexandria on 15th August, collected his staff and explained his plan to Admiral Seymour in great secrecy. He then set about an elaborate deception, intended to make Arabi Pasha believe that the British army would land at Abu Qir Bay. General Hamley, one of the Divisional commanders, was set to plan such a landing and its exploitation and so the press were duly informed of this. At noon on 19th August eight warships and seventeen transports sailed from Alexandria and anchored in Abu Qir Bay. After dark some small craft moved inshore and carried out a diversionary bombardment. The rest of the fleet sailed for Port Said. At 0200 on 20th August the Navy struck to secure the canal.

At Port Said a party of one officer and six Royal Marines were rowed ashore to silence the Egyptian sentries. These were found asleep and silenced. Then seamen and Royal Marines secured the docks and lock gates. Naval ships then sailed down the canal to Kantara taking possession of all barges and dredgers, and at Kantara landed a party to occupy the telegraph station. Just before dawn the Egyptian barracks in Port Said were surrounded and the occupants surrendered without offering any resistance.

At Ismailia, where HMS *Orion* had been joined by HMS *Carysfoot* and by contingents of sailors from HMS *Agincourt* and HMS *Northumberland* with additional field guns, a force of about 550 sailors and Royal Marines began to land from ships' boats. Initially there was some opposition quickly overcome after an exchange of rifle fire. Within two hours Ismailia was cleared of Egyptian troops.

The landing parties were deployed in a defensive perimeter around the town, and the telegraph office taken over. Amongst the telegrams found was one that revealed that there were, at Nefiche about two miles away, some 2000 Egyptian troops encamped at the railway station, and that an attack on the shipping at Ismailia was to be made as soon as the imminent re-enforcements arrived by rail. The telegraph line to Cairo was found to be open. A telegram was sent to Cairo, purporting to be from the traffic manager, reporting the landing of 5000 British troops. The War Minister acknowledged the telegram in due course. At dawn *Orion* and *Carysfoot* began a deliberate bombardment of Nefiche, controlled from the foremast of *Carysfoot* since the target was invisible from anywhere else in either ship. *Orion* had to be listed to starboard by shifting stores and ammunition and even by emptying her portside boilers to achieve the elevation necessary to clear the line of flight of her shot. The bombardment was successful — the troops in the camp were dispersed into the desert and an engine and rolling stock in the station were destroyed.

Through all this activity Ferdinand de Lesseps flitted in the unlikely role of Pantaloon. He had given Arabi Pasha his undertaking that neither France nor Italy would intervene in Egypt and that, therefore, Great Britain would never dare to attack the canal. He personally guaranteed its neutrality and that no troops would use it. He was entertaining a number of Egyptian officers when his party was disturbed by the news of the British landing. He rushed down to the landing place where, with Gallic theatrically, he stood, arms spread, declaiming that "les sacres anglais" would land over his dead body. He was pushed aside by a burly petty officer with the adjuration "We don't want no dead bodies 'ere Sir; all you've got to do is step back a little!" Discomfited he returned home. Next day he called upon the Senior Naval Officer and reiterated his claim to the neutrality of the canal. "I de Lesseps have guaranteed it!" Although accorded every respect and offered suitable refreshment as an emollient to a stern refusal, he stormed ashore in a towering rage denunciating the iniquities of the "sacre Anglais".

At Suez Admiral Hewett also moved at 0200. He landed a Naval Brigade and the 1st Battalion, the Seaforth Highlanders (from the Indian contingent). They marched out to the lock on the Sweet Water Canal that controlled the water supply of the port. In a smart engagement the Egyptian troops guarding the locks were driven off and the port and its water supply were secured. Hewett stopped all movement of shipping up the canal ready to pass the troopships with the Indian contingent when they were called forward.

The first reinforcements to reach Ismailia were a half battalion of the Royal West Kents who were rushed down the canal in torpedo boats from the fleet. They were quickly joined by a battalion of the Royal Marine Light Infantry. Major General Graham, their Brigade commander, advanced to and occupied Nefiche with these troops. By the evening of 23rd August 9000 men had been landed at Ismailia and Wolseley had set up his headquarters there. As the army took over the defence of Ismailia the Naval Brigade was moved to provide local defence along the length of the canal through a number of small parties of seamen with the field guns with which they had landed.

On 23rd August Wolseley became aware that the level in the Sweet Water Canal, on which he relied for water both for his army and for the port, was falling, and received intelligence that the canal had been dammed by the Egyptains at Magfar, ten miles west of Ismailia. Before dawn on 24th August Wolseley ordered a small force, under the command of Major General Willis, to advance to and secure Magfar. Wolseley's information was that the Egyptians had no large force nearer than Tel el Kebir, so he and his staff rode with the column to reconnoitre and expected to ride back to Ismailia for breakfast.

At about 0730 Wolseley, riding with the composite regiment of Household Cavalry (about to go into action for the first time since Waterloo) reached the dam. The Egyptian skirmishers at the dam were driven off by a spirited little charge and some prisoners were taken. Interrogated, they revealed that there was another dam guarded by a large body of infantry at Tel el Madure some thousands of yards ahead. Wolseley moved forward to reconnoitre the position and found that he was facing 9000 horse and foot with artillery support. Smoke on the railway indicated that further Egyptian reinforcements were on their way.

Wolseley's infantry had reached Magfar with two guns. He deployed them with their left flank secured by the canal, the two guns in the centre between the infantry battalion and the RMLI battalion, and the right flank, open to the desert, guarded by the cavalry and a squadron of mounted infantry. His gallopers he sent back to hurry forward the Duke of Cornwall's Light Infantry who were on the march behind him, to order forward the Guards Brigade and any other troops that had disembarked that morning. Wolseley, Willis and their staffs took post on a sandhill roughly in the middle of the position and awaited events.

At a little after 0900 the Egyptians, horse, foot and guns moved slowly down and closed the British line. The attack fell first on the British left and spread along the line, being checked by the controlled volleys fired from the British Martini rifles. A battery of four guns were then unlimbered and brought into action at a range of about 1000 yards. It was fortunate that most of the shells buried themselves in the soft sand before exploding. The opening salvoes were aimed at Wolseley, Willis and their staffs on the hillock. One shell passed close to Wolseley's head and others fell close to the group of staff officers. Only one horse had been killed before Wolseley ordered them to take cover on the reverse slope. When the horses had moved, the guns shifted target and engaged the cavalry on the right flank. Wolseley moved his cavalry back out of range. Finally at 1030 he allowed his two guns to open fire. There followed, for a period, an unequal artillery duel during which the first reinforcements, a battalion of Royal Marine Artillery, acting as infantry, came up. At about 1300 the Egyptians were reinforced by a column of infantry, cavalry and another six guns, all of which were placed to threaten the exposed flank. Wolseley's reply to the threat was, initially, to reinforce his gun crews with a party from the Royal Marine Artillery so as to increase the rate of fire. At this time two Gatlings were seen struggling up with their Royal Naval crews who were making heavy weather of manhauling their guns through soft sand. Two pairs of horses from the teams of the Royal Artillery were sent to help them and they were placed on the right flank. Here they engaged the six Egyptian guns at long range and silenced them. Throughout the afternoon the two armies faced each other and the Egyptians manoeuvred as though to attack both flanks. But further reinforcements reached Wolseley and the Egyptians withdrew into their former positions. When, at about 1800, the Guards Brigade arrived, the Egyptians withdrew to their trenches in the sandhills. Wolseley moved his force into a semi-circular bivouac, each flank resting on the canal and guarded by a Gatling.

At daybreak on 25th August Wolseley advanced to attack and found that the Egyptians had abandoned their positions and retreated toward Masamah. The cavalry were ordered in pursuit. They reached Masamah as a train was leaving the station. There was a brisk action before the station was secured together with seven guns, a large quantity of rifles and ammunition and 75 railway trucks loaded with supplies and stores. The cavalry reconnoitred forward to find that the Egyptians had abandoned the lock of the Sweet Water Canal at Kassassin undamaged. After a night in bivouac the infantry advanced to Kassassin.

There was a lull in the action for 24 hours then on 28th August Arabi Pasha led 12 000 men and twelve guns to attack the numerically inferior British troops at Kassassin. The Egyptians halted outside rifle range while their artillery fired a desultory and ineffective bombardment. At 1500 it appeared that the Egyptians were retiring. The British cavalry returned to camp, and the infantry stood down. Then at 1630 the Egyptians launched their attack. Major General Graham, who had been left in command when Wolseley and Willis returned to Ismailia, manoeuvred his troops to meet the various thrusts (the Royal Marine battalions distinguished themselves in this phase of the battle) and called on the cavalry to charge the flank of the Egyptian attack. In growing darkness and finally by moonlight the cavalry rode to the flank and then charged at the flash of the guns. The Egyptians retreated. At 2045 Graham ordered a general return to camp.

Wolseley was in no position to exploit these successes even if he wanted to. Although he had secured the Sweet Water Canal and its vital locks, the railway line and telegraph as far forward as Kassassin, he had less than half his troops ashore. Added to which the canal was blocked, his water supply was rapidly falling, and his transport was deficient. He had outrun his supplies and was only able to maintain troops as far forward as Kassassin because of the capture of Egyptian supplies at Masamah.

As Arabi Pasha showed no signs of advancing from his base at Tel el Kebir, Wolseley was content to consolidate his position. He left Major General Graham with his Brigade and the cavalry at Kassassin, stationed the Guards Brigade at Tel el Madura and the Naval Brigade at Magfar. While the disembarkation of troops and supplies at Ismailia continued, the Guards were charged with clearing the dam at Tel el Madura, and the Naval Brigade with clearing that at Magfar and the railway line.

If there was one thing at which the Egyptians proved adept it was the building of dams and the blocking of the railway. With sand bound by layers of papyrus reed and bullrush they had filled the canal (twice) and a convenient railway cutting for about thirty feet. It was found that neither the army nor the navy had any tool that was any use in excavating this, and when the navy tried demolition charges these too proved useless. The rushes had to be pulled out and the sand scooped away by hand. The rest of the army were delighted at the sight of the Guardsmen dressed only in helmets and shirts splashing about in the canal.

The Navy undertook two other tasks as well. They managed to pass boats onto the canal above the dams, and then ferried supplies up to the advance guard at Mahasmeh and Kassassin. They also constructed an armoured train equipped with a 40 pdr gun and six Gatlings. In this they patrolled the cleared and repaired railway line when it was brought back into use.

Wolseley took advantage of Arabi's immobility to complete his preparations. The Indian Division was called up from Suez, disembarked and moved up towards Kassassin. The Highland Brigade was called down from Alexandria. Wolseley's army would be complete and concentrated on 12th September, and his planning was almost complete. To tie up some loose ends, he made a reconnaisance in force of the Egyptian position at Tel el Kebir on 8th September.

Then, surprisingly, on 9th September Arabi Pasha, believing that only General Graham and his Brigade (which included the RMLI) were at Kassassin made what he thought was an overwhelming attack, launching 18 battalions of infantry with cavalry and artillery in two columns at the British positions. In fact Graham had 8000 men at Kassassin and the Guards Brigade and cavalry were encamped nearby. The cavalry rode out and got between the two enemy columns, threatening the inward flanks of both, and the Guards Brigade manoeuvred to attack the northern column in flank. At about 1000 the RMLI and the 3rd King's Royal Rifle Corps were ordered to take cover to avoid the fire of the Egyptian guns, which were firing case shot at them at 300 yards range. Suddenly the adjacent companies of the Marines and the Rifles (apparently without receiving an order to do so) rose and charged the guns. Three were taken and with the whole British line advancing, the Egyptians, in confusion, retreated towards Tel el Kebir. The British line followed until, just out of range of the guns of Tel el Kebir, Wolseley first halted them and then ordered them back to Kassassin.

Wolseley could probably have hustled the Egyptian army out of Tel el Kebir that day, but he was afraid that they would escape the crushing defeat he deemed necessary to permit the rapid advance on Cairo. This was essential if he was to occupy the capital before Arabi Pasha could organise further resistance or burn the city. So he spent the next three days in reconnaissance and planning while the final units of his army joined him. Amongst these was the Naval Brigade of 15 officers, 199 ratings, and with their armoured train were at last freed from their duties on the lines of communications.

The approach to Tel el Kebir was over a flat, open plain devoid of any cover. The Egyptian army was in a line of defences, four miles long and nearly two miles deep, covered by artillery. The outer defence was a deep ditch, ten feet wide and six feet deep, with a twelve-foot climb to the top of the parapet. Well-made redoubts were sited to command either flank. Cavalry vedettes rode out each morning at 0545 so that, by day, any approach would be seen and reported while still a long way off. Wolseley took the bold decision to attack just before 0545 after a night march, trusting to the darkness of the night and the well-known inefficiency of Egyptian sentries to give him the benefit of surprise.

Wolseley's planning was meticulous. Every divisional, brigade and battalion commander was personally briefed during a reconnaissance in which the route to Tel el Kebir was covered, and its defences and the individual points of attack were pointed out. The Royal Engineers marked out the start line in the desert about three and three quarter miles from Tel el Kebir and on it marked the assembly point for each unit. The army was to advance in three columns: two north and one south of the canal, with the cavalry so placed as to be able to ride round the flanks and take up the pursuit of the beaten enemy. Apart from two Royal Horse Artillery batteries with the cavalry, the artillery was massed between the two northern columns that were 1200 yards apart. The Naval Brigade with the 40 pdr gun and Gatlings in the armoured train were to advance down the railway on the north bank of the canal, and would be able to support the Indian Division, the third column, on the south bank. The advance was to be guided by Lieutenant Rawson RN on loan from the Royal Yacht to serve as Naval aide-de-camp to General Wolseley. Rawson was a practiced navigator who, having taken part in polar exploration, had developed some skill in steering by the stars. He rode at the head of the centre column, leading the Highland Brigade.

Leaving their campfires burning, the troops left camp at 1900 and formed up on the start lines. Here they underwent a rigorous arms inspection to ensure that no rifle was loaded and that no one had a loose round to load surreptitiously. They were then ordered to lie down and rest. At 0100 on 13th September the order to fall in was given and after some initial confusion the columns set off, marching for 40 minutes then halting for 20 during which the cohesion of the force could be checked. There was only one incident during the march. The centre of the Highland Brigade halted on a report of enemy horsemen ahead (probably Wolseley and his staff) while the wings, striving to keep in touch, edged inwards and were preparing to engage each other when the error was discovered. The imbroglio was sorted out and the advance continued. The march went so well that at 0300 the force was halted for about an hour so that the attack would be made at the planned time.

There had been intermittent cloud all night and Rawson had been unable to hold a true course. He had veered about seven degrees to the northward and was about 800 yards off course. This was a fortunate error for it brought the line of march clear of a strong redoubt mounting twelve guns, an advance work of the Egyptian lines which despite all reconnaissance remained undiscovered. So, by chance, surprise was achieved.

The Highland Brigade was discovered by the Egyptian pickets at 0445 at 200 yards from the Egyptian lines, and had covered another 50 yards before they were fired upon. They immediately charged the ditch and struggled up the twelve-foot slope to close with the defenders. Unfortunately Lieutenant Rawson, who had dismounted and joined in the rush for the ditch, was one of the first casualties, receiving a mortal chest wound. Bitter hand-to-hand fighting cleared the Egyptian first line but disorganised the Highlanders who were temporarily halted before the second line. Into the confusion rushed their Brigadier (the one armed veteran General Allison) and the Divisional Commander (General Hamley) leading the small reserve. Someone ordered the pipes to play and the advance began again.

At that moment, about 0505, the northern column (which had about 700 yards further to go) began to come into action. The first to be engaged were the Royal Marines, followed in turn by the other battalions of the Division, all played on by the Irish pipes of the 18th Royal Irish.

Then at 0510 the Indian Division south of the canal came into action. This Division and the Naval Brigade had been the most likely to be discovered on the approach march, for their route led through cultivated land and past the scattered huts of the fellaheen. They had, therefore, marched an hour later than the rest and had escaped detection until this moment when the Egyptian defences fired on them. The Naval Brigade brought their six Gatlings into action to cover the Seaforth Highlanders who made a frontal assault, supported by the 7th Bengal Native Infantry. The 20th Punjabis supported by the 29th Native Infantry swung round and attacked the Egyptian right flank. The Seaforths captured four guns and overran a fortified village with the bayonet. The Indian cavalry were passed over the canal to cut off the retreat of the Egyptians.

The British cavalry had by now worked round the Egyptian left flank, and their two batteries of Royal Horse Artillery were enfilading the Egyptian line. In the centre the artillery had forced their way over the ditch and into the Egyptian lines to engage targets of opportunity. The infantry were advancing steadily. By 0600 the Egyptian defence was crumbling and their troops were running in the open with the British and Indian cavalry riding them down.

Wolseley got his cavalry under control, and ordered the Indians to ride west to take Zagazig then south to rendezvous with the British cavalry at Belbeis, to which they were to ride directly southwest across the desert. The combined cavalry were then to ride direct for Cairo. By 1600 the Indian cavalry had secured Zagazig and captured six trains; a seventh had crashed when attempting to escape and had blocked the line. Late that night they reached Belbeis, made the rendezvous and bivouacked for a short night.

Before dawn the cavalry began the 39-mile ride for Cairo. At sunset the advance guard, which had left the main body out of sight, reached the suburb of Abbassieh and with barefaced effrontery demanded the surrender of the garrison. Arrangements were made for the surrender of the Citadel and for capitulation by Arabi Pasha who gave up his sword to the commanding officer of the cavalry. The midshipman, captured at Alexandria, was found and released unharmed.

Wolseley spent the night of the battle at Tel el Kebir having visited the wounded. Then he set off by train for Cairo. On 25th September Khedive Twekfik re-entered Cairo through streets lined by the British soldiers who had broken the Egyptian army, inflicting casualties of over 3000 dead, taking 60 guns from an army half as large again as themselves and all for the cost of 57 killed, 30 missing and 380 wounded.

The campaign had lasted 25 days.

Bibliography

Barthrop, M. (1986) *War on the Nile*. Blandford Press

Beresford, C. (1914) *Memoirs of Lord Charles Beresford*. Methuen

Bradford, E. (1923) *Life of AF Sir AK Wilson VC*. John Murray

Colomb, P. H. (1898) *Memoirs of Sir Astley Cooper Key*. (Publisher unknown)

De Cossen, E. A. (1990) *Fighting the Fuzzy-Wuzzy*. Greenhill Bodies

Emery, F. (1986) *Marching Over Africa*. Hodder and Stoughton

Keown-Boyd, H. (1986) *A Good Dusting: Sudan Campaign 1881–89*. Leo Cooper

Lehman, J. (1964) *All Sir Garnet*. Jonathon Cape

Marling, P. (1931) *Rifleman and Hussar*. John Murray

Gleichen, Count (1975) *With the Camel Corps up the Nile*. E P Publishing

James, L. (1985) *The Savage Wars*. Robert Hale

Preston, A. and Major, J. (1967) *Send a Gunboat*. Longmans

Smith, P. and Oakley, D. (1988) *The Royal Marines*. Spellmount

Symounds, J. (1974) *England's Pride*. White Lion

CHAPTER 8

THE SIEGE OF KHARTOUM

1884–1885

Egyptian rule in the Sudan, corrupt and brutal as it was, began in 1822 and by 1870 the boundaries of the country had been fixed as they are today. In 1877 General Gordon was lent to the Egyptian Government to become their Governor General in the Sudan, and for the two years that he held that appointment he did much to eradicate corruption and to suppress the slave trade. His Egyptian successor was less high-minded and the Sudan slid back towards anarchy.

In 1881 Mohammed Ahmed, a Dongola artisan turned Prophet, proclaimed himself the Mahdi, the one awaited by Islam, and began a revolt against Egyptian rule. In an early attempt to capture him, two companies of Egyptian soldiers were butchered by his followers, an event which began the myth of 'holy invincibility' which inspired his followers for the remainder of the revolt.

While it is doubtful that the Egyptian army would have had any success against the Mahdi and his growing following of armed religious fanatics, Arabi Pasha's actions in Egypt, which led to the breaking of the Egyptian army at Tel El Kebir, ensured that the Mahdi met no real resistance. So by the end of 1882 the Mahdi controlled the Southern Sudan up to about 40 miles below Khartoum. In January 1883 El Obeid, the chief town of the province of Kordofan, fell after a six-month siege and here the Mahdi set up his headquarters. Ten thousand rifles, five Krupp guns and ample ammunition were captured.

The policy of the British Government, headed by Gladstone, was one of non-intervention. The Khedive was advised by Sir Evelyn Baring (later Lord Cromer), the British Agent and Consul General in Cairo, that no British help would be forthcoming and that Egypt should evacuate its garrisons in the Sudan. Reluctantly the Khedive accepted this advice and wished to appoint Zobeir Pasha, a strong character but an infamous slaver, to implement it. Zobeir was, because of his profession, anathema to Gladstone who pressed for the appointment of General Gordon instead. Somewhat reluctantly the Egyptian Government accepted him and on 18th January 1884 Gordon made his idiosyncratic departure from Charing Cross Station. The Foreign Secretary bought his ticket, HRH the Duke of Cambridge (the commander-in-chief of the British Army) opened his carriage door, and General Wolseley presented him with a purse of 300 sovereigns which he had that evening borrowed from his friends and acquaintances round the London Clubs after discovering that Gordon was without ready cash for his journey to the Sudan.

Major General Charles G Gordon (Illustrated London News, January 26, 1884)

The borders of Egypt, Sudan and Abyssinia in 1877

In the Sudan Osman Digna had raised the Hadendoa tribe (the veritable Fuzzy Wuzzy) for the Mahdi and was besieging the Egyptian garrisons in Tolkar and Sinhat. This threatened the nearby Red Sea Port of Suakin, the key to the only route other than following the Nile, by which the evacuation of the Sudan was possible. This threat was taken so seriously that a large body of Egyptian Gendarmerie, commanded by a British Officer (Valentine Baker) had been sent to hold Suakin.

Baker Pasha thought that he could do better than that. He scraped together a force of 3500 Egyptian and Sudanese with four Krupp guns and two Gatling guns and marched to relieve Tolkar. On 4th February, at a place called El Teb, Osman attacked the marching square. Baker reported to Cairo:

"On the square being threatened by a small force of the enemy, certainly less than 1000 strong, the Egyptian troops threw down their arms and ran, carrying away the black troops with them, and allowing themselves to be

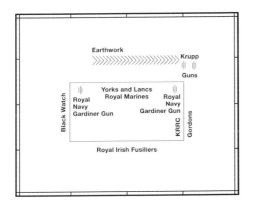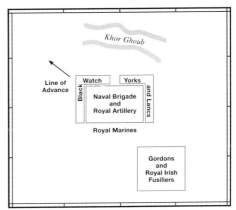

El Teb Tamai: plan of perimeter defence for Souakin

killed without the slightest resistance. More than 2000 were killed. They fled to Trinkitat."

Rear Admiral Sir William Hewett VC, KCB and the commander-in-chief, East Indies, had a portion of his fleet lying off Suakin. On learning of Baker Pasha's defeat Hewett landed a composite force of sailors and Marines and set up a perimeter defence for Suakin.

Were Suakin to fall to the Mahdi it could become a piratical base from which the Dervishes would prey on the Indian trade passing through the Red Sea. This threat was taken seriously in London. On 12th February Major General Graham was ordered to take the 1st Battalion of the Black Watch, the 1st Battalion of the Gordons and the 3rd Battalion of the 60th Rifles, together with the 19th Hussars, from Egypt to Suakin. There they were joined by the 1st Battalion of the Yorks and Lancs, the 2nd Royal Irish Fusiliers and the 10th Hussars, who were all diverted to Suakin whilst on passage home from India. Admiral Hewett added a Naval Brigade of 150 seamen and 400 Royal Marines landed by HM Ships *Hecla*, *Dryad*, *Briton*, *Carysfoot* and *Euryalus* with six Gardiner guns (a lighter version of the Gatling gun).

General Gordon had reached Khartoum on 18th February 1884. On 12th March the tribes along the Nile from Khartoum to Berber declared for the Mahdi and cut Gordon's telegraph link through Berber to Cairo. Gordon was now completely isolated except for the occasional smuggled message. In London, Gladstone continued to refuse to countenance any further intervention in Sudanese affairs or any move to rescue Gordon, although in the face of rising pressure.

To General Wolseley at the War Office it was plain that, in the end, there would be an expedition to relieve Gordon and that he would be called upon to command it. So, in early April, he began his planning. He disregarded the local recommendation that a railway across the desert from Suakin to Berber (the route of the Haj pilgrimage) be built. Wolseley decided that he would advance up the river and (recalling his exploits in the Red River campaign in Canada) that his troops would sail and row themselves up the Nile under the guidance of experienced Canadian boatmen (Voyageurs) to relieve Khartoum. The Admiralty, having conducted a survey of the Nile, advised Wolseley that this plan was impractical. Remembering Wolseley's hatred of the Admiralty it is not surprising that their advice determined Wolseley to go his own way.

Another of Wolseley's fixations was that British troops could not march long distances across the desert. Wolseley, therefore, decided that a camel corps might be useful. He again produced his old idea of syphoning off the cream of the best regiments into the new Camel Corps, allowing the regiments to form individual companies. The Camel Corps, of four regiments, was drawn from the Household and Line Cavalry and the Guards and Royal Marines. The Mounted Infantry, drawn from the 60th Rifles and the East Sussex, back in Egypt from Suakin, were also converted to camels.

By August the pressure on Gladstone, both in Parliament and from the general public, was becoming intense. Finally his hand was forced by Lord Hartington, the Secretary for War, who threatened resignation unless an expedition to relieve Gordon was mounted. Hartington's resignation on this issue would have brought down the Government so Gladstone authorised the mounting of the relief expedition, for which the orders were issued to Wolseley on 19th September.

Wolseley had had 'whalers' designed to his specifications, 30 feet in length, with a beam of 6½ feet and a draught of 2¼ feet, fitted for two dipping lug sails and six oars a-side. Each boat was to carry twelve men (ten soldiers and two voyageurs) together with their arms, ammunition and 1000 rations. Orders for these 'whalers', 800 in all, were placed with the Royal Dockyards and 47 private boat builders. In rather less than a month the first 100 were shipped to Egypt with the rest to follow. When complete the flotilla 'up the Nile' included eight steam pinnaces, two stern wheelers and some hired Egyptian government steamers.

The recruiting of the Voyageurs in Canada went ahead, though the selection process left much to be desired. When the recruits arrived in Egypt it was evident that not many of them were true Voyageurs. Most were not watermen but out of work lumberjacks, and there was a sprinkling of college men and the like who had signed on for the 'adventure'.

Wolseley's means of transportation up the Nile as far as Wadi Halfa (the railhead) was either by rail or by water, with a portage round the first cataract at Aswan. Beyond Wadi Halfa there was only the river with two cataracts before Dongola, another just past Korti and the fifth just before Berber. Stationed up the river at Aswan and Wadi Halfa were 29 Naval Officers and 190 ratings sent, on the initiative of the commander-in-chief, Mediterranean fleet, to help pass the various graft through the cataracts. There was also the bulk of the Egyptian army to provide manpower at Aswan where they were to carry 609 out of 700 whalers around the cataract as well as passing supplies up river. At Wadi Halfa the Egyptians provided the teams of men towing the boats through the cataract there.

The railway could not carry the volume of traffic required to carry the troops, the stores and the whalers up river to Wadi Halfa. Thomas Cook were therefore contracted to transport troops in their steamers as far as Wadi Halfa. Although the movement began very well it had to be halted for thirteen days because all available steaming coal had been burnt!

Wolseley established his headquarters at Wadi Halfa where his army was slowly assembling. He had brought with him as his naval aide-de-camp Commander Lord Charles Beresford RN whom he now ordered to take command of the naval parties strung along the river and to expedite the movement of the waterborne transport through the cataract. In particular Wolseley had been told that it was impossible to pass his steamers up the cataract and he consulted Beresford about this. Attempts had been made with towropes manned by 4000 natives but these had failed. Beresford rigged a system of purchases and with 1500 soldiers tailed on managed the job. He also established a boatyard at the head of the cataract to repair any damage suffered in passing up the rapids.

On 6th November the 1st South Staffs embarked in their whalers and set off for Dongola, 350 miles further upstream, designated by Wolseley as his advanced base. The other whalers followed in turn, but it was not until 19th December that the last would sail. On 12th November the Camel Corps, less the Royal Marine company which had not yet joined, trotted out to follow the left bank of the Nile up to Dongola.

Wolseley now decided to move his advance base to Korti, at the downstream end of the first great loop in its course. From here there was a known route across the desert to Metemmeh that had been surveyed as a possible route for a projected railway and on which there were two known sources of water.

Wolseley's first plan was for the Camel Corps to move across the desert from Korti to Metemmeh. It would then make a 96 mile dash to Khartoum while the 'River Column' worked their way upstream, took Berber and finally established a base at Shendi, opposite Metemmeh, from which the Camel Corps would be resupplied. To accompany the Camel Corps Beresford was ordered to raise a Naval Brigade of 10 officers and 100 ratings. Camels were provided as mounts for the officers and men and as transport for the two Gardiner guns with which they would be equipped. It required four camels to a gun: one for the barrels, one for the wheels, elevating and training gear, the trail on a third and the hoppers on the fourth. The gun could be offloaded, assembled and ready for action in less than four minutes. When it was assembled it was moved by drag ropes, muzzles forward with the train carried on a light pole. To go into action the trail was dropped, the drag ropes dropped and the gun was ready to fire.

Beresford had sent the first division of the Naval Brigade forward to Korti and was waiting down river for the second division to join him when he received his orders, which had taken seven days to reach him, to proceed by the shortest route and the quickest means to Korti. After a 32 hour camel ride he arrived in Korti to find preparations in full swing for the advance to Metemmeh.

On 26th December the Royal Marine company had arrived at Khorti to complete the Guards Camel Regiment, which was struck by their turn out and drill: "Excessively smart they looked as they came into camp and formed up correctly on their markers…they looked as if they had been turned out of a band box only the day before…their movements equalled their appearance." On 30th December the whole Camel Corps, and all available baggage camels loaded with ammunition and supplies, marched out for Jakdul Wells. They were accompanied by the 19th Hussars mounted on locally bred horses, a company of Royal Engineers, three screw guns and a camel borne medical 'hospital'. The column arrived at the Wells on 2nd January and dropped off the Guards Camel Regiment and the Royal Engineers to establish a camp. Taking all the camels, including the Guards' mounts, they then set off back to Korti where they arrived on 5th January with the intention of picking up the rest of the supplies for the forthcoming march, the Naval Brigade and the infantry (2 companies of the 1st Royal Sussex and 1 Company of the 2nd Essex) to garrison the semi-permanent camps to be established en route.

When General Stewart reported to Wolseley on his return to Korti he was told that, as a result of a verbal message received from General Gordon, the plan was modified. Stewart was now to capture and fortify Metemmeh that he was to hold until the River Column, having taken Berber on its way, arrived. The combined force would then advance and relieve Gordon. Whilst awaiting the arrival of the River Column, Stewart was to use the steamers that he would find at Metemmeh to make contact with him in Khartoum. He was also told that, according to Gordon, the sight of a British soldier in a red jacket would be sufficient to raise the siege!

Beresford spent these days in wheedling out of the army's Quartermaster General (Sir Redvers Buller VC) an assortment of stores that might be required to maintain the steamers at Metemmeh in a serviceable condition. Included in these were items such as boiler plate, Stockholm tar and oakum along with general engineering stores and tools.

At 1400 on 8th January the column set out from Korti: 1607 officers and men, 304 native camel drivers, 155 horses and one large white donkey, Beresford's chosen mount. (As a sailor, uncomfortable upon a camel, was heard to remark, "No wonder Charlie rides on a moke. He knows a thing or two does Beresford.") As the second division of the Naval Brigade had not reached Korti, Beresford had only five officers and 53 ratings with him and only one Gardiner gun.

The camels, when acquired, were not prime beasts and after the round trip of 196 miles in six days with inadequate food and insufficient rest had waned to an alarming extent and their condition was to deteriorate from now on. One effect of the loss of condition was the shrinking of their humps as they fed on their own fat. This destroyed the fit of their saddles, causing saddle sores that quickly became flyblown and alive with maggots. Only the Naval Brigade made any real attempt to deal with the problem. To the amusement of the army they 'caulked the seams' of their beasts, using Stockholm tar and pledgets of oakum from the ships stores that Beresford had acquired. Someone had remembered that Stockholm tar is an excellent disinfectant and fly repellent (still in use in modern veterinary practice) and the oakum gave some protection from further chaffing to the raw wound.

The column made a forced march to Jakdul that they reached on the morning of 12th January, where they found that the Royal Marines, Guards and Royal Engineers had established an ordered camp into which they settled immediately. The 13th was spent in watering the animals and at 1400 on 14th January the column set off for Metemmeh, marching until after sunset that night, then with reveille at 0330 marching off at 0400 with a break for breakfast at 1000, and marching on until after sundown again.

On 16th January the Hussars were sent ahead to secure the wells at Abu Klea, the objective of the day's march. During the breakfast halt the Hussars came back with the intelligence that there were a large number of Dervish massed in the hills between the column and the wells. Anticipating an immediate attack Stewart deployed the column for defence. He moved to a position on an area of ground between two hills and constructed a *zareba* close to the left hand hill which he picketted with the Mounted Infantry Camel Corps and the Naval Brigade, at extreme range for rifles on the right hand hill. No attack developed but the Dervish moved onto the right hand hill and began sniping. The screw guns were brought into action but to little effect and the column spent a sleepless night under intermittent rifle fire and the constant resonance of tom-toms "sometimes a distant throb and sometimes so loud and distinct that it appeared that an attack was imminent".

At daybreak on 17th January, under increasing rifle fire, the Mounted Infantry and the Naval Brigade were called into the *zareba* and the whole force stood to and awaited attack. At about 0900, as no attack had developed, Stewart decided to force the issue and advance on the wells that he urgently needed to reach. He left all his stores, baggage and camels (except for the 150 required to carry the guns, ammunition, water and the medical section) in the *zareba*, guarded by the detachment of the Royal Sussex. He formed his column into a marching square with the Hussars riding ahead, on the left flank Mounted Infantry and dismounted Scots Guards skirmishing behind them keeping down the Dervish sniping. In the rear face of the square marched the Naval Brigade. Beresford had been given discretion as to the siting of the Gardiner in case of attack.

The square moved off at 1000, holding to the lower slopes of the hills to their right that, though the going was bad, offered the least advantage to the Dervish.

The camels in particular found the rough ground difficult, and falling back, became entangled with the rear face that according to Beresford, "were all tangled up with a grunting, squealing, reeking mass of struggling animals". The Naval Brigade had to struggle manhauling the Gardiner forward amongst the chaotic rear face. After about an hour and a half three miles from the wells a line of green and white flags was sighted about 600 yards away and the square was halted to allow the rear face to close up and reform. Then from the direction of the flags a mass of Dervish appeared charging towards the left front corner of the square. Stewart advanced the square about 30 yards uphill to improve its field of fire though this increased the separation of the rear face.

The first 5000 of the Dervish were quickly followed by another 5000 who appeared from a nearby ravine and advanced upon the left face and the gap at the left rear of the square, towards which the ambulance section and the skirmishers were also making to find shelter. Beresford moved the Gardiner gun to a position in the gap ready to engage the Dervish but had to wait until the ambulance section and the skirmishers had cleared his field of fire. Then, after firing only 70 rounds, the base pulled off a cartridge case and the gun jammed (nearly 50% of the British rifles jammed for the same reason that day). Beresford and the gun's crew began the drill for clearing the stoppage and were overrun while doing so. Beresford was knocked under the gun, warding off a spear thrust with his open hand, which was badly cut. The rest of the gun's crew were killed.

Beresford struggled to his feet and was swept into the square:

"I can only compare the press to nothing but the crush of a theatre crowd alarmed by a cry of Fire! Immediately facing me was an Arab holding a spear above his head, the staff of the weapon being jammed against his back by the pressure behind him. I could draw neither sword nor pistol."

The mass of bodies surged on until it brought up against the ranks of kneeling camels. The front ranks of the leading and side faces of the square beat off attacks from the outside. The rear ranks faced about, and being on slightly higher ground were able to fire over the heads of their struggling comrades 'into the brown'. This eased the pressure on those fighting at the rear of the square who, with room to move, began to drive the Dervish back. Beresford managed to rejoin the Naval Brigade, sending out a new gun's crew to recover the Gardiner gun and bring it back into action, and led the rest in hunting down Dervish who remained inside the square. There was a last wild charge by a body of horsemen against the right rear which was quickly beaten off and the battle, which had lasted just ten minutes, was over. The Naval Brigade lost two officers and eight ratings, and two officers and seven ratings were wounded. Total casualties were nine officers and 68 men killed and nine officers and 85 men wounded. Over 1000 Dervish bodies were counted during the scavenging of the battlefield.

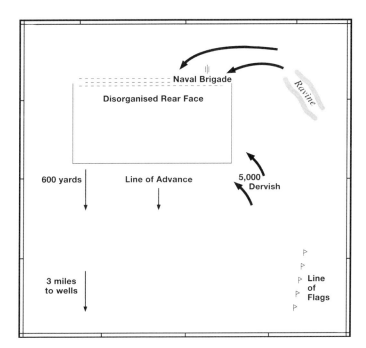

The advance of the marching square attempting to reach the wells at Abu Klea

At 1530 the square resumed its march to the wells, making painful progress over the rough terrain. The wells turned out to be a number of small pools that emptied quickly and filled slowly, the water yellow and thick as cream, inadequate to support the force and its animals. Soon after sunset a body of volunteers marched back to fetch in the camels and stores left behind. They were back by 0700 next morning and there was an immediate issue of rations. The force enjoyed its first meal for 36 hours: bully beef, ship's biscuit and water!

Although his men had had no sleep during the previous 48 hours, had suffered severely from thirst, spent 36 hours without food and had fought a battle, and his camels had had only 9 lbs of forage and no water for the last seven days, General Stewart decided that he must push on to the Nile, now about 25 miles away, as quickly as possible. Accordingly he ordered the march to begin at 1530 and to continue throughout the night. There was no moon and in the darkness confusion was compounded by the behaviour of the camels. Beresford described the march:

> "The camels, weary and famished, lagged and tumbled down, their riders went to sleep and fell off, the leading camels fell behind and the rear camels, most of them riderless, straggled up to the front...A longer and more exhausting nightmare I never suffered."

There is no doubt that the column lost its way and blundered about. At one point it fought its way through a wood of Acacia trees, suffering much from the sharp thorns (there was no Acacia wood on their planned route and it was never identified). At another point, Beresford halted the Naval Brigade, they brewed up tea (and from where did Beresford conjure up the water?) and then, much refreshed, marched on.

At dawn the column found itself at the foot of a long gravel slope that swept up, bare, to the sky line. When, after an hour, they breasted the summit they could see below them a wide valley and the Nile flowing between broad strips of green. Visible on their left was a chain of villages leading to Metemmeh, and out of Metemmeh a stream of Dervish heading to interpose themselves between the column and the Nile. And the tom-toms started again.

Stewart halted his column on the top of the rise and ordered the construction, out of camel saddles and biscuit boxes, of an enclosure some 300 yards square into which were led the camels which were knee haltered around the 'hospital'. Then he ordered his men to breakfast (bully, biscuit and for those that had any, water). Whilst at breakfast the force came under accurate sniper fire that could not be silenced even by 'smothering' fire from the Gardiner gun. There were casualties, one of which was General Stewart himself who was mortally wounded.

Command passed to Colonel Sir Charles Wilson, a brilliant Staff and Intelligence Officer who had no experience in commanding troops. Wilson was pressed by his advisors (including Beresford) in a council of war to form square and fight his way to the Nile. Wilson chose to construct a redoubt around the hospital before moving out. For two hours, under fire, everyone was employed shifting camel saddles, provisions and ammunition boxes to build the walls of the redoubt. Then Wilson split his force, leaving Beresford in command of the redoubt with the Naval Brigade, the Royal Artillery with their three screw guns, half the Heavy Camel Regiment and the sappers as garrison. As the square, formed from the remainder of the force moved off towards the Dervish, who were massed to their front, Beresford moved the screw guns and the Gardiner and engaged the Dervish until the square moved out of sight. Shortly after this happened the men in the redoubt heard disciplined volley firing. When this ceased, the volume of sniping slackened and finally died away and it was assumed that the square's volleys had dispersed the Dervish. In fact the Dervish had made another massed charge that was beaten off so decisively that the survivors fled, taking those threatening the redoubt with them.

The square moved on and reached the Nile at dusk, watered and slept the sleep of exhaustion, as did the garrison of the redoubt. Next morning, 20th January, Wilson occupied the deserted village of Gubat, left his wounded there under guard and then marched back to the redoubt, taking water with him. He was greeted with hearty cheers. There was a pause for a quick meal (bully, biscuit and tea) then the camels were loaded and the whole force marched back to Gubat.

On 21st January Wilson attempted to carry out Wolseley's orders to occupy Metemmeh (a walled town of some strength) but his operations were more in the nature of an armed reconnaissance; no real attack was made and after marching round the walls the column returned to Gubat. They had, however, made contact with four steamers sent down river by Gordon and there moved to Gubat.

Wilson called another council of war that night, one from which Beresford was absent (he was incapacitated by a fulminating carbuncle on his buttocks which required surgical intervention). It was decided that if it could be established that Gubat was safe from attack then two steamers would go to the relief of Khartoum. Reconnaissance on 22nd January established that the Dervish were in no position to attack Gubat and 23rd January was devoted to preparing two steamers for the trip to Khartoum. The engine room assistants (ERAs) from the Naval Brigade worked on the engines, wood was cut and loaded for fuel, and a cargo of grain was loaded into a nuggar (a native boat) to be towed. Wilson and two staff officers, Captain Trafford with 20 men of the Royal Sussex (with scarlet jackets) and the 240 Sudanese soldiers sent by Gordon in the gunboats also embarked.

The Naval Brigade was so weakened by casualties and sickness that they were not required to man the steamers though a petty officer and ERA sailed in one and an ERA in the other. With Beresford sick, they were now commanded by the war correspondent of the *Illustrated London News*, appointed acting Lieutenant RN by Colonel Wilson at Beresford's request. At 0800 on 24th January the steamers sailed for Khartoum.

For the week after Sir Charles Wilson sailed for Khartoum life at Gubat was almost tranquil. Daily the force sent out foraging parties seeking goats and cattle for slaughter, fresh vegetables for the sick and wounded and fodder for the camels. Beresford established himself onboard the *Safieh*, the larger of the two steamers remaining at Gubat and, commanding from a bed made up on the upper deck, made daily forays up and down the Nile to cover the foragers. On 26th January they shelled Metemmeh. On 31st January a large convoy of supplies was brought in from Jakdul. Amongst its escort was the second division of the Naval Brigade, two executive officers, an engineer, a surgeon and 47 ratings, a very opportune re-enforcement for Beresford.

At about 0300 on 1st February Beresford was sleeping on the upper deck of the *Safieh* when he was awoken by shouting from the river. One of the staff officers who had gone upstream with Wilson climbed on board to announce that Khartoum had fallen and Gordon was dead. On top of that, Wilson had lost both steamers, shipwrecked, and was marooned with all his men on an island 40 miles upstream, beyond a fort and battery that dominated the navigable channel.

Wilson's voyage had been a nightmare. On 25th January one of the steamers had run aground and it took most of that day to refloat her. On 26th that steamer ran aground again and after she had been refloated only three miles could be made good.

On 27th they were hailed from the left bank and told that Khartoum had fallen and Gordon killed. Believing this to be a false rumour they pressed on. On 28th January, with the minarets of Khartoum in sight over the banks of the Nile they were, again, told the news. But Wilson pressed on into heavy fire from artillery on both banks until Government House was identified with no flag flying and the Dervish uniform (white gowns with black patches) could be seen being worn in the streets of the city. Forty-eight hours too late, finally convinced, and having proved that the sight of the British Red Coat did not overawe, Wilson ordered the return to Gubat and the steamers turned and ran downstream. After four hours under fire they finally broke clear and tied up for the night some 30 miles downstream. Next day, 29th January, one steamer struck a rock and was abandoned, the British contingent transferring to the other steamer and the native contingent bivouacing on an island. On 30th January, with the natives embarked in the nuggar and going ahead all went well. But on 31st January, the remaining steamer hit a rock, began to fill and was beached on an island in mid-stream. Wilson landed guns, ammunition and stores, and after abandoning the idea of a night march, had sent one of his staff officers in a commandeered felucca to Gubat.

Beresford began immediate preparations to fight his way to the rescue of Wilson. The *Safieh* was the best steamer available and she was armed, stored, fueled, manned and under way in just over 13 hours. Two brass 4 pdr mountain guns, mounted fore and aft, were protected by turrets built of railway sleepers and boiler plate. The two Gardiner guns were mounted, in echelon, amidships and the wheel was protected by a barricade of railway sleepers. On board were all his officers and 45 ratings (28 as guns' crew, 14 to act as riflemen in close action, two ERAs and a chief stoker to supervise the Egyptian engineer) and six Sudanese stokers. Bolstering his firepower were 20 marksmen picked from the 60th Rifles under Lieutenant R L Power. Also onboard was Wilson's staff officer, Lieutenant Stuart Wortley.

The *Safieh* was conned upstream by a native pilot. Beresford (at his most emphatic) had told him that if the boat was successful in making the trip he would be rewarded but if there was any indication of treachery he would be shot forthwith! He was stood on a box so as to see over the barricade round the wheel and handcuffed to a staunchion. Beside him stood an iron-faced petty officer with a drawn revolver. Years later the Surgeon General of the Navy wrote to Beresford:

> "I always attribute our getting up and down when the river was so low and dangerous to your wise warning to the Pilot."

Safieh was incapable of making a 'dash' up the river. She could not navigate by night and would need to refuel at least once on each leg of the trip. So Beresford steamed upstream for what was left of daylight on 1st February, anchored overnight and steamed slowly upriver on 2nd February collecting wood, mostly (and with difficulty) by dismantling and cutting up the native irrigation wheels as they passed.

That evening they anchored for the night three or four miles short of the fort at Wad Habeshi, the main enemy position, before reaching Wilson.

Wad Habeshi was a strong earthwork mounting four guns and defended by about 5000 riflemen. The only practicable channel ran within 80 yards of the fort. Beresford's only hope of safe passage was "to maintain so overwhelming a fire upon the embrasures as to demoralise the guns' crews".

Beresford got under way at dawn and by 0700 Wad Habeshi was in sight, and beyond, in the distance, Mernat Island and the wreck of Wilson's steamer. At 0730, at a range of 1200 yards, the gun in *Safieh's* bows opened fire and soon the two brass guns, the starboard Gardiner and the rifles were firing steadily and accurately into the fort, ignoring the 500 to 600 tribesmen who were firing at them from the bank. The *Safieh* passed the fort and was about 300 yards upstream where none of her guns would bear and where only one gun of the fort could fire at her when a column of steam or smoke shot up the after hatchway. Uncertain whether the ship was on fire or had burst her boiler, Beresford steered towards the opposite bank and, as she lost way, anchored with a foot of water under her bottom, ordering all stores and ammunition to be brought on deck in case she settled.

Mr H Benbow, the chief engineer who had accompanied the 2nd division of the Naval Brigade, went below to find out what had happened. He returned to deck to report that a small shell had entered the hull above the waterline and then penetrated the boiler. There was no danger of sinking. Asked if he could repair the boiler, Benbow said that he could not be certain until he had examined the boiler when it had cooled. Taking with him a leading stoker from the party on deck (the two ERAs and the native stokers were all suffering from severe scalding) he drew the fires, pumped out the boiler and by 1100 had established that there was a three inch hole in the boiler with the plate bulged inward with torn and jagged edges. Benbow began to cut, shape and drill a plate 16 inches by 14 inches out of boiler plate, then to drill the boiler to take the bolts to secure the plate and then to make and fit a strongback to give added strength, necessary to withstand the steam pressure.

On deck, under constant rifle fire, one of the Gardiner guns was shifted to a newly built position at the stern and brought into effective action by acting Lieutenant W Ingram RN, the correspondent of the *Illustrated London News*. Sub Lieutenant Keppel and boatswain Webber modified the 4 pdr gun so that it could be trained on the fort. The turret built for it was so narrow that it was necessary to saw off the trail of the gun. Now the gun could be trained and fired at the fort, but every time it was fired it somersaulted onto its back. So, for every shot, between laying and firing, Keppel removed the sight to save it from damage. Keppel and Webber kept the gun in action all day, firing a total of 150 rounds. The shock of recoil eventually started the plates in the deck and hull. The combined effect of the Gardiner and the gun silenced the Dervish gun and prevented efforts to move it to a less exposed position.

Wilson could hear and see *Safieh* in action while he was busy with the Dervish on the left bank. He disengaged and moved downstream. His wounded, guns and ammunition floated down in the nuggar while he ferried his men to the right, unoccupied, bank using a felucca. All then moved down to a point opposite the *Safieh* and Wilson then began to shell Wad Habeshi in support of Beresford. After repeated attempts to communicate by signal had failed, Wilson's remaining staff officer began a ferry service in the felucca carrying messages to and fro until a plan of action was agreed.

Wilson, with one gun and 30 men, remained to keep Wad Habeshi under fire, diverting attention from *Safieh*. The remainder of his party marched on downstream to a spot, well below the fort, suitable for embarkation. The wounded remained in the nuggar that would slip down past the fort by night to join up. Wilson and his men remained until sunset and then moved down to join the rest of the party.

In the first trip in the felucca were the two ERAs who had sailed with Wilson. They immediately went below and joined Mr Benbow who had already been working for three hours. By 1700 everything was ready for the repair of the boiler though it was still too hot to enter. Mr Benbow hastened the cooling by pumping cold water through the boiler. At about 1830 a negro boy, well greased with tallow, climbed into the boiler and managed at the second attempt, to pass the bolts from the inside to secure the patching plate and strongbacks. By 1900 the work was complete. (Such was the quality of the repair that the *Safieh* remained in use on the Nile, first by Beresford who was to scuttle her, then, after salvage, by the Dervish until 1898 when Kitchener recovered the Sudan. Keppel, then in command of Kitchener's gunboats saw the patch still in place. It was then cut out and presented to him and is now in the possession of the National Maritime Museum).

As the action diminished at dusk Beresford began a plan to deceive the Dervish into believing that the *Safieh* had been abandoned. Boats were ostentatiously hauled alongside as though to take off the ship's company, all firing ceased, the ship was darkened and talking above a whisper was forbidden. Beresford made one gesture for the comfort of his men – a slow match was left burning in a bucket and smoking was allowed undercover. At about midnight the nuggar was seen as it drifted past and came under fire from the fort. As it drifted out of sight from the guns they shifted target to the *Safieh*. Firing soon ceased as the Safeih made no reply.

At 0500 on 4th February Mr Benbow lit the boiler, using the utmost care to prevent sparks flying up the funnel. For fifty minutes all went well and steam pressure rose to 10lbs. Then the native stokers suddenly increased the draught and sparks and hot ash showered out of the funnel. Shouts and a beating of tom-toms woke the fort from which quickly came gun and rifle fire. When steam pressure reached 20lbs Beresford weighed anchor and to the astonishment of the enemy steamed upstream to find room to turn in safety. Then at full speed and running with the current he raced past Wad Habeshi, plastering its guns as he passed. Now clear of danger and without suffering a casualty they sighted the nuggar aground about 400 yards below the fort and covered by one of its guns.

Beresford ran *Safieh* downstream to safety about a mile below the fort and ordered away a boat with Keppel and six ratings to assist. Keppel found the current too strong to pull against so he landed on the right hand bank where he and his crew towed the boat upstream to a point above the nuggar and moved down and across stream to board her. They lightened the nuggar, refloated her and with both boats drifted down to be picked up by *Safieh* under way. A mile further downstream Wilson and the rest of his party were picked up and at 1745 they arrived safely at Gubat.

Benbow received immediate promotion to Chief Inspector of Machinery. But Beresford was always to regret that, not knowing that a Victoria Cross could have been awarded for such services as those rendered by Benbow, he had not recommended him for that award. Mr Webber was promoted to Chief Boatswain and all the other officers were noted for early promotion.

On 4th February the news of the fall of Khartoum and the death of Gordon reached Wolseley at Khorti, and on 5th February the news reached London. Gladstone was vilified and blamed for the death of Gordon who became, overnight, a hero and a martyr. Such was the popular outcry that had Gladstore not announced that Wolseley had been ordered to avenge Gordon by the reconquest of the Sudan his government would have fallen.

Wolseley recast his plans. He now determined to seize Berber by a combined operation with the River Column continuing up the Nile and the Camel Corps down from Gubat. The army would then go into 'summer quarters' and he would fight an autumn and winter campaign to reconquer the Sudan. General Graham was ordered back to Suakin with orders to defeat Osman Digna and build a railway from Suakin to Berber. Major General Redvers Buller VC was ordered down from Korti to take command of the Camel Corps.

The River Column had made slow progress up the Nile. On 10th February they met a large force of Dervish at Kirbekan and, in the only battle of the campaign in which the British Infantry did not form a square, inflicted a smashing defeat on them. Major General Earle, in command, was killed while leading his troops. After the battle Wolseley finally appreciated that the River Column was consuming its supplies at such a rate that these would be exhausted before it could reach its objective. The column was ordered back and went into 'summer quarters' around Dongola.

Redvers Buller arrived at Gubat on 11th February with a convoy of much needed food and a reinforcement of six companies of the Royal Irish that had marched across the desert. Buller expected to remain at Gubat or to move on Berber but he found his command in deplorable condition. There was a shortage of stores and ammunition, there were wounded that should be evacuated, the camels were greatly reduced in number and those that remained were very nearly worn out, incapable of making the return journey to Jakdul necessary if the force was to be resupplied. Beresford, when consulted, recommended evacuation.

On 13th February Buller began his retirement. The wounded and sick marched out under escort of 300 men of the Camel Corps and the Sudanese from the steamers. Beresford had the melancholy task of scuttling the steamers, their guns spiked and thrown overboard. It would be possible to carry only three days rations (sufficient to get to Abu Klea) so, having been on short rations since arrival at Gubat, the force ate all it could and destroyed what was left. The hospital port and champagne were distributed throughout the force that evening.

At 0530 on 14th February the column left Gubat. The Hussars, whose native-bred mounts had proved hardy enough for the service required of them, were mounted; everyone else was on foot. There was a camel allocated to each four men to carry their kit and bedding rolls. The sailors of the Naval Brigade marched barefoot, carrying rifle, cutlass and 70 cartridges and manhauling the two Gardiner guns. On 15th February the column reached Abu Klea. There was insufficient water for both man and beast and no fodder for the camels, so next morning Buller sent all the camels off to Jakdul with his baggage and stores. The Sudanese troops and native camel drivers were also sent, all under the escort of the Hussars and the Light Camel Regiment. With the sick and wounded bedded down in the centre, Buller formed a fortified camp with the Naval Brigade and its Gardiners sited in a sand redoubt.

Here, in some discomfort, the column spent the next seven days. Overnight on 16/17th February, long range sniping with obligatory tom-tom heralded some Dervish action and on the forenoon of 17th February a field gun, brought up during the night, opened fire on the camp. After firing three or four rounds it was silenced by a Gardiner gun of the Naval Brigade. Desultory sniping continued day and night until 22nd February when a convoy of 782 camels arrived from Jakdul. Buller's departure was hastened by the intelligence that a force of 8000 Dervish with 6 guns had reinforced those already facing him. At 1400 on 23rd the sick and wounded were sent off under escort. At 1930, leaving all his campfires burning and a bugler to sound the Last Post at the routine time, the column began a night march. After four hours they caught up with the convoy of the wounded and bivouaced under arms for the remainder of the night. After three more days of hard marching, short rations and very little water the column arrived at Jakdul on 26th February. Kepple defined their arrival: "Water, mails, cigarettes!" The Naval Brigade could boast that not one man had fallen out on the march and that they were the only unit that could claim that honour.

After a day's rest at Jakdul they marched again for Korti, reached on 8th March. After an inspection by Wolseley on 9th March this Naval Brigade broke up and they returned to their stations on the Nile.

By the middle of March 1885, General Graham had assembled his army in Suakin. He had three infantry brigades, two British and one Indian, cavalry drawn from three British and an Indian regiment, three batteries of Field Artillery, a battery of Horse Artillery and a detachment of Royal Engineers (including a balloon section). To these were added a Naval Brigade landed from HMS *Carysfort*, *Dolphin*, *Sphinx*, *Condor* and *Coquette* equipped with Gardiner guns. This army was to be joined by a battalion of Australian infantry and a battery of Australian Field Artillery — a very important first!

The Hadendoa, led by Osman Digna and based on Tamaii, had conducted a number of night raids on the British lines round Suakin. Before Graham began his march towards Tamaii, on the line of the proposed railway to Berber, he cleared his flank, marching on the Hadendoa at the Wells of Hashin. He encountered the Hadendoa on the 20th March. The battle began with a massed charge of the Hadendoa that was beaten off by the combined fire of artillery, Gardiner gun and rifle. The advance on the wells continued, with the RMLI battalion and the Berkshires deployed in line skirmishing ahead. More Hadendoa were found in position on the forward slopes of the hills behind the wells and cleared away by the RMLI in a scrambling fight ending in a bayonet charge. The cavalry rode down the fleeing tribesmen. Graham left the East Surreys as garrison to the wells and marched back to Suakin.

On 22nd March Graham ordered Major General Sir John McNeill VC, KCB to establish the first of the chain of depots required for the construction of the railway. McNeill had the 2nd Brigade (less the East Surreys), the Indian Brigade, the 5th Lancers and the Naval Brigade to escort a large camel train loaded with stores. By 1000 the force had reached Tofrek and began to build a camp. Roughly aligned along the north/south axis there were three *zareba*s. Most southerly was a small *zareba* manned by half the Berkshires and half the Naval Brigade with two Gardiner guns. The main *zareba* contained the stores, protected by the Indian Brigade deployed by battalions to construct and cover the southeast, southwest and the northwest faces. At the northern corner another small *zareba* was manned by the RMLI and the other half of the Naval Brigade with two Gardiner guns. Further to the east were stationed the other half of the Berkshires. The camel trail train was halted beside the main *zareba* from whence the camels were being led into it to be unloaded and hobbled. The cavalry were disposed as a screen to the south.

At about 1400 the force was fully employed on the domestic chores of establishing itself (the RMLI, with arms piled around their square, had jackets off as well as their equipment and were drawing water and rations) when the cavalry screen came galloping in, closely followed by a howling mob of Hadendoa numbering about 5000. The left of the mob hit the southern square (Berkshires) which suffered badly; some men were swept away in the rush and the Naval Brigade's Gardiners were overrun, the officer in command and the guns' crews killed. The charge swept on

Major General J C McNeill VC, KCB
(Illustrated London News, December 6, 1873)

into the large *zareba*. The 17th Bengal Infantry deployed in line, two deep, on the left of the Berkshires, where the *zareba* wall had not yet been started, faced the heaviest concentration of the Hadendoa. Unable to fire for fear of hitting the cavalrymen, the Bengal Infantry were swept up by the impetus of the Hadendoa's charge and carried through the camel lines towards the RMLI *zareba*. The RMLI were already in difficulties for the Hadendoa had set about the camels, killing the Adendi drivers and hamstringing the beasts. A stampede resulted which broke through the thorn walls of the *zareba* and allowed the Hadendoa to infiltrate. The Marines were so squeezed that they ended up back-to-back firing controlled volleys.

The half battalion of the Berkshires beyond the Marines had time to form square and their steady volleys, together with those of the Sikhs and Bombay infantry whose rear ranks had turned about, stopped the Hadendoa though only at the cost of firing into the camel lines. There, unfortunately, some of the drivers and their camels were killed by 'friendly' bullets. After a very confused twenty minutes the attack died away and the tribesmen were driven off. Over 1000 Hadendoa had been killed for the loss of 130 British and Indian soldiers, 300 wounded, more than 150 civilian camel drivers and about 750 transport animals killed, maimed or lost. The Naval Brigade had suffered severely losing a quarter of its strength.

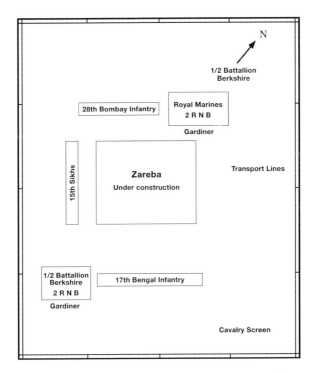

Plan of McNeill's zareba *protecting the railway that was under construction*

This battle, known as Tofrek (McNeills *zareba*), virtually ended the armed resistance of the Hadendoa. The tribesmen lost confidence in Osman Digna and dispersed.

General Graham built up his supplies at Tofrek before continuing his methodic advance on Tamaii. On 2nd April he tried to use his balloon for reconnaisance. The attempt is described in his diary: "…inflated balloon, which got torn in the bush and soon ignominiously collapsed." On 3rd April the force found Tamaii deserted and the wells filled in.

Graham maintained control of the area around Suakin by offensive patrolling, covering the construction of the railway by the civilian contractors, Messrs Lucas and Aird. It was pushed on undisturbed until 17 miles of track had been laid. On 5th May Graham led an attack on the village of Thakul. There was no resistance and 2000 sheep and goats were captured, a very welcome addition to the commissariat.

Then, on orders from the British Government, Wolseley had to cease all action and evacuate all British forces from the Sudan. The Russians had seized the village of Penjdeh on the disputed northern border of Afghanistan and Gladstone, who construed this as a possible prelude to an invasion of India, used this as an excuse to withdraw from the Sudanese adventure, of which he in any case did not approve.

On 27th May Wolseley handed over command to General Sir F Stephenson and left for the UK. On 20th June the Mahdi died in Khartoum while his armies were concentrating at Dongola for the invasion of Egypt. Power passed to the Khalifa who was to continue the fundamentalist fanaticism of his preceptor and continued preparations for the invasion of Egypt. On 30th December, at Ginnis near Wadi Halfa, General Stephenson led a dawn attack on the Dervish army. By 1000 the Dervish were in flight. The threat to Egypt was removed.

The future Field Marshal Lord Kitchener who had as a Major gathered intelligence in advance of the Desert Column, summed it all up:

"The memorable siege of Khartoum lasted 317 days and it is not too much to say that such a noble resistance was due to the indomitable resolution and resource of one Englishman. Never was a garrison so nearly rescued, never was a commander so sincerely lamented."

General Buller had a different opinion:

"The man wasn't worth the camels."

Bibliography

Barthrop, M. (1986) *War on the Nile*. Blandford Press

Bradford, E. (1923) *Life of AF Sir AK Wilson VC*. John Murray

Farwell, B. (1973) *Queen Victoria's Little Wars*. Allen Lane

James, L. (1985) *The Savage Wars*. Robert Hale

Lehman, J. (1964) *All Sir Garnet*. Jonathon Cape

Maxwell, L. (1985) *The Ashanti Ring*. Secker and Warburg

Molyneux, W. C. F. (1896) *Campaigning in South Africa and Egypt*. Macmillan

Marling, P. (1931) *Rifleman and Hussar*. John Murray

Padfield, P. (1981) *Rule Brittannia*. Routledge and Kegan Paul

(Author unknown) (1930) *A Midshipman in the Egyptian War*. RUSI Journal

Preston, A. and Major, J. (1967) *Send a Gunboat*. Longmans

Smith, P. and Oakley, D. (1988) *The Royal Marines*. Spellmount

Smith, P. (1987) *Victoria's Victories: Seven Classic Battles of the British Army, 1849–84*. Spellmount

Winton, J. (1981) *Jellicoe*. Michael Joseph

CHAPTER 9

THE SECOND BOER WAR

1899–1901

Enmity between the Boer and Britain smouldered on after the end of the first Boer War. Kruger remained President of the Transvaal and, with increasing age, more rigidly xenophobic than ever. The discovery of gold on the Rand brought a flood of immigrants, called Uitlanders by the Boers, to the Transvaal. Kruger determined that, numerous as they were, they should have no say in the government of 'his' Boer Republic and enacted a series of laws making it almost impossible for Uitlanders to acquire Transvaal nationality and obtain political rights. He imposed punitive taxation and introduced a system of trade monopolies that grossly inflated the operating costs of the goldmines.

Under Kruger's repressive regime the Uitlanders grew increasingly discontented and agitation for political reform intensified. Cecil Rhodes, despite his position as the Prime Minister of Cape Colony, gave support to his agent in Rhodesia, Dr Jamieson, who in December 1895 led an armed force of British South African Police from Rhodesia in an invasion of the Transvaal in support of a rising by Uitlanders which did not take place. Unsupported, Jamieson's force was surrounded at Doornkop and, after a show of resistance, surrendered. Kruger's position was strengthened, he was re-elected President for the fourth time and any real prospect of political reform vanished. A further result of this abortive raid was that Martinius Steyn, the President of the Orange Free State that up until then had remained neutral in the disputes between Great Britain and the Transvaal, concluded a military pact with Kruger.

The Transvaal could field 25 000 men in its Commandoes and a further 15 000 in the Orange Free State. The resulting force would be four times larger than the combined British garrisons in the Cape and Natal. Kruger also set about modernising his army. He set up an artillery corps (the only regular soldiers in the Transvaal) under a German mercenary equipped, initially, with four 155 mm guns and six 75 mm guns from Creusot, four 120 mm howitzers and eight 75 mm field guns from Krupps and 20 Maxim-Nordenfeld 1 pdr pom-poms made in Britain and not yet in service with the British army. He also ordered 37 000 of the new Mauser 7 mm magazine rifles with an ample supply of ammunition to be held in store. The Orange Free State acquired some 20 000 Mausers as well.

In December 1898 an Englishman was shot and killed by a Transvaal policeman (ZARP) who was tried for manslaughter and acquitted. The intense indignation of the Uitlanders at this acquittal led to a petition to Queen Victoria asking for her intervention on their behalf. This led, in May 1899, to a conference in Bloemfontein, the capital of the Orange Free State, between Steyn, Kruger and Milner, the British High Commissioner in South Africa. Neither Milner nor Kruger wished to reach an acceptable conclusion and the conference broke up within a week. The drift into war was now unstoppable.

The British garrisons in their scattered cantonments in the Cape and in Natal numbered 12 000 and Milner sought reinforcement. Wolseley, at the War Office, proposed to mobilise the 1st Army corps and a Cavalry Division (about 35 000 men in all) but was only authorised to send 10 000 men, to be drawn from British regiments in India and the Mediterranean garrisons, in September. After further pressure the mobilisation of the army corps was ordered on 7th October.

On 27th September President Kruger informed President Steyn that the Transvaal Commandoes had been called out. Steyn, after an unsuccessful attempt to obtain American mediation, called out those of the Orange Free State. On 2nd October the Volksraad voted for war and on 10th October an ultimatum demanding the stoppage of the movement of and withdrawal of the British reinforcements was delivered to the British Prime Minister. The ultimatum was rejected and the Boers, who had waited for the spring flush of grass on the veldt to provide forage for their ponies, invaded Cape Province, investing the small British garrisons in Mafeking and Kimberley, and advanced into Natal towards the main British base at Ladysmith where General White, just arrived to command both the peacetime garrison and the reinforcement from India, was attempting to organise his forces for the defence of the colony of Natal.

Concentrated at Simonstown were HM Ships *Doris* (Flag) and *Monarch* of the Cape Squadron and *Powerful*, diverted on her way home from China. HMS *Terrible*, her relief, diverted on her way to China and joined on 14th October. Admiral Harris, the commander-in-chief, was asked to form and hold at readiness a Naval Brigade on 13th October. On 20th October a Naval Brigade of nine Naval Officers, 53 Naval

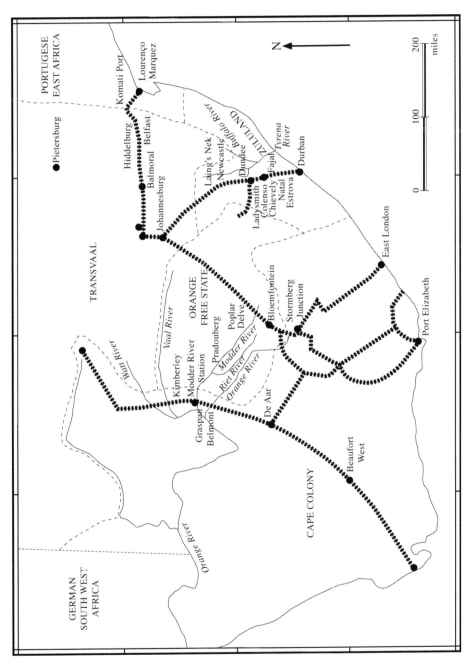

Map of Transvaal and Orange Free State

Ratings, seven Royal Marine Officers and 290 Royal Marines with two Naval 12 pdr field guns left Simonstown by train for Stormberg Junction. They were warmly welcomed by a battalion of the Berkshires who remembered the Naval Brigade that had shared the desperate fight at McNeill's *zareba* in the Sudan with them. The seamen had been issued with khaki uniform drawn from army sources and on the jackets, the high tight collars of which they found irritating and constrictive, they sewed the red woven badges of substantive and non-substantive rate. These red badges and their sennet hats, although with khaki covers, were the only distinguishing features of their dress. The Royal Marines stained their white webbing equipment with potassium permanganate.

Captain Percy Scott of the RN, commanding HMS *Terrible*, was one of the most inventive gunnery specialists then serving in the Royal Navy. He had already designed and tested a field mounting for 12 pdr guns dismounted from ships. This mounting consisted of a baulk of timber as a trail secured to the wheels and axle of a Cape cart onto which the gun was seated. It was fitted with a telescopic sight. The trail was not fitted with a spade so that the recoil was absorbed in the running back of the gun. It was necessary to run the gun back up after each shot and, for accuracy, match a peg driven into the ground to a painted mark on the gunwheel and to realign the gun after every shot. Elevation was by a simple screw mechanism and laying by shifting the trail. Spotting was by an officer with a large magnification telescope, taken from the flag deck and mounted on a tripod adjacent to the gun position. (These high-powered telescopes were to prove extremely popular with all ranks of the army. Officers, from General down, utilised them for reconnaissance and other ranks to catch a glimpse of a Boer.)

On 25th October Admiral Harris received an urgent telegram from the Governor of Natal:

> "Following from Sir George White, 24th October, in view of heavy guns being brought by General Joubert from the North I would suggest the Navy be consulted with a view of their sending detachments consisting of bluejackets with guns firing heavy projectiles at long ranges."

Made aware of the army's request for long range guns Percy Scott asked for all the resources of the dockyard to be made available to him and within 24 hours had produced two 'transportable' mountings for 4.7 inch guns consisting of four baulks of timber, fourteen-feet long and one foot square to be dug into the ground in the form of a cross to which the base plate was bolted. Onto this the mounting and gun were secured. Each gun required six wagons to transport it. Within 36 hours two of these 4.7-inch guns were on their way to Durban in HMS *Powerful*.

Later Percy Scott strengthened the 12 pdr mounting using a train axle and mounted 4.7 inch guns on wheels. He also mounted a 6 inch gun on wheels when General Buller asked for a 6 inch gun that could "move a mile or so across the flat. If possible I want it by Monday 12th February". The request was received on

8th February and by 11th February a gun had been dismounted in HMS *Terrible*, brought ashore by ship's boats and placed on a field mounting. It completed a test firing and started up to the front by train on Sunday evening.

Instead of limbers the trails of the guns were lifted and lashed onto Cape wagons that also carried some ammunition. The whole ensemble was towed, gun first, sometimes by mule teams and sometimes by oxen, eight span for a 12 pdr and 16 span for a 4.7 inch. These guns were affectionately nicknamed 'cow guns' by the army. Ammunition was carried in additional ox wagons as were provisions, stores, camp gear, bedding etc. Each team of oxen had its own native drivers who were supervised by conductors, local Europeans who also acted as interpreters.

General Sir Redvers Buller VC arrived in Cape Town on 31st October as commander-in-chief and to command the army corps in the field. He expected that General White would have obeyed instructions to abandon Natal north of the Tugela River and establish a defensive line on the south bank on which to stand to secure the remainder of Natal. Buller could then march from the Cape through the Orange Free State, capturing its capital Bloemfontein, and then through the Transvaal to capture Pretoria. Buller's march could be expected to draw off Boer forces in Natal. White could then advance, free northern Natal and invade the Transvaal from the rear. Instead Buller found that White had allowed himself, with an army of 12 000 men including a Naval Brigade, to be trapped in Ladysmith under siege. Natal north of the Tugela was in Boer hands and Natal south of the river was open to Boer invasion. In the north of Cape Province, near the Bechuanaland border, Mafeking was under siege as was Kimberley farther south. The Boers held the railway down to Belmont. On 1st November a Boer force crossed the Cape border further east and threatened Stormberg and the railway to East London.

Milner at Cape Town was afraid that the Cape Boers might rise in support of their compatriots at Kimberley and Stormberg and pressed Buller to use his army corps, when it arrived, to clear Cape Province of the invaders. The Governor of Natal was also pressing for action to secure his province. Buller decided to divide his Army Corps when it arrived. One force, under Lieutenant General Lord Methuen was to relieve Kimberley (where, incidentally, Cecil Rhodes was making a nuisance of himself) and to march on up the railway to relieve Mafeking. A second, under Lieutenant General Gatacre, was to operate around Stormberg. Buller would take the third, and largest, portion to Natal to relieve Ladysmith.

Equipped with their improvised weapons three Naval Brigades were to support the army. One, with General White, was already besieged in Ladysmith. The second was with General Buller in his efforts that led to the relief of Ladysmith, while the third fought under General Methuen in his attempt to relieve Kimberley and then marched and fought with Field Marshal Lord Roberts from the Cape through Bloemfontein and Pretoria to the borders of Portuguese East Africa (now Mozambique). The navy also provided two mobile searchlights, fitted with signal shutters, mounted on railway trucks which were used, one near Kimberley and one near Ladysmith, for long range communication between the relieving force and the besieged. There was one other strange detachment — a party of seamen was attached to the Army Balloon Section with Buller's force.

THE NAVAL BRIGADE AT THE SIEGE OF LADYSMITH

The northern part of Natal forms a finger of territory flanked by the Orange Free State on the west and the Transvaal on the east. This area had no strategic value though a British garrison was concentrated in the town of Dundee under General Penn-Symons and the reinforcements were concentrated on Ladysmith, further south, under General White. The first really defensible position was the line of the Tugela River where the railway crossed at Colenso. It was the intention that General White should withdraw Penn-Symons' force to Ladysmith and then move the whole force, with all the military stores accumulated at Ladysmith, behind the Tugela and hold this position pending the arrival of General Buller with the army corps from home. Penn-Symons was adamant that he could hold his forward position and the Governor of Natal, fearing the effect on morale of any surrender of territory, pressed White not to retreat to the Tugela. White vacillated and on 20th October the Boers attacked Dundee.

The British were surprised and, though they achieved a tactical victory, General Penn-Symons was mortally wounded. There was an unfortunate period during which the British artillery fired on their own infantry and half the cavalry allowed itself to be captured. Meanwhile another Boer force under General Kock was moving south aiming for the railway at Elandslaagte station which they occupied, cutting the rail and telegraph link between Dundee and Ladysmith. Major General French (with Major Haig as his chief staff officer) had been ordered to make a cavalry reconnaissance from Ladysmith and on 21st October discovered the Boers occupying Elandslaagte station. French asked White for reinforcements and three battalions of infantry (the Devons, Gordons and Manchesters) were rushed up the railway to meet him. In a hard fought fight the infantry drove the Boers out of their positions and the cavalry, catching them retreating, completed the destruction of Kock's force.

These two little victories had done nothing to stop the Boers' advance. At Dundee the four battalions of infantry were threatened by an army of 10 000 Boers led by General Joubert and were under fire from the first 6 inch Creusot guns (familiarly know as Long Toms) which far outranged the 15 pdrs of the British Field Artillery. On 22nd October General White realised the weakness of his position and telegraphed:

> "I cannot relieve you without sacrificing Ladysmith and the colony behind. You must try to fall back on Ladysmith."

Major General Yule, who had succeeded Penn-Symons was forced to abandon Dundee, leaving behind his wounded (including the dying Penn-Symons), supplies for two months and everything that could not be carried (including the officers' kit and the instruments and drums of the regimental bands) and begin a night cross country march to safety. The four mile long column passed undetected less than a mile from the Boer camp. Unmolested and not pursued they made their way across country to Ladysmith, which they reached after four days on 26th October.

Outnumbered by the Boer forces that were concentrated against him, General White believed that he could still inflict a heavy defeat on the Boers whose position was based on Pepworth Hill, four miles from Ladysmith. On this hill the Boers had placed at least one Long Tom that could fire into Ladysmith. White's plan was to despatch, by night, a small force of two battalions with a mule borne mountain battery to take up a position behind Pepworth Hill to block a Boer retreat, to outflank the main Boer position, and to take Pepworth Hill. He would then use his cavalry to destroy the Boers retreating in front of the infantry. The implementation of the plan on 30th October went disastrously wrong and by 1200, disheartened and disorganised, the infantry and cavalry were retreating on Ladysmith, covered by the artillery that held off the Boer infantry but could do nothing to silence the Boer artillery that was firing on them and the infantry.

HMS *Powerful* had arrived in Durban on 29th October and disembarked two 4.7 inch guns on transportable mountings, three 12 pdrs on improvised field mountings (known as Long 12 pdrs) and a Naval 12 pdr field gun. Under the command of Captain Hon Hedworth Lambton RN, a Naval Brigade of 17 officers and 267 ratings (gun crews and a rifle company of seamen together with a medical party and engine room ratings as stretcher bearers), they entrained and left for Ladysmith at 1900. At about 1200 on 30th October their two trains arrived in Ladysmith where they were greeted with shellfire from the Long Tom on Pepworth Hill and the unexpected confusion of a stream of ambulances and walking wounded making their way back from the front.

The Naval Brigade immediately began to unload the three Long 12 pdrs and somehow organised wagons as limbers and for ammunition and three eight span ox teams. Led by a local boy on a bicycle the three guns and the rifle company set out for the front. They reached the gun line, unlimbered and prepared to engage the 6-inch gun on Pepworth Hill. Before a round could be fired the order for all the artillery to retire was received and very reluctantly the three guns were limbered up. As they did so they came under fire from the 6-inch gun that increased in intensity as the guns began to move back.

When the range had increased to about 7000 yards a six-inch shell pitched very close to the leading gun. The gun was overturned with one wheel knocked off, the gun's crew were wounded and the ox team, broken loose, bolted and was lost. The remaining two guns unlimbered and covered by the rifle company came into action against the Long Tom that was quickly silenced. The Naval Brigade remained in this position, between the Boers and the retreating infantry, while the wheel was replaced on the damaged gun, the gun righted and another ox team was found to tow the gun back to camp. The unexpected intervention of the Naval Brigade and the silencing of the Long Tom checked the Boer advance and raised the morale of the British forces who were no longer subject to long range shelling to which they could make no reply.

Back in Ladysmith the unloading of the two trains continued. The 12 pdr field gun and the four Maxim guns were moved to a feature named Gordon's Hill, which was to become the main position for the Naval Brigade's guns, covering the northern side of the defences and the most likely line of attack for the Boers. The two 4.7 inch guns were then unloaded. Each gun needed six wagons to transport barrels, mountings, baulks of timber and the associated gear. When ready to move off the leading wagon dropped a wheel into a roadside gully and it was not until next day that it could be moved. The other eleven wagons were blocked in.

When the Long 12 pdrs were seen to be returning to the camp they were called to the Naval Brigade's position by a Naval Bugler sounding 'assembly'. This not only brought in the guns; mounted staff officers at the gallop and panting infantry officers at the double arrived to find why the 'alarm' had been sounded. There were some interesting and acerbic exchanges before the panic subsided.

Ladysmith, a small and unimportant township, was surrounded by a ring of hills which were occupied by 22 000 Boers under the command of General Joubert, the most experienced Boer commander but 66 years old and lacking aggression (it was he who had failed to follow up his victory at Majuba in the First Boer War). The 12 000 British occupied a 14 mile defensive perimeter round the town. To effectively oppose the 22 Boer guns, five Creusot 6 inch and seventeen 75 mm, there were only the guns of the Naval Brigade which were based on Gordon's Hill. The first 4.7-inch was assembled and ready to open fire at dawn on 2nd November and the second 24 hours later. Work then began on building protection for the gun positions. Parapets of sandbags, three or four layers thick, faced with four feet of loose earth with a *glacis* of rock were built round each gun. Then trenches were built to connect the gun positions, the ready use magazine and the main magazine. Finally barbed wire entanglements were rigged in front of the gun site.

With the tented camp nearby, Gordon's Hill became the 'home' of the Naval Brigade, though the campsite had to be moved to a sheltered position after a Boer gun found the range and ruined the wardroom lunch. The guns at Gordon's Hill could not provide artillery cover for the whole of the perimeter. The 12 pdrs being mobile were therefore moved to alternative sites around the perimeter to engage Boer guns when they fired at Ladysmith, returning home when the task was completed. From time to time one of the 4.7-inch guns was moved to a site to the south of the perimeter that gave cover to the most likely approach route of the expected relief column and from which one of the Long Toms could be engaged.

On the evening of 30th October, Captain Lambton telegraphed to Durban a request for more guns and ammunition. On 2nd November, before re-supply was possible, the Boers cut both the railway and the telegraph and the siege began. Lambton appreciated that the strictest economy in the use of ammunition was essential — he had only six hundred rounds for both 4.7-inch guns. Consequently, by his orders, fire was only opened in retaliation to Boer bombardments of the town. There was one exception. On 9th November, it being the birthday of the Prince of Wales, a royal salute was fired. So economical was the Naval Brigade that they still had ammunition in hand when the siege was raised on 28th February 1900, 117 days later.

Early in the siege there was a water crisis. The Boers had captured the town's water works, leaving only the very muddy water of the Tugela available to the besieged. The few water filters within the town were quite inadequate and the supply of alum, used for clearing the water was quickly exhausted. Mr Sheen, an Engine Officer with the Naval Brigade designed an extempore distillery capable of producing 1500 gallons of distilled water a day. Three of these distilleries provided

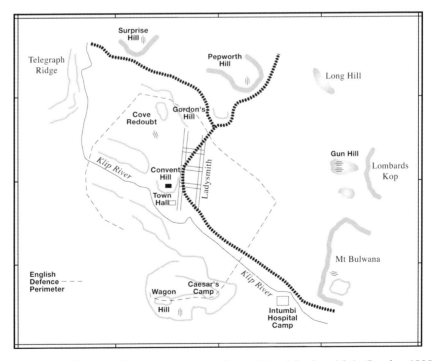

Plan of 14-mile defensive perimeter around township of Ladysmith in October 1898

the whole garrison with drinking water for the six weeks that the coal supply lasted.

The Boers made only two attempts to storm the defences of Ladysmith. They were, apparently, relying on starvation to bring about the surrender of the garrison. So, on the whole, life was dull and there was little to do to pass the time. Football was played until the ball burst, worn out by constant usage. Cricket was sometimes played, but the cricket pitch was overlooked by the Boers whose religious sensibilities were offended when a game was attempted on a Sunday. This game was unfinished — shellfire stopped play. Books were hard to come by and there only seemed to be about a dozen, including Shakespeare, circulating in the Naval Brigade. Even the packs of cards soon became greasy from overuse and eventually became almost unrecognisable. The Naval Brigade camp soon collected an assorted pack of dogs ranging from an underbred mastiff that hated shellfire, through pointer and spaniel to the wardroom's fox terrier bitch that whelped under the mess table and raised five pups.

The Naval Brigade was exceptionally fortunate in having fleet paymaster Kay in its ranks. Kay was a veteran, serving in his fourth Naval Brigade and very experienced in the vagaries of the army supply system. By his forethought, powers of organisation and his 'nose' for opportunity he was able to avoid unnecessary deprivation and discomfort for his 'brigade mates'. He foresaw the prospect of a long siege and from the first quietly acquired many of the simple foodstuffs like sardines that he knew would be looked on as luxuries in time to come. He located and purchased for £30 almost all the draught beer there was in the town and while it lasted the wardroom of the Naval Brigade could be hospitable to visitors. It was not until the 76th day of the siege that the Naval Brigade was reduced to siege rations – horsemeat and biscuit, the horsemeat in various forms: chevril (horsemeat soup or Bovril with a difference), horse sausage, potted horse tongue as well as minced, stewed and roast horse.

After the defeat of the first, rather half-hearted Boer attack on the night of 8th/9th November in which the Naval Brigade was hardly involved, action was restricted to the daily Boer shelling and the rationed reply from the Naval Brigade guns until 7th December when a sally from the British lines reached and destroyed a Long Tom. On 15th December the hopes of the British were raised by the distant sound of battle from the direction of the Tugela where General Buller was making his first attempt to relieve Ladysmith that resulted in the debacle at Colenso. Hopes were dashed by a message conveying the news that Buller could not make another attempt to relieve them for at least a month and suggesting that, when White's supplies were exhausted, as much ammunition as possible should be fired off and terms of surrender be sought. White replied that he could make food last much longer than a month and could not yet think of surrender. Buller also received a sharp communication from the War Office urging him to make another attempt to relieve Ladysmith, followed, later, by another informing him that Field Marshal Lord Roberts had been appointed commander-in-chief in South Africa over his head and ordering him to concentrate on relieving Ladysmith.

General White began preparations for a sally from the garrison in support of an attack or breakthrough by Buller's army. To this end he ordered one of the 4.7-inch guns and two of the 12 pdrs to be re-sited to command the southern approaches to his lines. Gunpits had been dug for the guns, which were to be moved on the night of 5th/6th January.

At 0240 on 6th January Mr Sims, Gunner, RN accompanied by Mr Sheen and with a party of thirteen ratings, Lieutenant Digby-Jones RE with 25 sappers and an escort of 70 Gordon Highlanders had brought the 4.7 inch and its ox drawn wagons to the bottom of the hill on which the gunpits were sited, had unloaded the baulks of timber and were constructing the gun platform by lantern light when the party was alarmed by the crack of bullets passing close overhead. There followed a period of much confusion. Some of the sappers and Gordons found their rifles, occupied the gunpits and a nearby sangar from which they resisted the attacks of several Boers of a Free State Commando who were silhouetted against the glare of a Boer searchlight intended for their assistance. The Imperial Light Horse, guarding this section of the perimeter, were extending along the crest to meet the attack. As their hats were similar to those worn by the Boers this added to the confusion. The first action of the sailors, led by Mr Sims was to immobilise their wagons by cutting loose and driving off the draught oxen, most of which were saved though some recalcitrant beasts broke back to the summit of the hill and set to grazing. These beasts remained browsing until the end of the battle next evening. Almost all were wounded and had, in the end, to be slaughtered. When the rest of the oxen were safe Mr Sims mustered his ratings and led them back to the gun pit, where he fell them in, numbered them off and detailed them into half-sections, right and left. He then conducted controlled volley fire by half sections. Everything was done strictly by the Whale Island drill book!

By daylight the attack had spread right along the southern face of the defences. A party of Boers was established on the crest of the hill flanking the gunsite and the position of the Imperial Light Horse. They were supported from first light by the Boer artillery, which opened fire on the British positions and in particular at the Royal Horse artillery batteries which had moved up into positions from which they could support the infantry. There developed a 'round robin' of artillery fire. The RHA fired at the Boer artillery, the Boer artillery fired at the British infantry and the naval guns on Gordon's Hill fired at the Boer guns. It was noted that the Boer artillery fire was generally inaccurate.

By 1100 the Boers were gradually being pushed back, the volume of fire had diminished and it was thought that the attack was over. General Hamilton, who had appeared and taken charge of the defence, felt it safe to thin out his line and at 1200 ordered some of his troops, including Mr Sims and his party, to retire down the hill and have a meal, leaving the sappers in the gun pit. Hamilton joined Major Miller-Wallnut of the Gordons and Lieutenant Digby-Jones in the gun pit. A party of Boers that had crept up unseen charged into the pit and a hand-to-hand scrimmage began. Mr Sims became aware of a sudden increase in the volume of fire and a body of men rushed down the hill and past him shouting that the Boers were in the gun pit. Mr Sims ordered his men to fix bayonets, extended them in line and led them in a charge into the gun pit where they joined in the melee. While Hamilton was rallying his troops they cleared the gun pit with the bayonet and then fired into the backs of the Boers that were escaping. By 1400 this attack was over and the position secure. At about 1430 the Boers launched another attack that was beaten off and by 1630 it was clear that the battle was won. The finale was 'a magnificent charge' by the Devons that cleared the last of the Boers from the ridge.

Next morning there was an armistice to allow the collection of the dead and wounded. The battle had cost the British 14 officers (including both Major Miller-Wallnut and Lieutenant Digby-Jones killed in the fight in the gun pit) and 135 other ranks killed and 31 officers and 244 other ranks wounded. The Naval Brigade lost one stoker and one able seaman was severely wounded. The total Boer casualties were uncertain, 79 bodies were so mangled by shrapnel that they were left to be buried where they fell and reports placed the total of Boer dead and wounded as at least 700. Mr Sims had a rifle blown out of his grasp and Mr Sheen sustained a slight facial wound. Mr Sims' conduct that day earned him direct promotion to Lieutenant.

Ladysmith had survived the heaviest attack to which it was subjected and life returned to the monotony of the siege as prosecuted by the Boers, with intermittent shelling to which the Naval Brigade made their rationed reply. But the morale of the garrison was dropping and sickness was taking a rising toll, with malnutrition developing as rations were stretched to prolong the defence. Hopes of relief were raised on 24th January when the sound of battle from Spion Kop was heard and on 25th January when wagons from the Boer laagers were seen moving off. But next morning the wagons were moving back and the garrison settled grimly to await relief whenever it would come.

The sound of gunfire was heard again on 5th and 7th February, on 14th and then intermittently until 28th February. At dawn that day the Boers could be seen in full retreat and in the afternoon they were rigging sheerlegs over the Long Tom on Bulwana Hill preparatory to moving it. The Naval Brigade came into action for the last time to engage this tempting target. A direct hit brought down the sheerlegs with a run and brought the Boer activities to an end. At 1815 that evening, two squadrons of cavalry rode in and Ladysmith had been relieved. The Naval Brigade was ordered back to their ship and on 9th March were accorded the honour of being played to the railway station by the pipes and drums of the Gordons. From Durban they sailed for

England. They took the Naval field gun and the Maxims with them, but handed over the 4.7-inch guns and the Long 12 pdrs to the Royal Garrison artillery.

In the course of the siege the Naval Brigade lost one officer and five ratings were killed or died of wounds but a further two officers and 25 ratings died of disease, mainly enteric fever caused by the infected water from the Tugela.

Sir George White wrote in his despatch:

"Captain the Hon. Hedworth Lambton RN commanding the Naval Brigade reached Ladysmith in the nick of time, when it became evident that I was not strong enough to meet the enemy in the open field. He brought with him two 4.7 inchs and four 12 pdr guns which proved to be the only ordinance in my possession capable of equalling the range of the enemy's heavy guns. Although the ammunition was strictly limited Captain Lambton so economised it that it lasted out till the end of the siege and under his direction the Naval guns succeeded in keeping at a distance the enemy's siege guns, a service which was of the utmost importance."

THE RELIEF OF LADYSMITH

On 31st October 1899, General Sir Redvers Buller VC arrived in Cape Town ahead of the Army Corps he was to command. His orders were to assemble his Army Corp and to advance on Bloemfontein and Pretoria to occupy the capital cities of the two Boer Republics, orders issued in London before Boer successes had brought three British garrisons under siege. Buller decided on a redeployment of his Army Corps, splitting it into three separate forces: one under Lieutenant General Lord Methuen to advance to the relief of Kimberley, the second under Major General Gatacre to clear the Stormberg area of Cape Colony while the third, under his personal command, would operate in Natal to relieve Ladysmith.

On 6th November HMS *Terrible* relieved HMS *Powerful* in Durban and Captain Percy Scott RN became the Military Commandant in the town which had been placed under martial law. Scott took energetic steps to place Durban in a state of defence. On 7th November, having collected 60 horses and 100 oxen as gun teams, he marched through the streets of Durban to take up defensive positions outside the town. He was headed by HMS *Terrible's* band, a Naval Brigade of 450 officers and men with two 4.7 inch guns on improvised field mountings (a further development of his 12 pdr mounting), sixteen 12 pdrs on field mountings and an assortment of smaller calibre guns.

Scott then constructed an armoured train, fitting it with Maxims and a 7 pdr gun, to be manned by sailors, with armoured trucks to carry a company of infantry. The train was sent forward to Estcourt and used to carry out a daily reconnaissance to Chieveley. On 15th November the Boers ambushed the train, derailing its three trucks and partially derailing the engine. Under heavy fire the railway track was cleared and the engine returned to the rails. Carrying 50 survivors, mostly wounded, the engine escaped leaving four dead, 14 wounded and 57 (one of whom was Winston Churchill) to become prisoners of war.

For the next ten days, while the vanguard of Buller's army arrived in Durban and moved forward to positions around Estcourt and Frere, the Boers, under Generals Joubert and Botha, raided down the railway towards Durban. Then on 26th November Joubert was injured in a fall from his horse and the raiding party of 2000 men with two guns retired behind the Tugela River. There, Botha prepared a defensible position of concealed rifle and gun pits, invisible to an attacker until well within range of the defending rifles.

General Buller arrived in Durban on 26th November and was greeted with a naval guard of honour and a demonstration of the 4.7-inch gun on wheels. From Pietermaritzburg, on his way up to Estcourt, Buller telegraphed to Durban for 'mobile guns' and at 1700 that day the first contingent of the Naval Brigade left Durban for Estcourt under the command of Captain Jones of HMS *Forte*. This contingent took two 4.7 inch guns and four 12 pdrs. By 8th December a further twelve 12 pdrs had moved forward to join Buller. The Brigade drawn from HM Ships *Terrible*, *Tartar*, *Philomel* and *Forte* was joined by two officers and 50 ratings of the Natal Naval Volunteers whose knowledge of the Zulu and Dutch languages were to prove invaluable throughout the coming campaign.

Buller concentrated his army at Frere where he established his base and railhead, with his outposts at Chieveley about four miles further up the railway (though the Boers had blown the railway bridge at Frere and until the replacement was built the line was cut). On 12th December the Naval Brigade marched from Frere to Chieveley where they established camp on a *kopje* (hillock) that was to become known throughout the army as Gun Hill. The column of guns, ammunition wagons and baggage wagons stretched for two miles and the seven-mile march, begun at 0400, was not complete until 2000. Next morning, 13th December, the guns were moved to another *kopje* about two miles nearer the Boer positions where the guns were dug in and the 4.7 inch guns fired a few rounds at what were presumed to be the Boer positions. The ceasefire was sounded when the heat haze obscured any targets beyond 7000 yards. This position became known as Shooters Hill.

Buller arrived at Frere on 6th December and took stock of the situation. He lacked adequate maps of the area and had only sketchy information of the Boers' defensive dispositions in terrain that he described as "ghastly country, exactly the sort made for the Boer tactics and they have strongly fortified it". There were two places at which Buller could pass his army over the Tugela. At Colenso, to his front, there were three passable drifts and an intact footbridge as well as the blown railway bridge; at Potgeiter's Drift, 15 miles to his left, there was also a passable crossing. At either crossing, having passed the river, it would be necessary to fight through a tangle of *kopjes* before reaching Ladysmith, though behind Potgeiter's Drift this

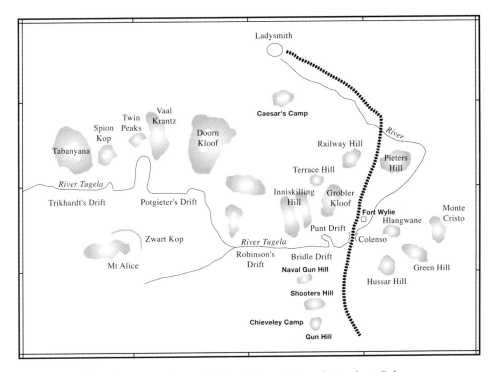

Buller's route to relieve Ladysmith, after initial attack at Colenso.

tangle was not as deep as at Colenso. Buller's initial plan was to attack at Potgeiter's but before he was ready to move he received the news of General Methuen's defeat at Magersfontein and General Gatacre's defeat at Stormberg. He decided that he could not afford the delay inherent in the flank march to Potgeiter's Drift and decided to attack at Colenso and fight his way to Ladysmith by the shortest route.

At Colenso the Tugela makes a sudden turn from its general west to east line and flows in a northerly direction between a line of *kopjes* and the eminence of Mount Hlangwane. About a mile to the west of Colenso the river made a deep ox bow bend beyond which lay Bridle Drift. General Botha had his men dig cleverly concealed trenches covering all three Drifts and the intact footbridge at Colenso, and had anchored his left flank with positions on Mount Hlangwane. On the *kopjes* behind Colenso there were a number of gun sites for the 75 mm guns and 1 pdr pom-poms between which the guns could be moved when threatened by counter battery fire. The 6 inch Creusots were further back, covering the Drifts to his right.

Buller planned a two-pronged attack with the Irish Brigade under General Hart on the left crossing the river at Bridle Drift, while General Hildyard moved to cross the river by the intact footbridge and the Wagon Drift beside it. Two naval 4.7 inch guns and four 12 pdrs were to provide general support, Hildyard had six naval 12 pdrs and two batteries of Royal Field Artillery, all under the command of Colonel Long, the CRA to support his advance. Two 12 pdrs were to remain in position on Shooters Hill to protect the camp.

At 0200 on 15th December reveille was sounded and at 0400 the two 4.7 inch guns and four 12 pdrs moved off to take up position on a slight eminence 4500 yards from the Boer centre. This position became known as Naval Gun Hill and from here Buller intended to conduct the battle. At about 0530 these guns began a preliminary bombardment. Hart began to move his Brigade towards Bridle Drift and Colonel Long his two batteries and six naval 12 pdrs towards the front. No Boers could be seen and there had been no return fire. There was nothing to show that the advance would be opposed.

Hart led his Brigade towards Bridle Drift which lay about a mile to the west of the loop in the river, then when about half way there altered his line of advance and headed straight into the salient formed by the loop. When all were inside his troops came under Boer rifle fire from their front and both flanks. For an hour there followed great confusion and the Brigade suffered very severely. Hart's only orders were to send more men into the loop. Buller, from Naval Gun Hill, watched the action. He sent a galloper to Hart with orders to withdraw and then emphasised it by riding down himself and repeating the order to Hart. Buller then rode back to Major General Lyttleton, whose Brigade was acting as the reserve for Hart, and ordered him to extricate Hart's Brigade as best he could. The Field Artillery Battery which had been detailed to support Hart, and which had not been called on, came under heavy fire from three 6 inch Creusot and were forced to move back. The Naval Brigade 4.7 inch guns shifted target to the Creusots which ceased firing shortly after being engaged.

Just before riding down to General Hart, Buller had seen that Colonel Long was moving his twelve 15 pdr guns and six naval 12 pdrs far closer to the Boer positions than he had intended and was well ahead of the infantry that should be covering him. Long led his 15 pdrs forward at the trot and they steadily drew ahead of the ox drawn naval guns. An 800-yard gap had formed when Long swung his guns into line to bring them into action about 500 yards from the Boer positions. This was the signal to the Boers to open fire and both the 15 pdrs, drawn up in line as though on a parade ground, and the 12 pdrs, which were struggling through a *donga* (gully) at the time, were subjected to a period of sustained and rapid rifle fire. The gun crews of the 15 pdrs took heavy casualties but fought on for an hour before their ammunition was exhausted. The survivors took cover with their wounded in a shallow *donga* close to the rear of the guns and waited for reinforcement and the re-supply of ammunition for which they had asked.

The longer range probably saved the naval guns from heavy casualties but the rifle fire was not without effect. The native drivers of all but two of the gun and wagon teams deserted and the ox teams became unmanageable. Two guns and their limbers were across the *donga* and these were brought into action. The rear two guns had not yet reached it and these too came into action. Numbers three and four guns were jammed into the *donga* with their ammunition wagons locked together and their panic-stricken ox teams mixed in an uncontrollable melee. With some borrowed artillery horses it was possible to extricate the guns which then came into action from behind using ammunition from numbers five and six's wagons. Efforts to extricate the wagons from the *donga* had to be temporarily abandoned because of the intensity of the shellfire and rifle fire directed at them.

Buller had been told of the position of Long's guns and rode up to find the naval guns in action and the 15 pdrs abandoned in their firing line in the open. He rode off to organise infantry support for them and back to organise the recovery of the guns. Three officers volunteered, and having hitched two gun teams to limbers for towing, cantered to the guns. Two of the three were wounded (one the only son of Field Marshal Lord Roberts mortally) but in the face of an increasing volume of fire two guns were hooked on and galloped away. Two further gun teams were despatched, suffered more than 50% casualties in both men and horses, and failed to reach the guns. An independent attempt from a battery on the right flank also failed. The naval guns were engaged in trying to subdue the Boer rifle fire.

While Buller was supervising the efforts to recover the guns a shell burst very close to him. He was struck and very severely bruised by a shell fragment and was probably concussed by the shockwave of the explosion. This may have affected his judgement for, suddenly, he ordered the army back to Chievely, abandoning the guns and the wounded on the battlefield, though he remained to see the rearguard move off to safety. He personally ordered the Naval 12 pdrs to retire.

This posed Lieutenant Ogilvie RN, in command of these guns, with a problem. He had two guns with their wagons over the *donga*, two wagons jammed in the *donga* and four guns with two wagons behind the *donga* and no means of traction. He 'borrowed' artillery gun teams with which he moved his guns out of range and while these were being moved had the guns' crews prepare the wagons for removal. The two in the *donga* were separated and manhandled out, then these two and the two beyond were turned ready to be hitched to teams of horses. One of the difficulties was the large turning circle of the heavy wagons that, initially, brought them closer to the Boer positions. Finally all were recovered and Lieutenant Ogilvie brought his detachment safely back to Chievely. It is surprising that after all the action the Naval Brigade had only three men wounded.

The withdrawal of the army was covered by the fire of the 4.7-inch guns and 12 pdrs on Naval Gun Hill. They remained in position until the infantry had passed them and then moved off to take up their old positions on Shooters Hill. The four naval surgeons were detached from the Brigade to assist in the care of the wounded brought back to the field hospital at Chievely.

Buller moved the army back to Frere, and Lieutenant Ogilvie with his six 12 pdrs was ordered to accompany it, leaving the 4.7 inch guns and the remaining 12 pdrs to move back to Gun Hill where they settled in. For the next 25 days the 4.7-inch guns carried out a daily task of harassing the Boers, usually shooting at dawn and dusk when the light was at its best. From time to time the guns indulged in night firing — laid at dusk they were fired blind during the night. On 19th December they were tasked with the demolition of the footbridge at Colenso. After a number of near misses by one gun the second, laid by the battery commander, secured a direct hit with the first round!

On 10th January 1900, having been reinforced with another Division, Buller renewed his attempt to relieve Ladysmith and began a flank march towards Potgeiter's Drift and Trikhardt's Drift beyond in a series of moves which led to the battle of Spion Kop. The Naval Brigade had been split into batteries attached to individual Brigades to give artillery support, which they did, using their long range to advantage. It was during these operations that the Naval Brigade began to demonstrate its ability to overcome obstacles and move its guns over almost any ground and up the steepest of slopes.

Buller had divided his army and had given command of the left column, heading for Trikhardt's Drift, to Lieutenant General Warren. He had joined him with the 5th Division and held a dormant commission to succeed to the command should Buller be killed or incapacitated. Buller retained command of the forces heading for Potgeiter's Drift. The hills behind Trikhardt's Drift were reported as lightly held by the Boers. Buller's plan was for Warren to cross the Tugela, brush aside the Boers in the hills, and threaten the flank of the Boer positions opposite Potgeiter's Drift. Then Buller would attack and together the two forces would join hands and advance to relieve Ladysmith.

Warren's advance was ponderous, two days to advance ten miles and cross the Tugela and a further two days to bring over the river his baggage wagons. Then he spent two days in indecisive and meaningless manoeuvres to his left. When Lord Dundonald's brigade of Mounted Infantry, guarding his left flank, penetrated the Boer defences and created an opportunity for a flank attack Warren, instead of reinforcing success, recalled Dundonald and set him closely to guard the left flank of the baggage train. On 20th January Warren launched an attack on Tabanyana, the range of hills to his front and in a day's fighting forced their way onto the southern summit. Warren stalled again and on 23rd January Buller rode into his headquarters and bluntly ordered Warren to advance or have his command withdrawn. Warren, in the face of this ultimatum, decided that he would attack Spion Kop on his right. Spion Kop was an extremely steep hill, almost precipitous in places but a position that, if he could take and hold, would force the Boers to retire.

Warren decided on a night attack. At 2300 on 23rd an assault force of 1500 men drawn from the Lancashire Brigade with 200 irregular (locally recruited) Mounted

Infantry began to climb the hill. Just after 0400 on the 24th, having driven off a small picket in thick mist, the force began to consolidate its position on what they believed to be the summit of the Kop. A staff officer was sent to Warren to report success and to request a naval 12 pdr be sent up as the sailors could take their guns where the artillery could not. At 0830 the mist cleared and the British found that they were on a false summit and that their position was overlooked at close range from two knolls held by Boers. There followed a day of homeric combat while the British clung to their position and tried to improve it while the Boers tried to drive the British from the summit. By sunset both sides had fought themselves to exhaustion and after dark both sides evacuated Spion Kop leaving the dead and wounded on the summit. Early on the morning of the 25th the Boers, driven by General Botha who had stopped a retreat during the night, reoccupied the summit. That day Buller rode over from his headquarters and relieved Warren of his command, though not of the 5th Division, and ordered the force to march back and join up with the rest of the army.

The army rested for a week then on 5th February Buller launched an attack on the lightly held feature of Vaal Krantz on which the Boer left flank was anchored. The guns were sited on the south bank of the Tugela to cover the attack. For the Naval Brigade this entailed much manhandling of the guns over rough country and up steep hillsides. The guns were, for three days, to keep up what one Boer General later described as "the heaviest bombardment I saw during the war". The infantry crossed the Tugela and secured and held a position on Vaal Krantz but it was found that not even the Naval Brigade could position its guns to support a further advance. After a council of war on the third day, Buller withdrew his troops across the Tugela and marched back to Frere. On 11th February the Naval Brigade arrived back at Gun Hill and reoccupied their old gun sites.

While Buller was operating to the west the Boers had strengthened their positions around Hlangwane. They were occupying a six mile semicircle of ground from the south round to the east of the Tugela running from Hussar Hill, a fold in the ground before Hlangwane, through Green Hill to the Cingola/Monte Cristo ridge. This six-mile semicircle protected the gorge through which the Tugela, the railway and the road to Ladysmith ran.

On 12th February Buller began to reconnoitre the ground and on 14th February began his operations by seizing Hussar Hill, using Lord Dundonald's Mounted Infantry supported by Lieutenant Ogilvie's 12 pdrs. When Hussar Hill was secured, the guns were dug in on it ready to support the infantry attack on Green Hill the next day. The guns back on Gun Hill took a full part in the action, firing steadily all day on both 15th and 16th while the infantry fought doggedly up Green Hill, which was cleared of the Boers by the end of 16th February.

That evening the Naval Brigade was reinforced by a 6-inch gun on an improvised travelling mounting that arrived from Durban and was dug in on Gun Hill. It soon came into action against a Boer Creusot 6-inch gun that out of range of the 4.7-inch guns had been firing at the naval gun positions on Hussar Hill. At a range of 16 000 yards it silenced the Boer gun. It was to dominate the Boer heavy artillery for the next ten days.

By the evening of 18th February, the Boers had been cleared from their positions on the south of the Tugela and Buller held one side of the road to Ladysmith. But to use it he had to clear the Boers from the hills that dominated the other side.

The Naval Brigade with its guns, except the 6-inch, was called forward from Gun Hill. They operated in close support of the infantry fighting an uphill battle in which after four days they gained only a toehold on the first two of the three hills that had to be taken to clear the road. On 25th Buller and Botha agreed a 24-hour truce for the treatment of the wounded and the removal of the dead.

Buller now shifted the direction of his attack. He pulled back over the Tugela then threw a pontoon bridge across the river in a position that would allow his forces to cross and attack on a wider front than before. The Naval Brigade was concentrated on Hlangwane, strengthened by two 4.7-inch guns on transportable (not wheeled) mountings that had to be dug in. "It was heavy and tiresome work in the dark and the glimmer of a lantern always, immediately, drew fire".

At 0700 on 27th February the guns opened fire, their initial targets being the Boer guns. The hundred-yard pontoon bridge across the river was in position by 1000 and the infantry began to cross, cheered by the news that General Cronje in the Transvaal had surrendered to Lord Roberts. They determined that they also would have something to avenge Majuba on the anniversary of that defeat.

Once across the river the troops defiled to the right and, as they reached their allotted position, turned and began to climb the hill facing them. By nightfall, and after hard fighting, all the Boer positions had been taken and the road to Ladysmith was open. The Boers were in disorganised retreat. Next morning Dundonald with his Mounted Infantry was sent forward to reconnoitre towards Ladysmith and that evening he rode into the town having brushed aside the Boer rearguard. On 2nd March the first convoy of supplies arrived in Ladysmith. Buller rode in on the 3rd.

There was now a pause in operations while the Ladysmith garrison, back on full rations, recovered their strength, re-equipped and reorganised. The Naval Brigade present at Ladysmith began to break up. The *Powerful's* returned to their ship on 7th March to resume their return to the United Kingdom and the *Terrible's* left on 11th March to resume their voyage to China. Reduced to ten officers and ninety men the Brigade could man two 4.7-inch guns and four 12 pdrs. All the remaining guns were handed over to the Royal Artillery.

The Boers, Joubert's men from Ladysmith and Botha's men who had held the Tugela, had retreated to positions 60 miles to the north near Dundee. On 21st March the Naval Brigade moved up the railway to Elandslaagte where they joined the advance guard facing the Boers. On 10th April the Boers brought four guns to bear on the wagon lines and when the Naval Brigade replied, on the guns. In the exchange one Boer gun was destroyed and the others silenced though two naval ratings were killed, two wounded and a wagon and gun limber destroyed. Eleven days later the Boers attacked again with infantry supported by guns. The Naval Brigade again destroyed a gun and the attack was beaten off.

On 11th May Buller began an advance intended to clear Natal of the Boers and then to march through the Transvaal to join up with Lord Roberts' army that would be advancing towards the border of Portuguese East Africa where the railway crossed at Komati Poort. The Naval Brigade marched with Buller as he manoeuvred the Boers out of successive positions back to Laing's Nek, clearing Natal of its invaders. On 22nd June *Forte*'s officers and men were recalled to their ship that was required for service in the Gambia. The 4.7-inch guns were handed over to the artillery and the 12 pdrs, manned from *Philomel* and *Tartar* were given defensive tasks on the lines of communication. The active participation of this Naval Brigade was over.

On 11th October the commander-in-chief, Cape Station ordered the return of the remnant of the Naval Brigade. On 24th October, having handed over their guns, they entrained for Durban flying a paying off pennant over their wagons. At 0800 they arrived in Durban, tired, grimy and wearing their campaign uniform, to be greeted with a civic reception and breakfast.

METHUEN'S ATTEMPT TO RELIEVE KIMBERLEY

Lieutenant General Lord Methuen had established his base and headquarters near the railway bridge over the Orange River. He had the Guards Brigade, the 9th Infantry Brigade and the Highland Brigade guarding the railway line upon which he was completely dependent for his supplies. He also had a regiment of cavalry (9th Lancers), a company of Mounted Infantry, irregular Horse nicknamed Rimington's Tigers and two batteries of Field Artillery equipped with 15 pdr guns. To this force was added a Naval Brigade of 400 officers and ratings with four 12 pdr guns on Scott's improvised mountings commanded by Captain Prothero of HMS *Doris* and drawn from HMShips *Doris*, *Powerful* and *Monarch*. The Naval Brigade from Stormberg had been withdrawn and, less the *Terrible*'s contingent sent to Durban, arrived at Simonstown one evening, was reinforced and entrained next morning for the Orange River.

The Naval Brigade arrived at Orange River Station as Methuen marched out of camp, beginning his advance on Kimberley. The Brigade detrained but there was some delay and confusion before its transport and the mules to draw both guns and wagons arrived. Consequently the Naval Brigade had to make a night march to catch up with Methuen and the main body. One officer commented, "The night march was a particularly trying one". Another heartfelt comment was, "A night march with obstinate mules is a very trying experience". When the Naval Brigade caught up with the main body at Belmont it was already in action with the Boers positioned high on the first range of *kopjes* covering the railway and the route to Kimberley.

Captain Prothero reported to Colonel Hall commanding the artillery. Hall sent the Naval Brigade to the right across the railway line, the crossing of which proved a difficult operation. The guns were brought into action but Captain Prothero was unable to spot the fall of shot and was not satisfied with the position. He ordered the guns to limber up, led them to the left between two *kopjes* and found himself with the Boers in sight 1700 yards away. After a short engagement these Boers vacated their position and as a part of a general withdrawal in the face of the infantry attack mounted their ponies and rode off. Methuen ordered the Naval Brigade forward to engage the retreating Boers, but as the going was very bad and with his officers, men and mules exhausted after their exertions of the previous 36 hours without food or sleep Prothero abandoned the pursuit.

After a night's rest the general advance along the line of the railway continued. On the line was an armoured train followed closely by another carrying the naval guns with the Naval Brigade marching abreast of them. Their mules had been taken to relieve the exhausted horses of the Royal Field Artillery that were being rested against the need of them in an actual engagement. At sunset the force halted and bivouacked about three quarters of a mile short of the two dams from which the force watered. The round trip took two hours and the water was very muddy. When the commissariat wagons finally came up, supper consisted of a meagre ration of tinned meat and ship's biscuit. After supper an ADC appeared with an order from Lord Methuen which began:

> "The enemy, about four hundred strong, hold a hill on our line of advance two miles to the North. The Naval Brigade will lead the attack supported by the KOYLI and a field battery..."

What Methuen did not know was that a contingent of Transvaal Boers under General Koos de la Rey had arrived and joined the Free State Commandos.

Leaving 50 sailors with the guns on the train the Naval Brigade stood to arms at 0300 on 25th November and led off the whole force, marching parallel to and about a mile from the right hand side of the railway track on which the armoured train and gun train kept level with them. At 0530 the scouts made contact with the Boers in position on three *kopjes* on the right of the railway. The two *kopjes* closest to the railway were low and from the right-hand *kopje* ran a spur towards the third and highest of the trio. The Boer positions were well concealed by bush and protective rock formations and dominated open ground that offered no cover to the advancing British troops. By 0700 the Naval Brigade, extended in a single line and supported by the 9th Brigade (also extended), were opposite the right centre of the Boer position and about 3500 yards away. A battery of field artillery and two 12 pdrs (all that the 50 seamen could unload from the train) were in action on the left, and the second battery was on the far right shelling the highest *kopje*. The Naval Brigade was ordered to move to the right and, supported by the King's Own Yorkshire Light Infantry and a half battalion of the North Lancs, began a diagonal march while the remainder of the 9th Brigade (Northumberlands and Northamptons) marched straight on towards the centre of the Boer position.

At 0745 the Naval Brigade was about 700 yards from the foot of the highest *kopje* when the field battery ceased fire. The Boers then opened fire on the Naval Brigade, which halted and turned half left to face the Boer positions. Captain Prothero then led the Brigade towards the Boers in a series of controlled rushes through the hottest zone of fire between 500 and 200 yards into the area of dead ground at the foot of the *kopje*. Here the Brigade paused to catch their breath and fix bayonets before beginning the climb up the face of the *kopje*. The steep climb in the face of the Boer fire was always difficult and in some places men were reduced to hauling themselves up on hands and knees. When the Naval Brigade was about 25 yards from the summit the Boer fire ceased, the summit was carried at a rush and the Boers ran from the bayonet to drop into cover a few hundred yards back and open fire again. Throughout the advance, and when holding the summit, the Naval Brigade had been enfiladed by the Boers on the Nek to their left. C company RMLI had suffered most severely. When the company of the KOYLI that followed the Brigade took ground on the *kopje* to dominate the Nek, the Boers were driven off and a general retreat began.

The Boers could be seen to mount their ponies, ride from the battlefield to their laager and drive off their wagons. The artillery was unable to interfere effectively with the retreat and the cavalry, as before at Belmont, failed to intercept the retreating column or even to cut up its rear.

Fleet surgeon Porter with a party of stokers acting as stretcher bearers had followed closely behind the advancing men so that the wounded were given first aid quickly and then moved back to the railway to be sent down to Simonstown by ambulance train. The casualties amongst the Royal Marines, whose line of advance had been closest to the enfilading fire, were particularly heavy. Two officers and nine Marines were killed and one officer and 72 Marines were wounded out of the five officers and 190 Marines in the Naval Brigade. Captain Prothero, who had led the advance and remained standing when the line had dropped to the prone position between rushes, had been seriously wounded. Two naval officers were killed as were two ratings and one officer, and five ratings were wounded out of the 50 in the attack. Six men serving the guns were also wounded by shrapnel.

Methuen rested his force for a day before resuming his advance. On 27th November the Naval Brigade moved forward by train as far as Kleinfontein where they bivouacked beside the railway. At 0430 on 28th they entrained again and moved on for about a mile and a half before detraining and joining the rest of the artillery on a low ridge to the west of the railway. This was about 5000 yards from the banks of the Modder River, beside which the Boers had dug concealed defensive positions covering the remains of the railway bridge that had been blown.

When about three miles from the river, Methuen deployed his infantry into three lines in open order and marched on over the veldt under cover of fire from the Naval Brigade's 12 pdrs. They engaged and silenced the Boer gun that at 0540 had opened the engagement by firing on Methuen's wagon train. That was the beginning of a one-day long artillery duel. The Boers had dug a number of concealed gun pits and, as a gun position was identified and brought under fire, shifted the gun to an alternative position. Although the Boer guns were temporarily silenced, they soon came into action again. Identifying the positions of the guns also proved difficult for they were using smokeless powder and the muzzle flash was difficult to spot. At one time the Naval Brigade moved its guns closer to the Boer lines hoping to find a position from which the identification of targets would be easier. In the new position, which offered no advantage, they came under heavy rifle and pom-pom fire. They retired to their previous positions gun by gun, keeping up a brisk fire from three guns while one moved.

The infantry, in line and open order, advanced steadily over the coverless veldt towards the Modder River, flanked by the Riet River on the right and stretching past the blown railway bridge to Rosmead Drift on the left. Along the Modder and Reit the Boers were entrenched with their left flank thrown forward so as to enfilade the British advance. The Boers remained concealed in their positions and then opened a rapid fire under which, caught in the open, the advancing infantry halted and went to ground. The British right and centre were to remain pinned down where they were to remain under a volume of fire that the artillery could not subdue for the rest of the day.

On the left flank, however, men of the 9th Brigade, led by General Pole-Carew, had after three hours fighting covered by the 62nd Battery RFA (which had marched for 28 hours non-stop to reach Methuen and foundered its horses to do so) forced the crossing at Rosmead Drift. They began to roll up the Boer defences, were counter-attacked and pushed back but held their position in a group of farm buildings on the north bank of the Modder. Methuen had been wounded and removed to the field hospital, and because of the break in the chain of command no action was taken to reinforce Pole-Carew and renew the attack next day. At dawn the Naval Brigade guns opened fire, there was no reply and the Boer positions were found deserted.

Having cleared the Boers from their positions on the Modder, Methuen began his preparations for his next move towards Kimberley. Whilst resting his forces he sent out reconnaissance patrols and brought up supplies and reinforcements, including the Highland Brigade commanded by Major General 'Andy' Wauchope. During the rest period reinforcements came up for the Naval Brigade drawn from HMS *Doris* and HMS *Monarch*. Captain Bearcroft of HMS *Philomel* arrived from Durban to command the Brigade.

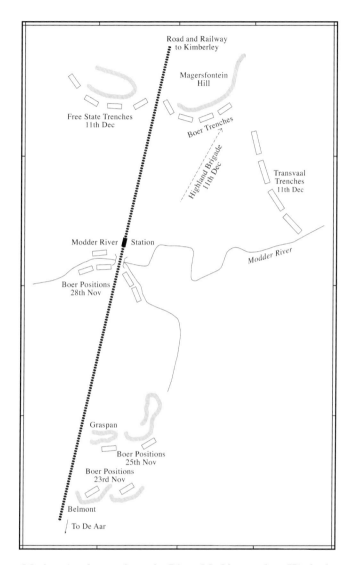

Methuen's advance from the River Modder north to Kimberly

Methuen requested the naval commander-in-chief at the Cape for heavier guns and with a longer range than the 12 pdrs. A 4.7-inch gun on a field mounting which was ready in the dockyard was sent up. On arrival it was sent to a position on the north bank and from there carried out daily bombardments of the Boer positions. On 9th December the 4.7-inch advanced as a part of a reconnaissance in force and, in the hope of provoking the Boers into revealing their positions, opened random fire. The Boers did not answer and the twelve mile long defence line dug at the foot of, and not as Boer custom dictated on the crest of, the Magersfontein ridge remained unsuspected.

That evening Methuen issued his orders for the attack on Magersfontein. His plan was for a night march followed by a dawn attack, and he selected the Highland Brigade that contained veterans of the night march to Tel el Kebir. As a preliminary move, on the afternoon of 10th December, the 4.7-inch gun accompanied five batteries of field artillery in an advance to within three miles of Magersfontein to bombard, until dark, the crest and forward slope. This bombardment did nothing, however, but alert the Boers to an impending attack.

At 0001 on 11th December, a moonless night in an African thunderstorm and facing into a gale force wind, the Highland Brigade formed up for the night march. They were formed into quarter column in close order, 3600 men packed into a column 45 yards in the face and 160 yards long, kept a cohesive whole by long ropes held by the right or left hand men of the flanking files. Led by Major Benson RA who had surveyed the route, they made slow though steady progress and about an hour later than planned, as the sky began to lighten, were 1000 yards from the foot of the ridge and at the point at which they were to extend. Here Wauchope made his fatal mistake. He decided to continue to advance in close order. It was not until the leading files were within 500 yards of the Boer trenches that the order was given. As the leading files began to extend the Boers opened fire and the Highland Brigade was thrown into momentary confusion as in the face of the intense fire they tried to extend and seek cover. Fortunately, because of the bad shooting light, the Boers were firing high.

For nine hours there was stalemate. The Highland Brigade lay out in the open, unable to move without attracting volumes of rifle fire. The Royal Artillery advanced their guns to within 1400 yards of the Boers to give support and from further back the naval 4.7-inch gun joined in. Then at about 1300 a party of Boers were detected working round the right flank of the Highland Brigade. The commanding officer of the Seaforths ordered two companies to move back to face this threat. This defensive move, seen and interpreted as a retirement by other tired, thirsty and painfully sunburnt men (particularly on the back of the knees, uncovered by the kilt), developed into a general retreat infused with panic under the unremitting, rapid fire from the Boers. The rest of the afternoon was spent in efforts to reform the Highland Brigade.

Methuen held his position until dawn next day in the hope that, as at the Modder, the Boers would retreat during the dark hours. A balloon reconnaissance at dawn showed the Boers still in position. Methuen, with grave problems in watering his force, did not feel strong enough to renew the attack and decided to return to the banks of the Modder. After a truce to allow for the burial of the dead and collection of the wounded, the army marched back to camp where Methuen received orders to remain on the defensive.

The army settled into camp where it would remain for two months, waiting, though it did not know it, for Field Marshall Lord Roberts who had been made commander-in-chief after the events of Black Week (the defeats at Stormberg, Magersfontein and Colenso). Initially the Naval Brigade was stationed north of the river and on 15th December began a routine of harassing the Boers, firing on their trenches and exchanging shots with their guns. But gradually the Naval Brigade was split up, a 4.7 inch gun which had just come up from the Cape was sited to cover the right rear of the army and two 12 pdrs were sited on the extreme right flank on the north bank, all in gun pits and protected by small detachments of Royal Marines.

Life in the camp was not comfortable. Drinking water was in short supply as it had to be boiled before use so thirst was always a problem. The ground was quickly reduced to a fine powder that was stirred up by any movement of man or beast, and sand storms and sand devils were frequent.

On 3rd February 1900, Commander Grant of HMS *Doris* with two more 4.7 inch guns manned from HMS *Doris* and HMS *Barrosa* arrived by rail and were sent back to Enslin, the station nearest to Belmont, where the wagons, water carts, 284 oxen with 42 native drivers and four colonial conductors were allocated to them and they began to work up for the coming campaign.

Lord Roberts' Campaign

Field Marshal Lord Roberts with his chief of staff, Lord Kitchener, landed in Cape Town on 10th February 1900. As further reinforcements arrived they were despatched up the railway towards the camp on the Modder. By 10th February Roberts was ready to advance. His army was strong enough to allow him to leave a force sufficient to guard his supply line up the railway, to move over the veldt to outflank the position at Magersfontein, attack the Boer supply depot at Jacobsdal and allow General French with the Cavalry Division to ride round Magersfontein and relieve Kimberley. When these preliminary moves were complete Roberts planned to advance over the veldt to the capital of the Orange Free State, Bloemfontein, the capture of which could be expected to force the Orange Free State out of the war.

On 11th February Roberts began his advance, leaving General Methuen with a Brigade to mask Magersfontein supported by two 4.7 inch guns and two 12 pdrs of the Naval Brigade. By 15th February French had relieved Kimberley and Roberts had secured Jacobsdal. That night General Cronje abandoned his positions at Magersfontein and around Kimberley and marched eastward in an effort to get ahead of the British and interpose his army between Roberts and Bloemfontein. On 16th February there was a skirmish between the British infantry and the Boers who managed to break contact and slip away at nightfall, leaving 78 loaded supply wagons in British hands. Next morning the cavalry made contact with the Boer column and drove it into a loop into the Modder River at Paardeberg where Cronje laagered his whole force together with his baggage train and the wagons of the wives

Lord Kitchener, Chief of Staff to Field Marshall Lord Roberts
(courtesy of Stromness Museum)

and families which had joined their husbands in the camp before Kimberley and at Magersfontein. Here Cronje was bottled up by the British 6th Division. By the evening of 17th February the Boers had entrenched their position.

On 17th February Lord Roberts was at Jacobsdal, recovering from a chill. Lord Kitchener was up with the troops at Paardeberg and assumed command of the operations there. On 18th February he launched an infantry attack on Cronje's perimeter supported by two naval 12 pdrs and the artillery attached to the 6th Division. Kitchener was without any staff, issued no written orders and without any overall view of the battle tried to control it himself, galloping about the field and issuing what he regarded as expedient orders to the officer nearest to him at the time regardless of rank, regiment or corps. At the end of the day British losses (including those of the 1st Royal Canadians) were the heaviest of any day of the war, totalling 1270 all ranks.

While Kitchener was launching the fruitless attacks on the Boer positions, the Naval Brigade was marching up from Magersfontein to join up with Grant's guns at Jacobsdal, which they reached on 18th February. Then, as they were settling down in the expectation of an 'all night in' they received orders and at 2130 moved off on an all night march halting at 1600. The oxen were turned out to graze and hands were at breakfast when Lord Roberts and his staff cantered up on their way to Paardeberg. Lord Roberts asked the Brigade, as soon as possible, to move on for another ten miles and thicken up the artillery with the troops surrounding Cronje. But the oxen had to be allowed to complete feeding and it was 1400 before the Naval Brigade could move again. At 2000 they bivouacked after covering 27 miles in 22 hours having been on the road for 15 of them. Reveille was at sunrise and after breakfast the Naval Brigade moved off at 0930. After having covered another five miles, they came into sight of the main camp and, beyond it, the tents and wagons of Cronje's laager.

The headquarters of the Naval Brigade with one 4.7 inch gun and three 12 pdrs was posted in a very exposed position, 1300 yards from the Boer trenches. Every time they fired, Boer rifles replied. This exchange went on for seven days. One sailor was killed and one wounded. Commander Grant with three 4.7 inch guns and one 12 pdr was ordered across the Modder to a position within 3000 yards of three Boer guns and a pom-pom. They opened fire at 1630 and their first shell burst among the Boer wagons. Strangely, and to the disappointment of the sailors, the Boer guns did not engage the Naval Brigade at any time in the next seven days. Grant's party established bivouac camp to the rear of the gun line, stretching tarpaulins between the wagons. They hung a fired 4.7-inch shell-case on a tripod and amazed the army by marking the passing of the hours in nautical fashion by bells!

On 19th February Roberts reached Paardeberg. Kitchener pressed for a resumption of the infantry attack but Cronje requested an armistice in which to collect and treat his wounded, demanding that British medical officers should enter his lines and undertake the treatment and then remain with the Boer laager, he having no doctors with him. Roberts would not accede to this demand (there were, after all, 800 of his own men wounded and requiring treatment).

On Wednesday 21st February, Roberts disposed his army in two concentric rings around Cronje and sited his artillery in preparation for the bombardment that he was to order the following day. Roberts also learnt that there were women and children in the laager and offered them safe conduct out of danger, an offer that Cronje refused. On 22nd February the bombardment began, directed at the Boer transport, food dumps and ammunition reserves. The British rate of fire was slow as ammunition was limited. The fall of shot was being observed from a balloon flying at 1000 feet and from which corrections were signalled down by flag to be passed to the guns. The Boers were, however, comparatively safe in their trenches or under the river bank and suffered mainly from the noise, the smell of the rotting carcasses of their dead oxen and horses (which penetrated to the British lines) and from the squalor created by their own lack of hygiene. The river was contaminated and became a source of infection. On Tuesday 27th February (the anniversary of Majuba), Cronje surrendered to Roberts.

The British had been operating throughout their siege of Cronje. Their only source of water was the Modder River, thick with mud and heavily contaminated from swollen and decaying animal carcasses. Boiled with a pinch of alum, which precipitated the mud, it cleared and became safe to drink but neither tea nor coffee in the quantities being issued could disguise the taste. Biscuit, sugar and jam were also issued in diminishing quantities and the ration meat was trek ox, so tough and unpalatable that it had to be made into soup. On 26th February the first wagon convoy arrived in camp and two and a half days rations (to last five days) were issued.

It was in this period that the seeds of the vendetta to be waged against the Naval Brigade by the Provost Marshal were sewn. There was a large flock of sheep grazing on the veldt about two miles from Grant's guns and this contingent of the Naval Brigade supped on fresh mutton each night (and there was always a leg of mutton for the wardroom!). To quote an officer with Grant:

> "The guileless bluejackets (the Stokers — good luck to them! — were the most successful criminals) seldom returned without one. Their invariable explanation was that 'it had followed them into camp' but this was a very elastic term and included, perfectly correctly, those occasions on which the unwilling animal was towed by a piece of rope; less accurately when it was pushed from behind by one and towed by the ears by another; and still less accurately, perhaps, when, as often happened, it was too dead beat from 'following' them so far, and was brought in on their shoulders."

When Grant was ordered to rejoin the rest of the Naval Brigade his line of march was through the remains of the Boer laager. There were quick eyes and light fingers amongst the guns' crews. "Oh! I picked that up in the laager" became the catch phrase within the Naval Brigade to explain 'acquisitions' of a certain type.

Two days after the surrender the whole army moved camp upriver, five miles eastward to a healthier situation, and to a position from which the Boers, who were concentrating to oppose the British advance on Bloemfontein at Poplar Grove, could be properly reconnoitred. Poplar Grove was the last defensible position before Bloemfontein and Boer Commandos were concentrating there, bringing their artillery with them. And, to encourage them, President Kruger of the Transvaal arrived in the Boer camp on the morning of 7th March to be greeted by the sound of Roberts' guns.

Roberts began his advance on 5th March. The Highland Brigade, to which were attached the three remaining 12 pdrs (the fourth, with a bulged barrel had been returned to Simonstown) formed part of the force advancing on the northern bank of the Modder. The four 4.7 inch guns were ordered to take up a position on a *kopje* 7000 yards from the Boer centre and to remain concealed until daybreak on 7th March. This section of the Naval Brigade spent 6th March constructing a roadway up the *kopje*. "How about the blooming sappers now?" was the question of one able seaman. The guns were hauled up to just below the crest where Grant's two guns were placed and to the right shoulder where the other two were sited. Then hands were piped to supper.

At 0400 on 7th the guns' crews fell in and, as the sun rose, ran their guns into position. Then they sat, uncomfortably exposed, for two hours until at 0600 Lord Roberts and his staff rode up to a position close to Grant's guns. At his signal the starting gun was fired from the right shoulder of the *kopje*, the signal for the cavalry under General French to begin a sweep round the left flank of the Boer positions. When the Boers saw the cavalry moving round their flank they began to abandon their trenches, mount up and ride off. Kruger was hustled into a light Cape Cart, in which, at a gallop, he led a general retreat. The 4.7-inch guns had little to do but towards the end of the action Lord Roberts personally directed the guns onto a target marked by some prominent anthills on the veldt below. As the second shell burst on target about 200 Boers broke cover and raced to the rear. There was just time for about two shots before the Boers vanished over a convenient ridge.

The three 12 pdrs with the Highland Brigade were in the open and were busy shelling the retreating Boer transport when a Krupp gun on the shoulder of a *kopje* to their left opened up on them. They shifted target to engage that gun and another, from the extreme right of the Boer position, joined in. In action to both right and left the 12 pdrs were very busy and having a warm time. Their transport was damaged but they incurred no casualties. Eventually the Boers were forced to abandon their guns that were subsequently taken though they had saved much of their transport.

After two days rest at Poplar Grove the army began its march on Bloemfontein, 70 miles ahead. On reduced rations and with uniform and particularly boots in deplorable condition (some men had bare feet protected by puttees wound round them) they covered the 70 miles in four days. On 13th March three war correspondents, riding ahead of the army, entered the town and found it unoccupied. That afternoon Lord Roberts accepted the formal surrender.

Lord Roberts had considerable administrative and logistic problems that required time to resolve. While the bridges on the railways from Cape Town, East London and Port Elizabeth were repaired, the whole army re-equipped and stocks of food and ammunition built up, the army remained encamped round Bloemfontein and for a while enjoyed a complacently relaxed routine. They were jolted from this when, on 31st March, De Wet raided the water works at Sannah's Post, 20 miles from Roberts' Headquarters, and from which Bloemfontein drew its drinking water. As a result the Naval Brigade was moved to a *kopje* two miles north of the town.

Early in the stay at Bloemfontein Lord Roberts reviewed the Naval Brigade and thanked them for their past services. He then called for the surgeons and their stretcher-bearers, mostly the stokers, and gave them separate and special praise. However good their bearing the Naval Brigade could not be commended on their turnout, for their khaki drill uniforms showed the wear and tear of four months campaigning and their sennet hats were disintegrating. These deficiencies were made good when the Naval Brigade were re-equipped with khaki serge uniform and bush hats, on the raised left brim of which the sailors embroidered a foul anchor and the marines a bugle. Those badges became almost the only marks by which to distinguish a member of the Naval Brigade.

On 22nd March, the day after Lord Roberts' inspection, the seamen of HMS *Powerful* left to rejoin their ship for its return home. Their Royal Marine attachment remained with the Naval Brigade. They had been replaced, partially, by a reinforcement that had caught up at the Poplar Grove. One of the officers to join was Midshipman A B Cunningham, the future Admiral of the Fleet Viscount Cunningham of Hyndhope.

While at Bloemfontein the army suffered an epidemic of enteric fever and the Naval Brigade was as badly affected as any other formation. Eighty-nine officers and men were taken to hospital and those that recovered were returned to Simonstown. As a result it was no longer possible to man all the 4.7-inch guns and the 12 pdrs with seamen. To the delight of the RMA, one of the 4.7-inch guns was handed over to them, leaving infantry duty to the RMLI. On 22ⁿᵈ April 'Grant's Guns' were ordered to join the Highland Brigade which was sent to prevent General De Wet and his men from joining with the Boer forces in the Transvaal and, if possible, to combine with another force pushing De Wet north, encircle him and force his surrender. At daybreak on 23ʳᵈ April 'Grant's Guns' numbering three officers, 50 seamen and stokers, three conductors, 42 native drivers with 13 wagons, three carts, four horses and 290 trek ox marched off with two 4.7-inch guns that had been manhandled down Naval Hill overnight.

'Grant's Guns' never rejoined the Naval Brigade. They enjoyed four months campaigning against a very mobile force of Boers. In nine days, from 22ⁿᵈ May to 30ᵗʰ May they marched 129 miles, fighting on five of them and ending the march on one-third rations. June and July were spent in and around Heilbron sparring with De Wet. At the beginning of August they began another series of marches, covering 250 miles in fifteen days, during which the gun wheels began to collapse. One gun was sent to Pretoria for repair, the other was dismounted and carried on wagons, Grant having promised the Brigade Commander that, if required, he could remount the gun and fire it within an hour. After a pause of a week, during which the first gun, repaired, replaced the second, sent for repair, another trek began lasting 20 marching days with minor skirmishes on ten of them during which 187 rounds were fired. 'Grant's Guns' arrived back at their base on 30ᵗʰ September, received orders to hand over its' equipment to the Royal Garrison Artillery and at 1500 on 2nd October entrained for Simonstown. General Hart in a farewell letter to commander Grant wrote:

> "Well assisted by your subordinates you have overcome serious campaigning difficulties with a ponderous gun which has deservedly become the terror of the enemy."

At 1300 on 2ⁿᵈ May the Naval Brigade received orders to march, leaving two 12 pdrs to garrison Bloemfontein. By 1700 the Naval Brigade had packed, loaded its wagons and inspanned its oxen ready to move off. Then, unsure of the way, without a guide and in deepening darkness they set off. After overcoming the initial setbacks caused by one gun having to be dragged out of a deep *donga* "which was not the short cut its' crew thought" and partly by the Brigade missing a turning, they settled to a steady march until 0100 when they were halted until daylight before crossing the Modder.

The Naval Brigade now settled into its own march routine, dictated by the need for their oxen to have sufficient time to graze during daylight and to keep closed up with the main column of troops which moved about a mile an hour faster than the ox drawn guns. The Naval Brigade moved off about two hours before the main body, halted for four hours at noon to allow the oxen to graze and then marched on until the camp of the main body was reached, usually about two hours behind. The Army Standing Orders laid down that ammunition wagons were never to be separated from the guns, and baggage wagons were to be a part of the baggage train. The Naval Brigade were determined, after their baggage wagons had been looted when entrusted to the baggage train, that they would not be separated from their baggage which, in any case they required at hand to expedite the rigging of camp and the cooking of supper after their late arrival in camp. So, whilst there was ammunition in every wagon there was also camp equipment, bedding, clothes and provisions. In this, as in their constant foraging for food and disregard for authority when it came to their comfort, the Naval Brigade annoyed the Provost Marshal.

On one occasion this 'vendetta' escalated until it involved Lord Roberts himself. A heated argument, which brought the column to a halt, developed between the Transport Officer of the Naval Brigade and the Provost Marshal about ammunitions and baggage wagons. The General commanding the division that was halted rode forward to find the reason for the delay, intervened in the argument, and maintained himself that the Naval Brigade's wagons always went with the guns. Not satisfied, the Provost Marshal reported the facts to Lord Kitchener who, in turn, reported to Lord Roberts who rode back. With the Divisional General explaining that all fifteen wagons contained ammunition Lord Roberts watched them pass. On one wagon the tarpaulin cover had slipped, exposing a case marked 'Van Houten's Cocoa'. Lord Roberts remarked, "Yes, they mark it very funnily!" and rode off. So did the Provost Marshall, though later he had his revenge when the officers of the Naval Brigade were caught shooting a flock of tame guinea fowl 'for the pot'.

In the advance to Johannesburg the Naval Brigade was in for hard marching, with periods of rest when Lord Roberts halted to clear the railway and bring up supplies. They only came into action once, on the third day of the march. When at Bandfort, Lord Roberts, in a brief action, forced General De La Rey to abandon his defensive position on the railway. Now the Boers dug defensive positions at each river crossing and abandoned each position in turn under threat of an outflanking movement by the British cavalry. When Lord Roberts was on the move the day's march was long: 20 miles in a day was not unusual. On 27th May the army crossed from the Orange Free State into the Transvaal and after a 22-mile march, camped beside the Klip River.

The 29th May was probably the worst day in the whole campaign for the Naval Brigade. They were ordered to cross the Klip by an old and rotten wooden bridge that the Royal Engineers had passed as strong enough to carry guns. The 12 pdrs with their mule teams crossed safely as did the leading (bluejackets) gun, although the bridge groaned audibly under the weight. The RMA gun was halfway across when its left wheel broke through the planking and the gun heeled over at 45° and stuck. The 7th and 11th Divisions were trapped behind and firing could be heard ahead. It took four hours to move the gun, first by cutting away the rest of the bridge and dropping the gun into the river bed where it needed a double team (64) of oxen and several hundred men to haul it up onto the river bank. Meanwhile the bluejackets' gun had marched to the sound of the firing but never caught up with the fleeing Boers. As dusk fell its crew were bringing it back to camp, following the tracks of a field artillery battery. The surface of a soft patch of ground could carry a piece of field artillery but could not take the seven-ton weight of a 4.7-inch gun and it got bogged down. Unable to extricate it, its crew spent a cold and hungry night. The 12 pdrs had pushed ahead, too far ahead, and found themselves behind the Boer lines in the outskirts of Johannesburg and had to make their way back through the Boer positions.

It was not until 1100 next day that the Naval Brigade succeeded in extricating the gun from the bog in which it had sunk, requiring the efforts of every officer, man, ox and mule! They returned to camp to await orders, which they received that evening. They were told that the town had surrendered and the following day, 31st May, they were to take place in a parade beginning at 1000 marching past Lord Roberts in Johannesburg before going into camp on the far side of the town. The march was an infuriating experience: it took four and a half hours with frequent unexplained halts to reach Johannesburg. It was not until 1500 that the Naval Brigade passed the saluting base and headed, hopefully, to camp. Their orders were to follow the Field Artillery but they never caught up with them and marched until dusk when they halted to spend another cold and hungry night. One officer, seeking the campsite, rode into the night, fell from his horse twice and finally found the camp three miles back. The Naval Brigade made their way there next morning.

At 0700 on Whit Sunday, 3rd June, the advance on Pretoria began with a 12-mile march after which the army went into camp fully expecting that the next day the Boers would make a desperate last ditch stand to save the capital of the Transvaal. The Naval Brigade left that camp at 0600 on 4th June, moved steadily forward until they came up with the army and halted at the foot of the Quaggapoort hills on which De La Rey had established a defensive line. The Naval Brigade was ordered to take post on the skyline and struggled up a steep hill to come under pom-pom fire as they deployed the guns on the summit. The only casualty, much to everyone's surprise, was the mounted Commander who was placing the guns and was hit in the foot by the fuse of a shell.

The guns came into action against several Boer guns on a long, low ridge to their left and against two of the famous Pretoria Forts on the right front. For the first hour of the action they were annoyed by rifle fire from behind a stone wall about 700 yards away that fortunately did no damage except to kill two mules of the 12 pdr gun teams. When the 12 pdrs fire could be diverted they dispersed the riflemen with a few rounds of shrapnel and then moved forward to the wall to again engage and silence the guns on the left. The infantry moved steadily forward until sunset when they bivouacked where they stood.

Under cover of this action General Botha had evacuated his men from the town, and taking most of his stores and ammunition, had retreated up the railway towards the Portuguese East African border. At 2200 Pretoria surrendered to Lord Roberts and he made a formal entry next morning. Once again there was a march past and the Naval Brigade, straight from their overnight bivouac passed through the streets which were lined by the Grenadier Guards, to the sound of 'A life on the Ocean Wave' played by the pipes and drums of that regiment.

Lord Roberts paused for a week in Pretoria confidently expecting that the Boers would sue for peace. When they did not he moved to attack General Botha in the positions he had taken up on Diamond Hill on his left flank. After a night march Roberts' attack began at dawn but the Naval Brigade, badly positioned and out of range of the Boers, had nothing to do on the first day. After moving forward some 7000 yards on the second day, they amused themselves playing 'long bowls' with a 6-inch gun mounted on a railway truck whenever it appeared in range on the track. This game ended when a lucky shot at extreme range destroyed the track in front of the gun. That evening the Boers evacuated their positions and retreated into the veldt.

The Naval Brigade was ordered into camp near Pretoria and after their fall from grace over the guinea fowl, they moved further from the town to a less comfortable situation with orders to guard the railway. They built themselves a hutted camp, utilising 'acquired' timber and corrugated iron sheet. Their main pastime was cricket, the necessary equipment having been bought in Pretoria.

On 22nd July Lord Roberts began the advance eastward along the railway towards the Portuguese border. By 25th August he had met General Buller from Natal near Belfast, and gave orders for the combined armies to attack General Botha who was occupying a defensive position straddling the railway protecting President Kruger's temporary capital. The flanks of the Boer position were anchored on impassable land, cut up deep ravines on the north and on a stretch of boggy land to the south. An outflanking movement was not practicable and the army was committed to assault the position. The Naval Brigade was stationed on Monument Hill (the monument marking the highest point of the Transvaal and offering a convenient aiming point and range marker for the Boers). There were, as far as the Naval Brigade was concerned, two days of confused action during which they engaged targets of opportunity when not engaging Boer Long Toms. When, on the second day the infantry penetrated the Boer position, the commandoes rode off: the larger section under Botha to the north, others broke to the south. Only a screen was left protecting the Presidents of the Orange Free State and the Transvaal as they moved up the railway to Portuguese East Africa.

After Belfast the Naval Brigade was, again, split up. The bluejacket 4.7-inch gun was attached to the Cavalry Division and took part in the march to Barberton. That proved to be the most difficult of the whole campaign, particularly a pass at Devil's Knuckles that was so steep that triple ox teams were needed to get the gun and wagons to the top of the pass. The way down the other side was a goat track and despite the greatest care Cape Carts and wagons capsized. One wheel of the gun collapsed and was replaced by a wagon wheel that, fortunately, lasted until Barberton where the armourer managed to repair and refit the gun wheel. The other 4.7-inch gun remained on Monument Hill.

The two 12 pdrs were attached to the 11th Division (Guards Brigade and 18th Brigade), commanded by General Pole-Carew. They were to reach the border at Komati Poort in pursuit of President Kruger who sought asylum in Portuguese East Africa and sailed into exile in Holland. The border was reached on 24th September. It was littered with the partially destroyed stores, ammunition and weapons of the Boer Army that had crossed into Portuguese territory the previous day. On 30th September, handing over their transport to the Army Service Corps, the guns and gun crews entrained for Pretoria where, after a five-day journey they rejoined the Naval Brigade. The train journey had all the elements of farce: the train driver was an alcoholic, the stokers had to improvise brushes and clean the boiler, it was necessary to push the train up any steep gradient, and the drunken driver opened the throttle when he should have braked. The train was in a collision and it took the naval party two and a half hours to clear the line, "the never failing drag ropes proving most useful".

The Naval Brigade was reunited in Pretoria. They were inspected and thanked by Lord Roberts and by General Pole-Carew (with whom they had been connected since Belmont and Graspan). They handed the guns over to the Royal Artillery and entrained for Simonstown, pausing at Bloemfontein to collect the large consignment of stores for which they had been waiting. The Naval Brigade arrived in Simonstown at 1400 on 12th October to an enthusiastic reception. The Royal Navy's share of the war on land was over; they played no part in the guerrilla war that was to last for eighteen months.

Bibliography

Bacon, R. (year unknown) *A Naval Scrap Book, 1877–1900*. Hutchinson

Barthrop, M. (1987) *The Anglo–Boer Wars*. Blandford Press

Baring-Pemberton, W. (1964) *Battles of the Boer War*. Batsford

Burne, E. A. (1902) *With the Naval Brigade in Natal*. Edward Arnold

Doyle, A. C. (1900) *The Great Boer War*. Smith, Elder & Co.

Cunningham, A. B. (1951) *A Sailor's Odyssey. The autobiography of Admiral of the Fleet Viscount Cunningham of Hyndhope*. Hutchinson

Hamilton, I. (1966) *The Happy Warrior*. Cassell

Jeans, T. T. (1901) *Naval Brigades in the South African War 1899–1900*. Samsoulow and Marston

Kruger, R. (1959) *Goodbye Dolly Grey*. Cassell

Marling, P. VC (1931) *Rifleman and Hussar*. John Murray

Padfield, P. (1966) *Aim Straight*. Hodder and Stoughton

Pakenham, T. (1979) *The Boer War*. Weidenfeld and Nicolson

Smith, P. C. and Oakley, D. (1988) *The Royal Marines*. Spellmount

Symounds, J. (1963) *Buller's Campaign*. Cresset

Wilson, H. H. (1900) *With the Flag to Pretoria*. Harmsworth

CHAPTER 10

THE BOXER REBELLION

1900

By the end of the 19th century, China's self-imposed isolation from the outside world had been broken in so far as foreign diplomatic representatives were established in Peking. Certain ports and cities were designated as foreign trading concessions with extra-territorial rights for the foreigners living in them. The grant of each successive concession came only after a humiliating surrender to force by the Chinese imperial government and deepened the inbred, paranoiac hatred of the 'foreign devils'. There was also a significant missionary effort within China that, though gaining converts to Christianity, was deeply offensive to and resented by most Chinese.

At that time China was ruled by the Dowager Empress Tz'u Esi who had entered the Imperial Hareem in 1852 at the age of 17, had progressed from junior through the positions of favourite, wife and mother of the heir, regent and, de facto, absolute despot. She was brought up with an absolute contempt for foreigners. This stemmed from various events during her lifetime: the burning of the summer palace in 1860 when she, as a part of the court, was forced to flee to Peking and the political concessions that she had had to make, culminating in the recent defeat at the hands of the Japanese. Her dealings with foreign diplomats were marked by dilatoriness and chicanery. The Dowager Empress' attitude and behaviour were reflected in the attitude of her officials.

In 1896 a Chinese secret society, I Ho Ch'uan (the Society of Righteous and Harmonious Fists) became active in the northern provinces of Shantung and Chihli, murdering Christian converts, looting and destroying Christian property and aiming at the total ejection of all foreigners from China. Before joining action each member was taught to perform a series of ritualistic movements or stylised posturing in pugilistic attitudes that, if properly performed would make the practitioner immune to bullet or blade. Whether from a canting reference to harmonious fists or because of their aerobic activities this society became known as the Boxers. The Boxers enjoyed the patronage of the father of the heir-apparent, Prince Tuan, and possibly of the Dowager Empress, as well as sponsorship from high Manchu officials in the provinces. However, they lacked any controlling body to exercise leadership of command. Recruited from the poorest classes of Chinese society, coolies, landless peasants, discharged soldiers and the riff-raff of the towns and cities, their uniform consisted of a red cincture, sash, neck scarf and a turban or headband. They were armed with sword, pike, and a peculiar three-bladed spear or bludgeon.

The initial activities of the Boxers were aimed at the congregations of small, isolated, up-country missions in Shantung and were only intimidating. Then, incidents began to occur with increasing frequency and violence. The murder of Chinese converts and the looting and arson of their homes became commonplace. As missionaries reported incidents to their legations, the protests were lodged with the Chinese foreign office, where they were acknowledged and ignored. The inaction of the authorities emboldened the Boxers and in the autumn of 1899 a party of about 300 Boxers massacred an entire congregation. In December 1899, the first missionary was murdered in Chihli, the province in which Peking lay, and by May 1900 the Boxers were operating with impunity within about 60 miles of the capital. At the end of the month the Boxers began to move along the railway line from Pao Ting Pu towards Peking, destroying the permanent way, rolling stock and station buildings, and murdering railway staff. The foreign diplomats in Peking, while not realising the full danger of the situation, were becoming alarmed for their own safety and obtained authority from their home governments for armed guards for the legations. On 26th May permission was sought from the Chinese foreign ministry for armed guards to be brought to Peking. After the usual prevarication and delay permission was obtained on 30th May. The British minister, Sir Claude MacDonald, cabled to the commander-in-chief of the British China Fleet requesting a guard for the British Legation.

Admiral Sir Edward Seymour was with a part of his fleet at Wei-hai-wei when he received this request. He ordered the cruiser HMS *Orlando* and the sloop HMS *Algerine* to embark a party of three officers and 76 Royal Marine Light Infantry for passage to Taku at the mouth of the Pie-Ho where they would proceed by train to Peking. Anchored off the Taku Bar was an international fleet and on 31st May, having added a leading signalman, an armourer's mate and a sick berth steward, the detachment joined the other national contingents for the journey to Peking, which was completed without incident. HMS *Algerine* landed her field gun and gun's crew of ten men at Tongku.

Victoria's contribution to the British forces in China: the Governor of Victoria addressing the British contingent (Illustrated London News, September 22, 1900)

The Taku Bar lay some twelve miles off the mouth of the Pie Ho River with a depth of water of two feet at low and 17 feet at high tide. The mouth of the Pie Ho was guarded by the Taku forts, two on each bank. Upstream was the town of Tongku, from which the railway ran. Tientsin was the major town in the area with two international concessions (one French and one British) outside the walled Chinese city adjacent to the railway station.

Admiral Seymour, in HMS *Centurion*, arrived off the Taku Bar on 1st June where he found assembled Russian, German and American ships under their respective Flag Officers and Austrian, Italian and Japanese private ships. As the senior Admiral, Seymour invited the senior officers of the six nations on board his flagship for consultations. He obtained complete agreement that, should the situation warrant, an International Brigade would be landed under his personal command. While preparations to land the International Naval Brigade were being made, Seymour, having made a personal reconnaissance as far as Tongku on 3rd June, relieved *Algerine's* party by a field gun and crew and a landing party of 100 men from HMS *Centurion*. Captain J R Jellicoe, RN, his Flag Captain, was sent to Tientsin to establish contact with the British Consul General and to discover the best method of getting the International Naval Brigade to Peking if it should be required.

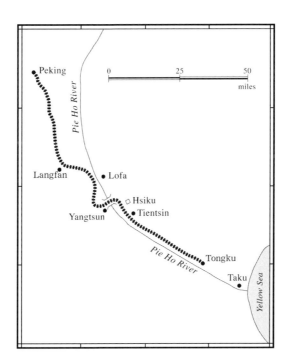

The location of the Taku forts at the mouth of the Pie Ho River

Jellicoe arrived back in Tongku on 9th June to be told that, whilst he was on his way back, the situation in Peking had deteriorated quickly. Riots had broken out, the grandstand at the racecourse and Chinese Christians' property were in flames and a Chinese Christian had been burned alive. Awaiting him too was Sir Claude MacDonald's message appealing for further aid. Jellicoe passed this information, by searchlight, to HMS *Centurion*. He then arranged for all available tugs and lighters to be sent out to the fleet when the tide allowed. He alerted the railway company and ordered trains for 1000 men to be ready at dawn and at 2100 started downriver in an American launch, taking a local pilot with him. Finding HMS *Whiting* and HMS *Fame* anchored in the stream he ordered them to come to immediate notice for steam and dropped off the pilot in HMS *Whiting*. He got back to HMS *Centurion* at 2330 and reported to the Admiral. Seymour had earlier received Sir Claude's alarming telegram and, consequently, had called a meeting of Flag and Senior Officers. He told them that he was prepared to land and personally lead the maximum available force to Peking. He hoped for the greatest possible co-operation from them as representatives of their nations.

By 0100 on 10th June the British contingent had started upstream, HMS *Centurion*'s party in a tug, those from HMS *Endymion* and HMS *Aurora* in HMS *Fame* and their own boats under tow by HMS *Fame*. The British contingent caught the tide — the other nations followed on the next. The British contingent reached Tongku at 0400, were entrained by 0500 and reached Tientsin by 0730. Here, while waiting for the rest of the force, they assisted in making up the five trains that were to be their transport. Four were made up of a flat car, protected by a boiler plate and baulks of timber, mounting a machine gun and accommodating 30 riflemen, the locomotive and tender, passenger cars, a freight car for field guns and ammunition and finally a wagon carrying rails, ties, sleepers and tools for repairing the track. The fifth train was loaded with repair materials.

By mid-afternoon on 10th June, Seymour's command began to move off for Peking on what was expected to be a three to four hour trip. The force numbered 116 officers and 1956 men with seven field guns and twelve machine guns; the British Naval Brigade was 62 Naval and Marine officers, 640 seamen and 213 Royal Marines with four field guns and eight machine guns. Before dark they had covered some 25 miles to Lofa where they halted for the night.

On 11th June HMS *Barfleur*, flying the flag of Rear Admiral Bruce, arrived in the anchorage off Taku. Captain Burke of HMS *Orlando*, who had been the Senior British Naval Officer in the anchorage, immediately waited upon Rear Admiral Bruce to brief him. The orders from Admiral Seymour were that HMS *Barfleur* should land 100 seamen and her remaining Royal Marines to reinforce the garrison left to guard the international concessions at Tientsin. With eleven other officers, 100 seamen and 68 Royal Marines, the Commander of HMS *Barfleur*, Commander D Beatty DSO, RN, reported to the Senior Naval Officer in Tientsin, Captain E H Bayly, RN and joined up with the 248 seamen and Royal Marines from HMS *Orlando* already there. Together with 400 sailors from the ships of other nations and the 1600 Russian soldiers who arrived on 13th June, they defended the French and British concessions and the railway station. This was in all a five mile perimeter with defences improvised by an American mining engineer and future President of the United States, Herbert Hoover, using bags of sugar, rice and peanuts and bales of wool, silk and cotton taken from the warehouses.

Seymour left a party of 60 seamen at Lofa, the overnight stop, in a quickly built fortification (nicknamed Fort Endymion) and pressed on, making slow progress towards Peking. The lines and its bridges were much damaged but repairable. The first encounter with the Boxers came at about 1900 when a large body armed with swords and spears appeared out of a village about a quarter of a mile away, performed their ritual callisthenics and charged the leading train. The charge wilted under disciplined volley fire and, leaving a quarter of their number dead, the rest dispersed. A quick search of the village yielded a few chickens and some eggs which did not go far to bolster the somewhat meagre rations of the force. Progress on the next two days was disappointingly slow, delayed by severe damage to the line and by further attacks from the Boxers in increasing numbers. By the evening of the second day they had reached Langfan, about half way to Peking, where the station buildings had been severely damaged and the water tanks destroyed.

On 13th June, sending a party of Royal Marines to reconnoitre the state of the line ahead of him, Seymour began to construct a fortified post at Langfan, water the railway engines (a tedious business passing buckets down a long human chain from nearby wells) and relay the railway track which had been torn up for at least three miles. In the evening the reconnaissance party returned. They had encountered a large force of Boxers that had been held off and eventually forced back. The marines, now short of ammunition, had returned.

The forenoon of 14th June was quiet and the relaying of the railway track progressed. Hands were piped to dinner at noon and as they settled to the meal were surprised by a mob of about 500 Boxers charging from an adjacent wood, having silenced the Italian picket therein. The Royal Naval Brigade brought the Maxim on their train into action but some of the Boxers broke in amongst the surprised diners and a hand-to-hand scrimmage took place. The Boxers were driven back with heavy casualties. Surprisingly, apart from the overwhelmed Italian picket, Seymour's men were unharmed.

When that action was just over a hand trolley from Lofa rattled into Langfan with the news that Fort Endymion was under attack from about 2000 Boxers equipped with two field guns. Seymour took the rear-most two trains back to Lofa and arrived in time to beat off the last attack of the day. Leaving one train at Lofa, Seymour returned to Langfan that evening.

Seymour remained at Langfan for two days until 17th June, sending back a train to ferry forward supplies of food and ammunition as rations were almost exhausted and reserves of ammunition were dangerously low. On 15th and 16th June the Boxers had swept in on the railway between Tientsin and Lofa and between Tientsin and Tongku. They also destroyed the railway bridge over the Pie Ho at Yangstun and the station with its telegraph office and had cut Seymour's communications with Tientsin and Tientsin's with Tongku and the fleets outside Taku. The return of the empty train alerted Seymour to his predicament.

The Admirals of the allied fleets off Taku were also aware of this and knew that the Boxers had broken into the French concession at Tientsin and had torched a large part of it. They could see that the Chinese Imperial troops were moving into and reinforcing the garrison of the Taku forts and that torpedo tubes were being placed to cover the mouth of the river. They realised that the Taku forts were the key to the situation, for if they were not secured there would be nothing that could be done either to succour the Legations in Peking or to re-establish contact with and reinforce Seymour, the garrison at Tientsin or the garrison at Tongku. They therefore issued an ultimatum, delivered to the commander of the forts at 2000 on 16th June demanding the surrender of the forts by 0200 on 17th. They positioned upstream of the forts two British destroyers, HMS *Fame* and HMS *Whiting* with orders to take the four Chinese destroyers alongside in Taku dockyard. Accompanying them was a bombarding force of sloops and gunboats from all the nations present except the United States whose Admiral received specific orders from Washington not to take part. Landing parties totalling 900, of whom 320 men were British, were embarked in the gunboats. No reply to the ultimatum had been received by 0100 on 17th, and an hour before it expired the guns of the four forts opened fire as simultaneously as the Chinese could manage.

The sloops and gunboats thereupon began to bombard the forts and to land the assault parties. HMS *Fame* and HMS *Whiting* moved upriver to close, board and take the four new German-built Destroyers of the Chinese Navy lying alongside in Taku dockyard. The assault force was landed about 1300 yards from the first fort and moved towards it under cover of the bombardment, which seemed to be having little effect until a lucky shot exploded the magazine of one fort. At 0430 the bombardment lifted and the assault began, becoming something of a race over the flat muddy approach between the British and Japanese contingents that swept into the fort and quickly secured it. It took only fifteen minutes to re-group and the assault swept on towards the other fort on the north bank of the river. A lucky shot from HMS *Algerine* detonated its magazine and the fort was quickly captured with little opposition. The serviceable guns of the captured forts were turned on the two forts on the southern bank, and under cover of this and the fire from the bombardment an assault force crossed the river in captured small craft and seized those two forts. In six hours four forts and four destroyers had been captured and the vital base for further operations against Tientsin and ultimately Peking was secure.

The Chinese reacted strongly to this pre-emptive strike. The Chinese Imperial Army, which had maintained hostile neutrality, began actively to support the Boxers, adding artillery and small arms to the primitive weaponry that until then, had not been available to them. The threat to Seymour at Langfan, the garrison at Tientsin and to the Legation at Peking was greatly increased.

In Peking the news of the taking of the Taku forts precipitated the crisis. The situation had remained threatening. There had been rioting and arson against Chinese Christians and their property in the Chinese part of the city. Although a Japanese Diplomat had been killed by the mob when outside the Legation quarter, no attack had been made on that quarter itself. At 1600 on 19th June, every foreign minister received a document demanding that they, their staffs and Legation guards should leave Peking and proceed to Tientsin within 24 hours. The Diplomats attempted to negotiate; the German Minister, Baron Von Kettler, was set upon and murdered on his way to the Chinese Foreign Ministry. At 1600 on 20th June Sergeant Murphy, RMLI, marched up to Captain Strouts, RMLI, who was standing on the lawn of the British Legation, and reported, "Firing has commenced, Sir!" The siege of the Legations had begun.

Admiral Seymour was concentrating the men of his command back down the railway at Yangtsun. He was convinced that he could make no progress by rail; that morning, the 18th June, the German train was cut off and had to be rescued, an action that cost the lives of seven and left 57 wounded. With the railway line cut and the iron bridge destroyed, Seymour decided that he must retire downriver to Tientsin. At 1600 on 19th June, four junks were commandeered to carry the wounded and the gins and, having spent the forenoon and afternoon destroying what could not be carried, the force began to march down the riverbank. Each man was loaded with a rifle and ammunition, a blanket and two days ration of biscuit. The junks were awkward under tow by parties of sailors on the bank and, the Pie Ho being shallow and with many sandbanks, frequently took the ground. Progress was slow.

On 20th June troops of the Chinese Imperial Army made contact with the left flank and the march became a fighting retreat under intermittent artillery fire from light guns on the left, small arms fire from each flank and active opposition from each village passed, every one of which had to be cleared of the enemy before the retreat could continue.

The force moved out of its overnight bivouac at 0530 the following morning, and at about 1000 were approaching mutually supporting villages at Pietsang, one on each bank of the river. Both were strongly held, the defence supported by two field guns. Action began when the Chinese field guns opened fire on the British and French on the left bank. The French attempted to rush the village, made a lodgement and were then trapped by intense crossfire from the right bank. Captain Jellicoe brought up a 9 pdr field gun that fired a couple of rounds into the village. He then led the British contingent in a charge which pushed the Chinese back to a convenient bank outside the village where the Chinese reformed and kept up a hot fire which, in combination with the cross fire from over the river, pinned down the British and the French. About this time Captain Jellicoe was severely wounded. The Germans, across the river, broke into the village before them, the crossfire stopped and slowly both villages and the bank were cleared.

In Seymour's own words the position was

"…an anxious one; it appeared quite possible we might be surrounded and a disaster occur; the Chinese never give quarter and any of our officers or men who fell into their hands were at once killed."

He discussed the position with Captain Von Usedom, who commanded the German contingent and who, now that Jellicoe was wounded, he had invited to become his chief of staff and second in command. Still under intermittent shellfire and random rifle shot, the force bivouacked, commandeered two more junks, embarked the new wounded and re-embarked the field guns. Then at 0100 on 22nd June the force began a night march, moving down the left bank of the Pie Ho. After about two hours they came on the first village. This was immediately rushed by the Royal Marines and taken, but this success was offset by the sinking of the junk carrying the field guns that were lost.

Shortly after that, Seymour and the advance guard found themselves passing a large walled enclosure on the opposite bank. Challenged by the Chinese on the wall Seymour tried to bluff his way past, claiming to be a friendly force making for Tientsin. The bluff failed and heavy and small arms fire from the Chinese halted the march. Seymour considered it essential to take the Chinese position. He ordered the Royal Marines and a company of seamen from HMS *Centurion* to cross the Pie Ho and attack from the northeast, and the German contingent to move down the river, cross and attack from the southwest. These complimentary, dashing attacks were successful. No one was more surprised than Seymour to find that he had captured the main arsenal of the Chinese Army at Haiku, the existence of which was unknown to him. The arsenal was well stocked with field guns, machine guns, rifles and ammunition of varied types and calibre, explosives, medical stores and an abundance of rice. There was, however, no meat either fresh or preserved, and the water supply, of very dubious quality, was barely adequate.

Under sporadic gunfire the whole force moved into the arsenal and almost immediately faced a heavy counter-attack during which some 7000 Chinese launched a series of massed charges. In daylight none of these charges got within 500 yards of the walls and the Chinese suffered heavy casualties. One of these was a mounted officer who led the first charge. His mount was shot under him and in between charges was hauled into the arsenal, butchered to make a welcome supplement to a boiled rice supper. When the counter-attack had been beaten off, Seymour sent a party of two officers and 100 Royal Marines to march down the railway to Tientsin to inform the authorities there of his position. This small party met heavy opposition and had to fight its way back to the arsenal.

In the pre-dawn darkness of 23rd June, the Chinese launched another heavy attack and succeeded in penetrating the defences. There was fierce fighting on and within the walls before the attack was beaten off as the light increased. Chinese trapped within the walls were hunted down during the day. Seymour continued his efforts to communicate with Tientsin, entrusting cyphered messages to Chinese camp followers. Of the three messengers dispatched two vanished. The third, after an adventurous trip during which the Boxers captured him twice, ate the message then was recaptured in the outskirts of the French concession of Tientsin by French troops who had to be persuaded of his bona fides. The messenger gave a verbal report at the British Consulate on 24th June.

The 24th was a very anxious day in Haiku arsenal. In Seymour's words:

"It was marked by a very bad dust storm; you could only bear to look leeward and then could see but a few yards, and had we been attacked from windward, the enemy would have had a very great advantage."

To add to the anxieties caused by the storm were the worries of wondering whether a messenger had reached Tientsin with which they had been out of touch for seven days, during which they had heard the distant, but continuous growl of gunfire from the town's direction.

There had indeed been sporadic fighting at and around Tientsin since before the Taku forts were seized on 17th June, beginning on the night of the 15th when the Boxers broke into the French concession, set fire to many of the buildings there and then established themselves within the walls of the Chinese city. By 17th the position had been established. There was an ominous quiet until, at 1300, the Chinese artillery opened fire. Commander Beatty, with permission from Captain Bayly, organised a sally. In a smart little action, in which the Royal Marines distinguished themselves, fired houses and buildings to clear the British front and create a field of fire.

A detachment of 400 Russians and Frenchmen were guarding a railway bridge on the line outside Tientsin and, at the urging of the Russians, it was decided to bring them in to join the main body. A train, carrying 600, was organised to leave Tientsin at 0800 on the 18th for this purpose. At 0600 the Chinese began a three-pronged attack on the allied positions aimed particularly at the railway station from which, however, the 'rescue' train left on time. Very heavy fighting developed round the station where an allied force of roughly 650, including about 200 British, 50 French and 50 Japanese sailors were holding back about 5000 Chinese. The Chinese artillery was particularly effective and drove off a Russian battery of four guns that attempted to return fire from the open and without protection. Beatty brought forward a naval 9 pdr field gun for which he built an emplacement from bales of freight from the station warehouse. This gun proved most effective in breaking up the Chinese attacks but, despite the protection, the gun's crew were very vulnerable to rifle fire and in one period of ten minutes all but two were wounded. Fighting continued throughout the day until at 1600 a train's whistle was heard. The Chinese made a final desperate effort to take the station that was unsuccessful and the men from the station, combining with the men from the train, fixed bayonets and charged the Chinese. After a short period of wild firing the Chinese bolted for safety. The activity for the day was over except for some sporadic shellfire.

The following morning the bombardment began again at 0430. At 0600 two guns that the Chinese had brought up to within 1000 yards during the night opened up on the Town Hall and the adjacent club, the refuge for women and children and the hospital respectively. Beatty led a sortie that, in the face of heavy rifle fire, drove off the guns but at the cost of four officers and twelve ratings wounded. Beatty himself was wounded twice, high in the left arm and again in the left wrist. After two days Beatty talked the surgeons into discharging him from hospital and with his arm in a sling he resumed his duties with the Naval Brigade.

Tientsin was now cut off from Tongku and subjected to daily bombardment and heavy rifle fire that were causing a steady number of casualties. The defenders'

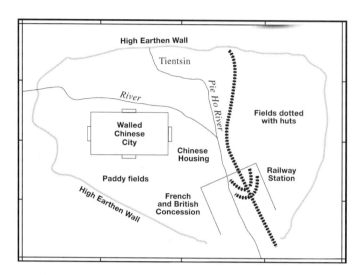

High Earthen Wall

Tientsin

River

Pie Ho River

Fields dotted
with huts

Walled
Chinese
City

Chinese
Housing

Railway
Station

Paddy fields

High Earthen Wall

French
and British
Concession

Tientsin while under daily bombardment during June 1900

reserves of ammunition were being used at an alarming rate. Indeed on 22nd June the Russians proposed an evacuation, a proposal that received no support. Fortunately, the following morning at 0800, troops identified as friendly were sighted moving up the Pie Ho River towards the concessions and at 1100, led by Commander Craddock with a party of seamen from HMS *Alacrity*. They broke through the Chinese and entered the British lines. Surprisingly, the bombardment ceased as the reinforcements, in which a company of the Welsh Fusiliers were the forerunners of a British Army presence, marched in.

There was no bombardment on 24th June, which facilitated the preparations for the relief of Seymour. A multi-national force of 2000 under the Russian Colonel Schivinsky, in which Commander Craddock commanded a British contingent of 600 seamen and Royal Marines and 150 Welsh Fusiliers, made an overnight march to Haiku, brushing aside Chinese resistance, to arrive at about 1030 on 25th June. The rest of the day was spent in preparations to evacuate and then destroy the arsenal. Stretchers had to be made to carry the 266 wounded men, all of whom had to be transported across the Pie Ho. Demolition charges were rigged throughout the arsenal and incendiary devices planted. By 0200 on 26th all was ready and as the march back to Tientsin began Lieutenant Lowther-Crofton, RN, of HMS *Centurion* had the satisfaction of initiating a series of explosions and igniting fires that burnt for over 24 hours. Without a shot being fired, Tientsin was reached at 1000 that day.

Seymour settled himself in Tientsin, hiring a house as his headquarters, and began to re-equip his officers and men, arrange for the treatment of his wounded, hire transport back to the fleet when they could be moved and thence to Wei-Hai-Wei where hospitals and accommodation for convalescence were established. Then he organised the evacuation of the women and children from Tientsin, where necessary arranging accommodation for them in their national ships off Taku. Although frequently consulted about operations he refused to take command, holding that it was improper for a naval officer to command army units ashore. Once the Chinese tailor that he had retained had made uniforms to replace those left at Yangtsun, he was out and about each day amongst Tientsin's defenders. He was hit and severely bruised by a spent bullet and had a member of his staff, his Intelligence Officer, Lieutenant G M K Fair, RN, of HMS *Endymion* wounded at his side when watching the Japanese attack a Chinese position. As military reinforcements arrived he sent his seamen back to their ships. He returned to his flagship when the operations at Tientsin were concluded.

The situation in Tientsin became easier. Communication with Tongku was re-established, the railway link was secured and reinforcements were arriving almost daily. The Chinese continued the bombardment of the railway station and the concessions and to counter this some of the 4-inch and 4.7-inch guns were sent up from the fleet to be mounted as part of the defences. There was as yet no central command of the varied national contingents and any co-ordination of operations depended on informal arrangements between individual national commanders. Such an informal operation took place on 28th June when the Russians, supported by a British contingent of seamen and Royal Marines and soldiers of the Welsh Fusiliers, assaulted and took the eastern of the two small arsenals at Tientsin.

This proved to be the last flicker of the Russian effort in the defence of Tientsin. They had held the railway station since the beginning of the siege and on 2nd July they marched back to their camp. The Royal Naval Brigade was rushed into the empty position. For the next eleven days the British held this vital post under increasing Chinese pressure from the trenches, which the Chinese had advanced to within 300 yards and from a battery of nine guns that concentrated their fire upon the station from close range.

On 6th July Commander Beatty led two companies of seaman to rescue HMS *Orlando's* 9 pdr field gun which, supported by the Wei-Hai-Wei Regiment (Chinese recruited from the environs of Wei-Hai-Wei for its protection, under British Officers) had been sent to silence a Chinese piece which was causing much damage to the hospital and gas works. The 9 pdr was found stuck, with its crew and the Wei-Hai-Wei regiment sheltering nearby from heavy small arms and shellfire. Quickly the 9 pdr was cleared and run back to safety. It proved more difficult to extricate the Wei-Hai-Wei regiment that were somewhat demoralised by the shell fire and rifle fire which caused them casualties, including their Commanding Officer. Once they could be got moving they stampeded back to safety. Sadly Midshipman Esdaile, acting as Beatty's 'Dogie', was accidentally shot by one of them and at 17 was to be the youngest fatality of the Boxer Rebellion.

At 0200 on 11th July the Chinese launched their heaviest and most determined attack on the railway station that led to an urgent appeal from the Royal Naval Brigade for reinforcements and more ammunition. The Hong Kong regiment (Sikhs specially recruited in India for service in Hong Kong) came up and in a bloody hand-to-hand melee drove back the Chinese who had, in places, penetrated the defensive positions.

This event was the catalyst that started the action to take total control of Tientsin and to remove the threat posed by the Chinese Imperial Army and the Boxers. All day on 12th July Commanding Officers of the national contingents conferred and Brigadier General Dorwood, who had arrived from Wei-Hai-Wei to command the British military force of the Welsh Fusiliers, Hong Kong Regiment and Wei-Hai-Wei Regiment, co-ordinated the individual plans. Two thousand five hundred Russians were to attack the eastern gate of the city at 1000 on the 13th. Three columns, 500 yards apart, consisting of 900 American Infantry and 800 British including the Naval Brigade on the left, 1500 Japanese in the centre and 900 French (colonial troops from French Indo-China and of poor quality) on the right were to attack the south and cover the west gate. Covering fire would come from the 4.7 inch and 4 inch naval guns in their fixed emplacements and three 12 pdrs on field mountings from HMS *Terrible* (just arrived from South Africa).

The guns opened fire at 0530 on the 13th and at 0630 the advance began. The Japanese in the centre began to get ahead of the flanking columns and presented an unprotected left flank to a strong Chinese force that included cavalry. Brigadier General Dorwood received a request for support and directed the 9th (American) Infantry to move up on the left (the American right) of the Japanese to counter the threat. The Americans moved up onto the right of the Japanese and were caught in the open under heavy fire from the walls of Tientsin. Dorwood moved the Welsh Fusiliers and Royal Marines to replace the Americans and counter the Chinese threat. This move left the seamen of the Naval Brigade exposed in the open and suffering casualties. Commander Beatty, still suffering from his wounds and with his arm in a sling, led the Brigade forward to shelter under the walls of Tientsin and then, taking a stretcher, with two others went back into the open to rescue a wounded seaman. Midshipman Guy, who had tried on his own to bring the man into shelter, joined them in the attempt. Beatty recommended Guy for the Victoria Cross, which he was later awarded.

At about 1300 Dorwood received another communication from the Japanese General requesting that the artillery barrage be lifted as (erroneously as it turned out) his men were in the city. When the gunfire ceased the Chinese left shelter and opened a withering fire on the Americans, who were still deployed in the open and now suffered heavy casualties. The bombardment was quickly re-instituted and with some difficulty the Americans were extricated from their position and their wounded brought in.

It was stalemate with no news from the Russians. This was not broken until, at about 0300 on 14th, Japanese sappers blew the south gate and an assault penetrated the city. There was a period of street fighting in which the Japanese, supported by the Naval Brigade, played a conspicuous part. The bulk of the Chinese army and Boxers escaped through the unguarded north and west gates which would have been covered had not events drawn the British column to the support of the Japanese. The Russians who "had been delayed by unforeseen circumstances" entered through the east gate at about 1000 in time to join the orgy of plunder, rape and murder as the city was ransacked.

A period of inaction followed the fall of Tientsin while reinforcements flowed in. Lieutenant General Sir Alfred Gaselee, commanding a division from the Indian Army, superseded Brigadier General Dorwood. A Japanese division, a Russian division and more American Infantry also arrived. The Royal Naval Brigades were run down until only 260 seamen, required to man the guns, and 300 Royal Marines remained.

In Europe an agreement was reached that the German Field Marshal Graf Von Waldersee be appointed as commander-in-chief, Allied Forces in North China, and together with a German reinforcement, he sailed to China after a valedictory exhortation from the Kaiser:

> "Just as the Huns a thousand years ago under the leadership of Atilla gained a reputation by virtue of which they live in such a manner in China that no Chinese will ever dare again look askance at a German."

On 30th July the Japanese, carrying out a reconnaissance in force with six battalions, an artillery battery and a squadron of cavalry re-established contact with the Chinese, well dug in at Pietsang. By the evening of 3rd August Gaselee had persuaded the other allied commanders that a relief force of 18 000 all ranks, made up of the troops under his command and of American, Japanese, Russian and French troops, should march on Peking, leaving about 23 000 men, mainly Russian and Japanese to garrison Tientsin. The Naval Brigade, commanded by Captain G A Callaghan RN of HMS *Endymion*, of 260 seamen and 300 Royal Marines with four 12 pdr guns from HMS *Terrible*, formed part of Gaselee's command.

On the 5th August the allied advance began, the first objective being to clear Pietsang. The Japanese were marching in two columns, one on each flank covering a British and American column on the right bank and a Russian and French column on the left bank of the Pie Ho. By chance, the brunt of the fighting fell on the Japanese. First the left hand column deployed to attack a powder magazine, taken at the point of the bayonet, then the right hand column met with unusually stiff resistance in the outskirts of Pietsang. Supported by the fire of the Naval Brigade's 12 pdrs, the resistance was broken at 0830 and after two hours Pietsang was clear of the Chinese and the advance could continue.

Next day Yangtsun was reached after a fighting advance during which the Chinese were driven from a series of fortified positions. By the end of the day the force had lost cohesion as, thirsty in a temperature of 110° F individual units straggled along the line of march. The unfortunate incident when the American 14th Regiment came under shellfire from friendly artillery, both the Russians and the British were blamed, did nothing to improve morale.

After a day of rest around Yangtsun the march resumed on 8th August. Formed in one column, in the order Japanese, Russian, American and British, this became most unpleasant for the Americans and British who, moving off last were marching in the worst of the heat and in the dust clouds created by the troops ahead of them. On 12th August the force reached Tungshu, about ten miles from Peking and the national commanders held a council of war to agree a plan. The Russian General stated that his men were exhausted and proposed that the force should advance next day to within about two or three miles of the city, halt for a day to rest their men and reconnoitre the ground before making an attack on the 15th. Each nation would then assault a designated gate in the eastern wall of the city. This plan was agreed.

By 0001 on the 14th the Russians, having marched diagonally across the lines of advance agreed for the Japanese, French and American attacks, launched an assault on the gates designated as the American target. The Russians managed to cross the moat and break down the outer gate to find themselves trapped in a bailey before the inner gate, subjected to close range fire from the front and both sides. At the news of the Russian action the individual Generals hustled their commands into attacks on their designated targets. The Japanese and French attacks met strong resistance from the Chinese. The Americans found the Russians in confusion around the 'American gate' and it was not until 1400, after a bold escalade of the wall, that they extracted the Russians.

General Gaselee was probably the last General to hear what was happening and the British, having the furthest to march to their gate, did not arrive until noon. Fortunately for them the assaults on the other gates had drawn off the Chinese who should have been on guard. The British column passed through unopposed, advancing along the lanes of the Chinese City towards the Legations where the flags of Great Britain, the United States of America and of Russia were flying. At the feet of their masts leading signalman Swannell stood semaphoring the message: "Come in by the sewer".

At 1500, wading through mud and sewage, the first troops broke through to the Legations to be welcomed by Sir Claude MacDonald "in immaculate tennis flannels backed by the ladies in garden party dresses and carrying parasols". At first the uncharitable wondered whether the siege of the Legations had justified the exertions of the relief, an opinion that quickly changed when the details became known.

Gaselee's troops began to clear the Chinese from their positions round the Legations and to push them back out of range. The Americans fought their way through to join up with Gaselee's men at about 1700. It was not until after dark that the Japanese captured their gate and entered the city. After the rigours of the march to Peking the artillery horses were in very poor condition. Six horses of the 12th Field Battery RFA foundered at the beginning of the approach to the city and, to save the remainder, the men of the Naval Brigade and Wei-Hai-Wei Regiment towed the guns forward joining the infantry at the Legations at about 1700. The sailors' language was reported as 'remarkably profane'. There is no record of that of the Chinamen of the Wei-Hai-Wei Regiment.

The Legations had been under siege since the 20th June, with improvised defences making up a perimeter and each nation holding the portion of the defences nearest their own Legation. The British Legation, by far the largest building with a range of outbuildings and extensive grounds (which also contained the wells of sweet water on which all the garrisons depended), provided shelter for the European civilians. It was also a command post for Sir Claude MacDonald, the British Minister, who, before adopting a diplomatic career, had served in the 74th (Highland Light Infantry) and had seen active service in Egypt, the Sudan and West Africa. He had been elected to command the defence when a Captain in the Austrian Navy (a visitor who had allowed himself to be trapped in the Legations) had assumed command as the Senior Officer present but proved himself incapable of conducting the defence. The total garrison consisted of the 400 officers and men sent up to Peking on 31st May and about 100 civilian volunteers, known as the carving knife brigade because, in their enthusiasm, they had initially tied carving knives, as bayonets, to the muzzles of their rifles. Sir Claude equipped himself with a Martini-Henry rifle, in the use of which weapon he had instructed, and, whenever he was free to do so, freelanced as a sniper.

There were some 400 non-combatant Europeans, including women and children, housed in the British Legation and 2000 Chinese Christians who had fled within the perimeter for protection. The Legations' ladies were organised to sew sandbags for the defensive works (curtains, sheets, and double damask dinner napkins were all sacrificed) and the Chinese were organised into pioneer gangs to fill and place the sandbags. Apart from private stocks of food, the merchandise of the two European shops and the cellar of the European hotel within the Legation area there were over one hundred ponies and draught mules available for slaughter and 230 tons of grain belonging to the Chinese court and stored in a warehouse within the defensive perimeter.

There was, however, a lack of artillery. The Russian commander had started out for Peking with a field gun but, when changing trains at Tientsin, left the gun and his reserve of small arms ammunition behind but brought the field gun ammunition with him. The Austrians had a 1 pdr with a limited supply of ammunition. Armourer's mate Thomas reloaded the used shell cases using powder from the Russian shells, percussion caps taken from the .45 pistol cartridges and shot made by melting down domestic items like teapots and candles sticks. The gun fired seventy 'Thomas' shells without a misfire. Thomas also worked on an old, dismounted, muzzle loaded canon found in the Legation grounds. With the assistance of the Chief Machinist and Gunner's mate from the American detachment this was mounted on a spare set of 1 pdr wheels. More of the Russian ammunition was adapted and the 'International Gun', nicknamed 'The Dowager Empress' or 'Betsy' served effectively throughout the siege. The Americans had a Colt Machine Gun and the Austrians a Maxim but to conserve ammunition these were, until the last days of the siege, only fired in an emergency.

For the first three days of the siege the Chinese contented themselves with desultory rifle fire at the Legation lines that were hastily being strengthened. At about 1000 on 23rd June the Boxers launched their first major attack, torching buildings abutting the walls of the Legations, hoping to burn their way through the defences; any attempt to extinguish the fires brought down heavy rifle fire and the occasional shell. The most serious of these fires was in the Han Lin Institute and library, the depository of Chinese culture that housed among other books the Chinese Encyclopaedia, a great and ongoing work of nearly a million pages. The Han Lin backed onto the British Legation wall and the fire could easily have spread to the Legation buildings. The Royal Marines broke through the wall into the library and were able to protect the fire-fighters who managed to prevent the fire from spreading, although the library was burnt out.

The Boxers, now strengthened by the inclusion of some Imperial troops, attacked the next day. They crept up to and fired at the stable gate of the Legation, taking cover in a group of buildings against the wall outside, ready to rush in when the gate fell. The Royal Marines again broke through the wall, led by Captain Halliday of the RMLI, and made a sortie. Halliday, leading, was first through the wall and was shot through the left shoulder and lung. In turn he shot three or four of his assailants with his revolver, allowing his men to come through the wall. When they were through, Halliday ordered them to carry on with the sortie and made his way back for medical treatment. The Chinese attack was beaten off and the buildings demolished to clear a field of fire. Halliday was awarded the Victoria Cross for his actions. At 1600 there was an abortive effort, perhaps from the Dowager Empress, to communicate with the Legations. Sir Claude had gone so far as to order a temporary ceasefire but when a company of mandarins approached, escorted by soldiers, they were fired upon by the Boxers and scuttled away.

The siege continued in unmethodical fashion with the Chinese making occasional un-coordinated attacks or remarkably ineffective bombardments, usually from a single gun, most shots being 'overs'. There was one burst of activity at the beginning of July when the Germans were surprised and driven from their defences that lay on the top of a part of the ancient wall of the Tartar city. The wall was 60 feet thick at the base, 52 feet wide at the top and 40 feet high. It was adjacent to the German and American Legations and dominated the entire Legation area. The Americans, whose defensive position above their Legation blocked access at the other end of this stretch of wall, were exposed to attacks from front and rear and were forced from their position. Reinforced by Royal Marines and Russians they launched a counterattack and re-established themselves, building a barricade to protect what had been their rear. Shortly after midnight on the 3rd a combined force of 50 men drawn from the American Marines, the Royal Marines and the Russians assaulted the barricade built by the Chinese on what had been the German position. The American Marine officer leading the assault was wounded in the opening stages, and there followed a period of confusion in the dark before the Chinese position was taken and secured.

The next real alarm came on 13th July when there was an attack on the Japanese/Italian sector that came close to success. The position was re-established after a counterattack. Then there was another attack on the German position that was repulsed only after a bayonet charge. The culminating event of the day was the explosion of two mines under the French position, killing two and burying the French Commanding Officer who was dug out bruised and shaken. In fact the mines blew prematurely and killed 30 of the Chinese sappers.

News of the fall of Tientsin seemed to have reached Peking on the 16th July and led to a lull in the martial action while the diplomats exchanged notes. The Dowager Empress even sent gifts of fresh fruit and vegetables to the ladies of the diplomats.

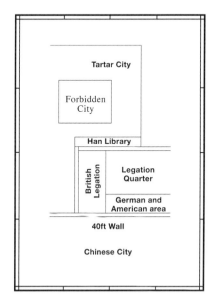

Location of defensive positions within the ancient Tartar city

The lull lasted until 23rd July when the Chinese were seen to have begun building a 'tortoise', their form of advancing barricade.

It was about that that an exchange of messages between Tientsin and the Legations began, smuggled through the Chinese lines by volunteer messengers. The first message, from the British Consul General was ineptly worded, but the second, from American sources, showed that relief was on its way. On the 8th August a cyphered dispatch from Sir Claude reached General Gaselee enclosing a plan of Peking and of the Legation defences. The key to the cypher was held by the British Consul at Tientsin and not by Gaselee. An officer of the British Lancers galloped back to Tientsin and returned on the 10th with a decoder. This message crossed with one to Sir Claude and one to the Japanese giving possible dates for the relief of the 13th or 14th August.

The Union Flag, the Stars and Stripes and the Imperial Eagle of Russia were raised on the Tartar wall in spite of a greatly increased volume of fire from the Chinese whose efforts to take the Legations increased as relief drew near. The Colt machine gun and the Maxim were now used by the defenders as there was no further need to conserve ammunition. The flags were an irresistible target for the Chinese and the Union Flag was shot away, to be replaced by Armourer's mate Thomas and leading signalman Swanell who were to be on the wall to direct the relief when it arrived.

After the relief was effected the allied forces settled down to clearing Peking and then the surrounding countryside of armed Chinese. Peking was systematically looted, each country was allocated a sector of the city and trespass was subject to instant punishment. The diplomats and other civilians who had endured the siege joined enthusiastically in the looting. Field Marshall Graf Von Waldersee arrived with his German troops and fulfilled the Kaiser's injunction. The Naval Brigade returned to their ships.

There was one more Naval contribution to be made. The Chinese still occupied the forts at Shan-Lai-Quan at the foot of the Great Wall and very close to the Manchurian border, a jealously guarded Russian sphere of influence. Seymour, chairing a series of international conferences finally obtained agreement to a plan that satisfied the national pride of the participating nations. Very shortly before the combined fleet was to sail to carry out the plan HMS *Pigmy*, a gunboat, joined the flag and reported that the forts had surrendered to her!

Bibliography

Bodin, L. E. and Warner, C. (1979) *The Boxer Rebellion*. Osprey

Brodie, J. B. and Ray, A. F. (1903) *The Commission of HMS Goliath 1900-03*. Westminster

Chalmers, W. S. (1951) *The Life and Letters of David, Earl Beatty*. Hodder and Stoughton

Fleming, P. (1995) *The Siege of Peking*. Hart Davis

Harfield, A. (1990) *The Indian Army of the Empress 1861–1903*. Spellmount

Keown-Boyd, H. (1991) *The Fists of Righteous Harmony*. Leo Cooper

Padfield, P. (1966) *Aim Stright*. Hodder and Stoughton

Padfield, P. (1981) *Rule Britannia*. Routledge and Kegan

Seymour, E. (1911) *My Naval Career and Travel*. Smith Elder

Smith, E. C. (1944) *A China Flagship*. (Publisher unknown)

Smith, P. C. and Oakley, D. (1988) *The Royal Marines*. Spellmount

Winton, J. (1981) *Jellicoe*. Michael Joseph

EPILOGUE

Queen Victoria's death in 1901 coincided with the last use of Naval Brigades in the theatre of war. During her reign, Queen Victoria noted the exploits of the Naval Brigades. When the siege of Ladysmith was lifted, she sent a telegram:

> "Pray express to the Naval Brigade my deep appreciation of the valuable services they have rendered with their guns."

On their return to Britain the crew of HMS *Powerful* were greeted with a hero's welcome. They pulled their guns through the streets of Portsmouth and London where flag waving crowds cheered them on. They even took their guns to Windsor Castle where they had lunch with the Queen.

And it did not end there. Fresh from their Boer War exploits, the sailors of the Naval Brigade attended the Royal Tournament of 1890, where they treated the audience to a display with their 4.7-inch guns. In 1907 this became the Royal Navy Field Gun Competition, where teams competed against the clock around a course designed to represent the natural obstacles over which the Naval Brigades had to manhandle their guns in order to get them to Ladysmith. This long-lasting tribute to their achievements ended in 1999 with the final year of the Royal Tournament.

Winston Churchill briefly revived the concept of using under-employed naval ratings in land operations in 1914 when he realised that there were a large number of naval reservists with no sea roles. Consequently, the Royal Naval Division (RND) was formed, seeing action throughout the battlefields and trenches of World War One and serving with some distinction. It should be noted that during the war, more Royal Navy personnel assigned to the RND were killed or wounded than in the sea-going arm of the service.

The RND was disbanded in 1919.